BLUEPRINTS: *A Problem Notebook*

FINANCIAL MANAGEMENT

Theory and

Practice

Ninth Edition

EUGENE F. BRIGHAM
UNIVERSITY OF FLORIDA

LOUIS C. GAPENSKI
UNIVERSITY OF FLORIDA

MICHAEL C. EHRHARDT
UNIVERSITY OF TENNESSEE

HARCOURT COLLEGE PUBLISHERS

Fort Worth   Philadelphia   San Diego   New York   Orlando   Austin   San Antonio
Toronto   Montreal   London   Sydney   Tokyo

Printed in the United States of America
ISBN: 0-03-023368-2

PREFACE

Blueprints has become an integral part of the material we provide to students. To get students more involved, we have developed a set of Mini Cases which cover the key points in each chapter and which we use as the basis for our lectures. For our classes, we use the computer slideshow to present the material that is summarized in each Mini Case. Early on, students began asking us to make copies of the slides available to them. We did so, and that improved the class considerably. With paper copies of the slides, students could focus on what was being said in the lecture without having to copy things down for later review. *Blueprints* includes a copy of each Mini Case, copies of the slides, and space to write down additional notes. Since, we frequently use the blackboard, both to explain the calculations which lie behind some of the numbers and to provide different examples, our students end up with lots of marginal notes which clarify various points.

We consider the current version quite complete. However, the <u>optimal</u> product varies from instructor to instructor, depending on how the class is conducted. Therefore, instructors are encouraged to modify *Blueprints* to suit their own styles and interests. For example, if one covers chapters in a different order, or does not cover certain chapters, or covers only part of some chapters, or has additional materials not covered in the text, or anything else, the *Blueprints* chapters can be rearranged, added to or subtracted from, or modified in any other way.

One thing has become crystal clear over the years—the best lecture notes, and materials related thereto, are instructor-specific. It is difficult to use someone else's notes verbatim. However, there is no point in reinventing the wheel, and if the *Blueprints* wheel fits a particular instructor's wagon, he or she might do well to use it, spending time adapting it to his or her own style and coverage rather than taking the time to develop lectures notes *de novo*. Therefore, you are encouraged to look over the *Blueprints* package, decide if and how you might use it, and then go to it. If you are like us, you will change things from semester to semester—there is no such thing as static optimality!

We would like to thank Dana Aberwald Clark for riding herd on all of us, and making sure *Blueprints* was completed on time and was consistent with the text of *Financial Management*. Susan Purcell Whitman and Tina Goforth took care of the massive typing job; their care and dedication are much appreciated.

If you do use the package, and find some modifications that work well for you, we would very much appreciate hearing from you—your modifications might well help us and others. Please send any comments or suggestions to Michael Ehrhardt at the address given below.

Eugene F. Brigham
Louis C. Gapenski

Michael C. Ehrhardt

P.O. Box 117167
College of Business
University of Florida
Gainesville, Florida 32611-7167

Finance Department, SMC 424
University of Tennessee
Knoxville, TN 37996-0540

June 1998

SUGGESTIONS FOR STUDENTS USING BLUEPRINTS

1. Read the textbook chapter first, going through the entire chapter rapidly. Don't expect to understand everything on this first reading, but do try to get a good idea of what the chapter covers, the key terms, and the like. <u>It is useful to read the chapter before the first lecture on it.</u>

2. You could also read the *Blueprints* chapter material before class, but that is not necessary.

3. *Blueprints* was designed as the basis for a lecture—the most important material in each chapter is covered, and the material most likely to give you trouble is emphasized. As your instructor goes through *Blueprints*, you should (1) see what we regard as the most important material and (2) get a better feel for how to think about issues and work relevant problems.

4. You could read *Blueprints*, in connection with the text, and get a reasonably good idea of what is going on in the course. However, the real value of *Blueprints* is as a vehicle to help the class lecture make more sense and to help you get a good set of notes. In class, your instructor will discuss various points raised in *Blueprints* and elaborate on different issues. Also, he or she will explain how formulas are used, where data in tables come from, and the like. <u>You will end up with lots of marginal notes on your copy if you use *Blueprints* as it is supposed to be used.</u> Indeed, these marginal notes will constitute your class notes.

BLUEPRINTS

TABLE OF CONTENTS

BLUEPRINTS: CHAPTER 1
AN OVERVIEW OF FINANCIAL MANAGEMENT

Suppose you went home for a quick visit early in the term, and, over the course of the weekend, your brother, who received his MBA three years ago, asked you to tell him about the courses you are taking. After you told him that financial management was one of the courses, he asked you the following questions:

a. What kinds of career opportunities are open to finance majors?

b. What are the most important financial management issues of the 1990s?

c. What are the primary responsibilities of a corporate financial staff?

d. (1) What are the alternative forms of business organization?

   (2) What are their advantages and disadvantages?

e. What is the primary goal of the corporation?

   (1) Do firms have any responsibilities to society at large?

   (2) Is stock price maximization good or bad for society?

   (3) Should firms behave ethically?

f. What factors affect stock prices?

g. What determines cash flows?

h. What factors affect the level and riskiness of cash flows?

i. What is an agency relationship?

   (1) What agency relationships exist within a corporation?

   (2) What mechanisms exist to influence managers to act in shareholders' best interests?

   (3) Should shareholders (through managers) take actions that are detrimental to bondholders?

1 - 1

CHAPTER 1
An Overview of Financial Management

- Career opportunities
- Issues of the 1990s
- Forms of business organization
- Goals of the corporation
- Agency relationships

---

1 - 2

Career Opportunities in Finance

- Money and capital markets
- Investments
- Financial management

---

1 - 3

Financial Management
Issues of the 1990s

- Use of computers and electronic transfers of information
- The globalization of business

Responsibilities of the Financial Staff

1 - 4

- Forecasting and planning
- Investment and financing decisions
- Coordination and control
- Transactions in the financial markets
- Managing risk

Alternative Forms of Business Organization

1 - 5

- Sole proprietorship
- Partnership
- Corporation

Sole Proprietorship

1 - 6

- Advantages:
  - Ease of formation
  - Subject to few regulations
  - No corporate income taxes
- Disadvantages:
  - Limited life
  - Unlimited liability
  - Difficult to raise capital

Partnership

■ A partnership has roughly the same advantages and disadvantages as a sole proprietorship.

Corporation

■ Advantages:
- ● Unlimited life
- ● Easy transfer of ownership
- ● Limited liability
- ● Ease of raising capital

■ Disadvantages:
- ● Double taxation
- ● Cost of set-up and report filing

Goals of the Corporation

■ The primary goal is shareholder wealth maximization, which translates to maximizing stock price.
- ● Do firms have any responsibilities to society at large?
- ● Is stock price maximization good or bad for society?
- ● Should firms behave ethically?

1 - 10

Factors that Affect Stock Price

- Amount of cash flows expected by shareholders
- Timing of the cash flow stream
- Riskiness of the cash flows

---

1 - 11

Three Determinants of Cash Flows

- Sales
  - Current level
  - Short-term growth rate in sales
  - Long-term sustainable growth rate in sales
- Operating expenses
- Capital expenses

---

1 - 12

Factors that Affect the Level and Riskiness of Cash Flows

- Decisions made by financial managers:
  - Investment decisions
  - Financing decisions (the relative use of debt financing)
  - Dividend policy decisions
- The external environment

Agency Relationships

- **An agency relationship exists whenever a principal hires an agent to act on his or her behalf.**
- **Within a corporation, agency relationships exist between:**
  - **Shareholders and managers**
  - **Shareholders and creditors**

Shareholders versus Managers

- **Managers are naturally inclined to act in their own best interests.**
- **But the following factors affect managerial behavior:**
  - **Managerial compensation plans**
  - **Direct intervention by shareholders**
  - **The threat of firing**
  - **The threat of takeover**

Shareholders versus Creditors

- **Shareholders (through managers) could take actions to maximize stock price that are detrimental to creditors.**
- **In the long run, such actions will raise the cost of debt and ultimately lower stock price.**

BLUEPRINTS: CHAPTER 2
FINANCIAL STATEMENTS, CASH FLOW, AND TAXES

Donna Jamison, a 1993 graduate of the University of Florida with four years of banking experience, was recently brought in as assistant to the chairman of the board of Computron Industries, a manufacturer of electronic calculators.

The company doubled its plant capacity, opened new sales offices outside its home territory, and launched an expensive advertising campaign. Computron's results were not satisfactory, to put it mildly. Its board of directors, which consisted of its president and vice-president plus its major stockholders (who were all local business people), was most upset when directors learned how the expansion was going. Suppliers were being paid late and were unhappy, and the bank was complaining about the deteriorating situation and threatening to cut off credit. As a result, Al Watkins, Computron's president, was informed that changes would have to be made, and quickly, or he would be fired. Also, at the board's insistence Donna Jamison was brought in and given the job of assistant to Fred Campo, a retired banker who was Computron's chairman and largest stockholder. Campo agreed to give up a few of his golfing days and to help nurse the company back to health, with Jamison's help.

Jamison began by gathering financial statements and other data.

Assume that you are Jamison's assistant, and you must help her answer the following questions for Campo. (Note: We will continue with this case in Chapter 3, and you will feel more comfortable with the analysis there, but answering these questions will help prepare you for Chapter 3. Provide clear explanations, not just yes or no answers!)

Balance Sheets

	1998	1997
Assets:		
Cash	$ 7,282	$ 9,000
Short-term investments	0	48,600
Accounts receivable	632,160	351,200
Inventories	1,287,360	715,200
Total current assets	$1,926,802	$1,124,000
Gross fixed assets	1,202,950	491,000
Less accumulated depreciation	263,160	146,200
Net fixed assets	$ 939,790	$ 344,800
Total assets	$2,866,592	$1,468,800
Liabilities and Equity:		
Accounts payable	$ 524,160	$ 145,600
Notes payable	720,000	200,000
Accruals	489,600	136,000
Total current liabilities	$1,733,760	$ 481,600
Long-term debt	1,000,000	323,432
Common stock (100,000 shares)	460,000	460,000
Retained earnings	(327,168)	203,768
Total equity	$ 132,832	$ 663,768
Total liabilities and equity	$2,866,592	$1,468,800

Income Statements

	1998	1997
Sales	$5,834,400	$3,432,000
Cost of goods sold	5,728,000	2,864,000
Other expenses	680,000	340,000
Depreciation	116,960	18,900
Total operating costs	$6,524,960	$3,222,900
EBIT	($ 690,560)	$ 209,100
Interest expense	176,000	62,500
EBT	($ 866,560)	$ 146,600
Taxes (40%)	(346,624)	58,640
Net income	($ 519,936)	$ 87,960
EPS	($5.199)	$0.880
DPS	$0.110	$0.220
Book value per share	$1.328	$6.638
Stock price	$2.250	$8.500
Shares outstanding	100,000	100,000
Tax rate	40.00%	40.00%
Lease payments	40,000	40,000
Sinking fund payments	0	0

Statement of Retained Earnings, 1998

Balance of retained earnings, 12/31/97	$203,768
Add: Net income, 1998	(519,936)
Less: Dividends paid	(11,000)
Balance of retained earnings, 12/31/98	($327,168)

Statement of Cash Flows, 1998

OPERATING ACTIVITIES
Net income	($ 519,936)
Adjustments:	
Non-cash adjustments:	
Depreciation	116,960
Changes in working capital:	
Change in accounts receivable	(280,960)
Change in inventories	(572,160)
Change in accounts payable	378,560
Change in accruals	353,600
Net cash provided by operating activities	($ 523,936)

LONG-TERM INVESTING ACTIVITIES
Cash used to acquire fixed assets	($ 711,950)

FINANCING ACTIVITIES
Change in short-term investments	$ 48,600
Change in notes payable	520,000
Change in long-term debt	676,568
Payment of cash dividends	(11,000)
Net cash provided by financing activities	$1,234,168
Sum: Net change in cash	($ 1,718)
Plus: Cash at beginning of year	9,000
Cash at end of year	$ 7,282

a. What effect did the expansion have on sales, net operating profit after taxes (NOPAT), net operating working capital, capital, and net income?

b. What effect did the expansion have on net cash flow, operating cash flow, and free cash flow?

c. Jamison also has asked you to estimate Computron's EVA. She estimates that the after-tax cost of capital was 11 percent in 1997 and 13 percent in 1998.

d. Looking at Computron's stock price today, would you conclude that the expansion increased or decreased MVA?

e. Computron purchases materials on 30-day terms, meaning that it is supposed to pay for purchases within 30 days of receipt. Judging from its 1998 balance sheet, do you think Computron pays suppliers on time? Explain. If not, what problems might this lead to?

f. Computron spends money for labor, materials, and fixed assets (depreciation) to make products, and still more money to sell those products. Then, it makes sales which result in receivables, which eventually result in cash inflows. Does it appear that Computron's sales price exceeds its costs per unit sold? How does this affect the cash balance?

g. Suppose Computron's sales manager told the sales staff to start offering 60-day credit terms rather than the 30-day terms now being offered. Computron's competitors react by offering similar terms, so sales remain constant. What effect would this have on the cash account? How would the cash account be affected if sales doubled as a result of the credit policy change?

h. Can you imagine a situation in which the sales price exceeds the cost of producing and selling a unit of output, yet a dramatic increase in sales volume causes the cash balance to decline?

i. In general, could a company like Computron increase sales without a corresponding increase in inventory and other assets? Would the asset increase occur before the increase in sales, and, if so, how would that affect the cash account and the statement of cash flows?

j. Did Computron finance its expansion program with internally generated funds (additions to retained earnings plus depreciation) or with external capital? How does the choice of financing affect the company's financial strength?

k. Refer to the income statements and the statement of cash flows. Suppose Computron broke even in 1998 in the sense that sales revenues equaled total operating costs plus interest charges. Would the asset expansion have caused the company to experience a cash shortage which required it to raise external capital?

l. If Computron started depreciating fixed assets over 7 years rather than 10 years, would that affect (1) the physical stock of assets, (2) the balance sheet account for fixed assets, (3) the company's reported net income, and (4) its cash position? Assume the same depreciation method is used for stockholder reporting and for tax calculations, and the accounting change has no effect on assets' physical lives.

m. Explain how (1) inventory valuation methods, (2) the accounting policy regarding expensing versus capitalizing research and development, and (3) the policy with regard to funding future retirement plan costs (retirement pay and retirees' health benefits) could affect the financial statements.

n. Computron's stock sells for $2.25 per share even though the company had large losses. Does the positive stock price indicate that some investors are irrational?

o. Computron followed the standard practice of paying dividends on a quarterly basis. It paid a dividend during the first two quarters of 1998 then eliminated the dividend when management realized that a loss would be incurred for the year. The dividend was cut before the losses were announced, and at that point the stock price fell from $8.50 to $3.50. Why would an $0.11, or even a $0.22, dividend reduction lead to a $5.00 stock price reduction?

p. Explain how earnings per share, dividends per share, and book value per share are calculated, and what they mean. Why does the market price per share *not* equal the book value per share?

q. How much new money did Computron borrow from its bank during 1998? How much additional credit did its suppliers extend? Its employees and the taxing authorities?

r. If you were Computron's banker, or the credit manager of one of its suppliers, would you be worried about your job? If you were a current Computron employee, a retiree, or a stockholder, should you be concerned?

s. The 1998 income statement shows negative taxes, that is, a tax credit. How much taxes would the company have had to pay in the past to actually get this credit? If taxes paid within the last 2 years had been less than $346,624, what would have happened? Would this have affected the statement of cash flows and the ending cash balance?

t. Working with Jamison has required you to put in a lot of overtime, so you have had very little time to spend on your private finances. It's now April 1, and you have only two weeks left to file your income tax return. You have managed to get all the information together that you will need to complete your return. Computron paid you a salary of $45,000, and you received $3,000 in dividends from common stock that you own. You are single, so your personal exemption is $2,650, and your itemized deductions are $4,550.

   (1) On the basis of the information above and the 1998 individual tax rate schedule, what is your tax liability?

   (2) What are your marginal and average tax rates?

u. Assume that a corporation has $100,000 of taxable income from operations plus $5,000 of interest income and $10,000 of dividend income. What is the company's tax liability?

v. Assume that after paying your personal income tax as calculated in Part t, you have $5,000 to invest. You have narrowed your investment choices down to California bonds with a yield of 7 percent or equally risky Exxon bonds with a yield of 10 percent. Which one should you choose and why? At what marginal tax rate would you be indifferent to the choice between California and Exxon bonds?

CHAPTER 2
Financial Statements, Cash Flow, and Taxes

- Balance sheet
- Income statement
- Statement of cash flows
- Accounting income versus cash flow
- MVA and EVA
- Personal taxes
- Corporate taxes

Balance Sheets: Assets

	1998	1997
Cash	7,282	9,000
Short-term inv.	0	48,600
AR	632,160	351,200
Inventories	1,287,360	715,200
Total CA	1,926,802	1,124,000
Gross FA	1,202,950	491,000
Less: Depr.	263,160	146,200
Net FA	939,790	344,800
Total assets	2,866,592	1,468,800

Liabilities and Equity

	1998	1997
Accts payable	524,160	145,600
Notes payable	720,000	200,000
Accruals	489,600	136,000
Total CL	1,733,760	481,600
Long-term debt	1,000,000	323,432
Common stock	460,000	460,000
Retained earnings	(327,168)	203,768
Total equity	132,832	663,768
Total L&E	2,866,592	1,468,800

Income Statement

	1998	1997
Sales	5,834,400	3,432,000
COGS	5,728,000	2,864,000
Other expenses	680,000	340,000
Deprec.	116,960	18,900
Tot. op. costs	6,524,960	3,222,900
EBIT	(690,560)	209,100
Interest exp.	176,000	62,500
EBT	(866,560)	146,600
Taxes (40%)	(346,624)	58,640
Net income	(519,936)	87,960

Other Data

	1998	1997
No. of shares	100,000	100,000
EPS	($5.199)	$0.88
DPS	$0.110	$0.22
Stock price	$2.25	$8.50
Lease pmts	$40,000	$40,000

Statement of Retained Earnings (1998)

Balance of retained earnings, 12/31/97	$203,768
Add: Net income, 1998	(519,936)
Less: Dividends paid	(11,000)
Balance of retained earnings, 12/31/98	($327,168)

Statement of Cash Flows: 1998

OPERATING ACTIVITIES

Net Income	(519,936)
Adjustments:	
Depreciation	116,960
Change in AR	(280,960)
Change in inventories	(572,160)
Change in AP	378,560
Change in accruals	353,600
Net cash provided by ops.	(523,936)

L-T INVESTING ACTIVITIES

Investments in fixed assets	(711,950)

FINANCING ACTIVITIES

Change in s-t investments	48,600
Change in notes payable	520,000
Change in long-term debt	676,568
Payment of cash dividends	(11,000)
Net cash from financing	1,234,168
Sum: net change in cash	(1,718)
Plus: cash at beginning of year	9,000
Cash at end of year	7,282

What can you conclude about the company's financial condition from its statement of cash flows?

- Net cash from operations = -$523,936, mainly because of negative net income.

- The firm borrowed $1,185,568 and sold $48,600 in short-term investments to meet its cash requirements.

- Even after borrowing, the cash account fell by $1,718.

What effect did the expansion have on net operating working capital (NOWC)?

$$NOWC = \begin{array}{c} \text{Non-interest} \\ \text{bearing CA} \end{array} - \begin{array}{c} \text{Non-interest} \\ \text{bearing CL} \end{array}$$

$NOWC_{98} = (\$7,282 + \$632,160 + \$1,287,360)$
$\qquad - (\$524,160 + \$489,600)$
$\qquad = \$913,042.$

$NOWC_{97} = \$793,800.$

What effect did the expansion have on capital used in operations?

$$\begin{array}{c} \text{Operating} \\ \text{capital} \end{array} = NOWC + \text{Net fixed assets.}$$

$\begin{array}{c} \text{Operating} \\ \text{capital}_{98} \end{array} = \$913,042 + \$939,790$
$\qquad\qquad = \$1,852,832.$

$\begin{array}{c} \text{Operating} \\ \text{capital}_{97} \end{array} = \$1,138,600.$

Did the expansion create additional net operating profit after taxes (NOPAT)?

$$NOPAT = EBIT(1 - \text{Tax rate})$$

$NOPAT_{98} = -\$690,560(1 - 0.4)$
$\qquad\qquad = -\$690,560(0.6)$
$\qquad\qquad = -\$414,336.$

$NOPAT_{97} = \$125,460.$

What is your initial assessment of the expansion's effect on operations?

	1998	1997
Sales	$5,834,400	$3,432,000
NOPAT	($414,336)	$125,460
NOWC	$913,042	$793,800
Operating capital	$1,852,832	$1,138,600

What effect did the company's expansion have on its net cash flow and operating cash flow?

$NCF_{98} = NI + DEP = -\$519,936 + \$116,960$
$= -\$402,976.$

$NCF_{97} = \$87,960 + \$18,900 = \$106,860.$

$OCF_{98} = NOPAT + DEP$
$= -\$414,336 + \$116,960$
$= -\$297,376.$

$OCF_{97} = \$125,460 + \$18,900$
$= \$144,360.$

What was the free cash flow (FCF) for 1998?

$FCF = NOPAT - \text{Net capital investment}$
$= -\$414,336 - (\$1,852,832 - \$1,138,600)$
$= -\$414,336 - \$714,232$
$= -\$1,128,568.$

How do you suppose investors reacted?

**What is the company's EVA?
Assume the firm's after-tax cost of
capital (COC) was 11% in 1997
and 13% in 1998.**

$$EVA_{98} = NOPAT - (COC)(Capital)$$
$$= -\$414,336 - (0.13)(\$1,852,832)$$
$$= -\$414,336 - \$240,868$$
$$= -\$655,204.$$

$$EVA_{97} = \$125,460 - (0.11)(\$1,138,600)$$
$$= \$125,460 - \$125,246$$
$$= \$214.$$

**Would you conclude
that the expansion increased or
decreased MVA?**

$$MVA = \frac{Market\ value}{of\ equity} - \frac{Equity\ capital}{supplied}$$

**During the last year stock price has
decreased 73%, so market value of
equity has declined. Consequently,
MVA has declined.**

**Does the company pay its suppliers
on time?**

■ **Probably not.**

■ **A/P increased 260% over the past
year, while sales increased by only
70%.**

■ **If this continues, suppliers may cut
off trade credit.**

Does it appear that the sales price exceeds the cost per unit sold?

- No, the negative NOPAT shows that the company is spending more on it's operations than it is taking in.

What effect would each of these actions have on the cash account?

1. The company offers 60-day credit terms. The improved terms are matched by its competitors, so sales remain constant.

    - A/R would ↑
    - Cash would ↓

2. Sales double as a result of the change in credit terms.

    - Short-run: Inventory and fixed assets ↑ to meet increased sales. A/R ↑, Cash ↓. Company may have to seek additional financing.
    - Long-run: Collections increase and the company's cash position would improve.

2 - 22

How was the expansion financed?

- The expansion was financed primarily with external capital.
- The company issued long-term debt which reduced its financial strength and flexibility.

2 - 23

Would external capital have been required if they had broken even in 1998 (Net income = 0)?

- Yes, the company would still have to finance its increase in assets.

2 - 24

What happens if fixed assets are depreciated over 7 years (as opposed to the current 10 years)?

- No effect on physical assets.
- Fixed assets on balance sheet would decline.
- Net income would decline.
- Tax payments would decline.
- Cash position would improve.

Other policies that can affect financial statements

- Inventory valuation methods.
- Capitalization of R&D expenses.
- Policies for funding the company's retirement plan.

Does the company's positive stock price ($2.25), in the face of large losses, suggest that investors are irrational?

- No, it means that investors expect things to get better in the future.

Why did the stock price fall after the dividend was cut?

- Management was "signaling" that the firm's operations were in trouble.
- The dividend cut lowered investors' expectations for future cash flows, which caused the stock price to decline.

What were some other sources of financing used in 1998?

- Selling financial assets: Short term investments decreased by $48,600.
- Bank loans: Notes payable increased by $520,000.
- Credit from suppliers: A/P increased by $378,560.
- Employees: Accruals increased by $353,600.

What is the effect of the $346,624 tax credit received in 1998.

- This suggests the company paid at least $346,624 in taxes during the past 2 years.
- If the payments over the past 2 years were less than $346,624 the firm would have had to carry forward the amount of its loss that was not carried back.
- If the firm did not receive a full refund its cash position would be even worse.

INCOME TAXES

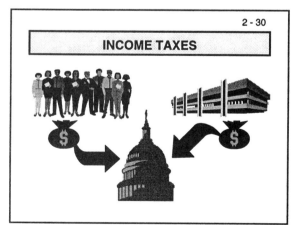

1997 Tax Year Single Individual Tax Rates

Taxable Income	Tax on Base	Rate*
0 - 24,650	0	15%
24,650 - 59,750	3,697.50	28%
59,750 - 124,650	13,525.50	31%
124,650 - 271,050	33,644.50	36%
Over 271,050	86,3480.50	39.6%

*Plus this percentage on the amount over the bracket base.

Assume your salary is $45,000, and you received $3,000 in dividends. You are single, so your personal exemption is $2,650 and your itemized deductions are $4,550.

On the basis of the information above and the 1997 tax year tax rate schedule, what is your tax liability?

Calculation of Taxable Income

Salary	$45,000
Dividends	3,000
Personal exemptions	(2,650)
Deductions	(4,550)
Taxable Income	$40,800

$40,800 - $24,650

- **Tax Liability:**

  TL = $3,697.50 + 0.28($16,150)

  = $8,219.50.

- **Marginal Tax Rate = 28%.**
- **Average Tax Rate:**

  Tax rate = $\dfrac{\$8,219.5}{\$40,800}$ = 20.15%.

1997 Corporate Tax Rates

Taxable Income	Tax on Base	Rate*
0 - 50,000	0	15%
50,000 - 75,000	7,500	25%
75,000 - 100,000	13,750	34%
100,000 - 335,000	22,250	39%
...	...	...
Over 18.3M	6.4M	35%

*Plus this percentage on the amount over the bracket base.

Assume a corporation has $100,000 of taxable income from operations, $5,000 of interest income, and $10,000 of dividend income.

What is its tax liability?

Operating income	$100,000
Interest income	5,000
Taxable dividend income	3,000*
Taxable income	$108,000

Tax = $22,250 + 0.39 ($8,000)
    = $25,370.

*Dividends - Exclusion
  = $10,000 - 0.7($10,000) = $3,000.

Taxable versus Tax Exempt Bonds

State and local government bonds (municipals, or "munis") are generally exempt from federal taxes.

■ Exxon bonds at 10% versus California muni bonds at 7%.

■ T = Tax rate = 28%.

■ After-tax interest income:

Exxon = 0.10($5,000) - 0.10($5,000)(0.28)
        = 0.10($5,000)(0.72) = $360.

CAL = 0.07($5,000) - 0 = $350.

At what tax rate would you be indifferent between the muni and the corporate bonds?

Solve for T in this equation:

Muni yield = Corp Yield(1-T)

$$7.00\% = 10.0\%(1-T)$$
$$T = 30.0\%.$$

Implications

- If T > 30%, buy tax exempt munis.
- If T < 30%, buy corporate bonds.
- Only high income, and hence high tax bracket, individuals should buy munis.

The first part of the case, presented in Chapter 2, discussed the situation that Computron Industries was in after an expansion program. Thus far, sales have not been up to the forecasted level, costs have been higher than were projected, and a large loss occurred in 1998 rather than the expected profit. As a result, its managers, directors, and investors are concerned about the firm's survival.

Donna Jamison was brought in as assistant to Fred Campo, Computron's chairman, who had the task of getting the company back into a sound financial position. Computron's 1997 and 1998 balance sheets and income statements, together with projections for 1999, are shown in the following tables. Also, the tables show the 1997 and 1998 financial ratios, along with industry average data. The 1999 projected financial statement data represent Jamison's and Campo's best guess for 1999 results, assuming that some new financing is arranged to get the company "over the hump."

Jamison examined monthly data for 1998 (not given in the case), and she detected an improving pattern during the year. Monthly sales were rising, costs were falling, and large losses in the early months had turned to a small profit by December. Thus, the annual data look somewhat worse than final monthly data. Also, it appears to be taking longer for the advertising program to get the message across, for the new sales offices to generate sales, and for the new manufacturing facilities to operate efficiently. In other words, the lags between spending money and deriving benefits were longer than Computron's managers had anticipated. For these reasons, Jamison and Campo see hope for the company--provided it can survive in the short run.

Jamison must prepare an analysis of where the company is now, what it must do to regain its financial health, and what actions should be taken. Your assignment is to help her answer the following questions. Provide clear explanations, not yes or no answers.

Balance Sheets

	1999E	1998	1997
Assets:			
Cash	$ 14,000	$ 7,282	$ 9,000
Short-term investments	71,632	0	48,600
Accounts receivable	878,000	632,160	351,200
Inventories	1,716,480	1,287,360	715,200
Total current assets	$2,680,112	$1,926,802	$1,124,000
Gross fixed assets	1,197,160	1,202,950	491,000
Less accumulated depreciation	380,120	263,160	146,200
Net fixed assets	$ 817,040	$ 939,790	$ 344,800
Total assets	$3,497,152	$2,866,592	$1,468,800
Liabilities and Equity:			
Accounts payable	$ 436,800	$ 524,160	$ 145,600
Notes payable	600,000	720,000	200,000
Accruals	408,000	489,600	136,000
Total current liabilities	$1,444,800	$1,733,760	$ 481,600
Long-term debt	500,000	1,000,000	323,432
Common stock	1,680,936	460,000	460,000
Retained earnings	(128,584)	(327,168)	203,768
Total equity	$1,552,352	$ 132,832	$ 663,768
Total liabilities and equity	$3,497,152	$2,866,592	$1,468,800

Note: "E" indicates estimated. The 1999 data are forecasts.

Income Statements

	1999E	1998	1997
Sales	$7,035,600	$5,834,400	$3,432,000
Cost of goods sold	5,728,000	5,728,000	2,864,000
Other expenses	680,000	680,000	340,000
Depreciation	116,960	116,960	18,900
Total operating costs	$6,524,960	$6,524,960	$3,222,900
EBIT	$ 510,640	($ 690,560)	$ 209,100
Interest expense	88,000	176,000	62,500
EBT	$ 422,640	($ 866,560)	$ 146,600
Taxes (40%)	169,056	(346,624)	58,640
Net income	$ 253,584	($ 519,936)	$ 87,960
EPS	$ 1.014	($5.199)	$0.880
DPS	$ 0.220	$0.110	$0.220
Book value per share	$ 6.209	$1.328	$6.638
Stock price	$12.17	$2.250	$8.500
Shares outstanding	250,000	100,000	100,000
Tax rate	40.00%	40.00%	40.00%
Lease payments	40,000	40,000	40,000
Sinking fund payments	0	0	0

Note: "E" indicates estimated. The 1999 data are forecasts.

Ratio Analysis

	1999E	1998	1997	Industry Average
Current		1.1×	2.3×	2.7×
Quick		0.4×	0.8×	1.0×
Inventory turnover		4.5×	4.8×	6.1×
Days sales outstanding (DSO)		39.0	36.8	32.0
Fixed assets turnover		6.2×	10.0×	7.0×
Total assets turnover		2.0×	2.3×	2.6×
Operating capital requirement		31.8%	33.2%	29.5%
Debt ratio		95.4%	54.8%	50.0%
TIE		-3.9×	3.3×	6.2×
Fixed charge coverage		-3.0×	2.4×	5.1×
Operating profit margin after taxes		-7.1%	3.7%	4.4%
Profit margin		-8.9%	2.6%	3.5%
Basic earning power		-24.1%	14.2%	19.1%
ROA		-18.1%	6.0%	9.1%
ROE		-391.4%	13.3%	18.2%
Price/earnings		-0.4×	9.7×	14.2×
Market/book		1.7×	1.3×	2.4×
Book value per share		$1.33	$6.64	n.a.

Note: "E" indicates estimated. The 1999 data are forecasts.

a. Why are ratios useful? What are the five major categories of ratios?

b. Calculate the 1999 current and quick ratios based on the projected balance sheet and income statement data. What can you say about the company's liquidity position in 1997, 1998, and as projected for 1999? We often think of ratios as being useful (1) to managers to help run the business, (2) to bankers for credit analysis, and (3) to stockholders for stock valuation. Would these different types of analysts have an equal interest in the liquidity ratios?

c. Calculate the 1999 inventory turnover, days sales outstanding (DSO), fixed assets turnover, operating capital requirement, and total assets turnover. How does Computron's utilization of assets stack up against other firms in its industry?

d. Calculate the 1999 debt, times-interest-earned, and fixed charge coverage ratios. How does Computron compare with the industry with respect to financial leverage? What can you conclude from these ratios?

e. Calculate the 1999 operating profit margin after taxes, profit margin, basic earning power (BEP), return on assets (ROA), and return on equity (ROE). What can you say about these ratios?

f. Calculate the 1999 price/earnings ratio and market/book ratio. Do these ratios indicate that investors are expected to have a high or low opinion of the company?

g. Use the extended Du Pont equation to provide a summary and overview of Computron's financial condition as projected for 1999. What are the firm's major strengths and weaknesses?

h. Use the following simplified 1999 balance sheet to show, in general terms, how an improvement in the DSO would tend to affect the stock price. For example, if the company could improve its collection procedures and thereby lower its DSO from 44.9 days to the 32-day industry average without affecting sales, how would that change "ripple through" the financial statements (shown in thousands below) and influence the stock price?

Accounts receivable	$ 878	Debt	$1,945
Other current assets	1,802		
Net fixed assets	817	Equity	1,552
Total assets	$3,497	Liabilities plus equity	$3,497

i. Does it appear that inventories could be adjusted, and, if so, how should that adjustment affect profitability and stock price?

j. In 1998, the company paid its suppliers much later than the due dates, and it was not maintaining financial ratios at levels called for in its bank loan agreements. Therefore, suppliers could cut the company off, and its bank could refuse to renew the loan when it comes due in 90 days. On the basis of data provided, would you, as a credit manager, continue to sell to Computron on credit? (You could demand cash on delivery, that is, sell on terms of COD, but that might cause Computron to stop buying from your company.) Similarly, if you were the bank loan officer, would you recommend renewing the loan or demand its repayment? Would your actions be influenced if, in early 1999, Computron showed you its 1999 projections plus proof that it was going to raise over $1.2 million of new equity capital?

k. In hindsight, what should Computron have done back in 1997?

l. What are some potential problems and limitations of financial ratio analysis?

m. What are some qualitative factors analysts should consider when evaluating a company's likely future financial performance?

CHAPTER 3
Analysis of Financial Statements

- Ratio analysis
- Du Pont system
- Effects of improving ratios
- Limitations of ratio analysis
- Qualitative factors

Balance Sheet: Assets

	1999E	1998
Cash	14,000	7,282
ST investments	71,632	0
AR	878,000	632,160
Inventories	1,716,480	1,287,360
Total CA	2,680,112	1,926,802
Gross FA	1,197,160	1,202,950
Less: Deprec.	380,120	263,160
Net FA	817,040	939,790
Total assets	3,497,152	2,866,592

Liabilities and Equity

	1999E	1998
Accounts payable	436,800	524,160
Notes payable	600,000	720,000
Accruals	408,000	489,600
Total CL	1,444,800	1,733,760
Long-term debt	500,000	1,000,000
Common stock	1,680,936	460,000
Retained earnings	(128,584)	(327,168)
Total equity	1,552,352	132,832
Total L & E	3,497,152	2,866,592

Income Statement

	1999E	1998
Sales	7,035,600	5,834,400
COGS	5,728,000	5,728,000
Other expenses	680,000	680,000
Depreciation	116,960	116,960
Tot. op. costs	6,524,960	6,524,960
EBIT	510,640	(690,560)
Interest exp.	88,000	176,000
EBT	422,640	(866,560)
Taxes (40%)	169,056	(346,624)
Net income	253,584	(519,936)

Other Data

	1999E	1998
Shares out.	250,000	100,000
EPS	$1.014	($5.199)
DPS	$0.220	$0.110
Stock price	$12.17	$2.25
Lease pmts	$40,000	$40,000

Why are ratios useful?

- Standardize numbers; facilitate comparisons
- Used to highlight weaknesses and strengths

What are the five major categories of ratios, and what questions do they answer?

- ■ Liquidity: Can we make required payments as they fall due?

- ■ Asset management: Do we have the right amount of assets for the level of sales?

(More...)

- ■ Debt management: Do we have the right mix of debt and equity?

- ■ Profitability: Do sales prices exceed unit costs, and are sales high enough as reflected in PM, ROE, and ROA?

- ■ Market value: Do investors like what they see as reflected in P/E and M/B ratios?

Calculate the firm's forecasted current and quick ratios for 1999.

$$CR_{99} = \frac{CA}{CL} = \frac{\$2,680}{\$1,445} = 1.85x.$$

$$QR_{99} = \frac{CA - Inv.}{CL}$$

$$= \frac{\$2,680 - \$1,716}{\$1,445} = 0.67x.$$

Comments on CR and QR

	1999	1998	1997	Ind.
CR	1.85x	1.1x	2.3x	2.7x
QR	0.67x	0.4x	0.8x	1.0x

- Expected to improve but still below the industry average.
- Liquidity position is weak.

What is the inventory turnover ratio as compared to the industry average?

$$\text{Inv. turnover} = \frac{\text{Sales}}{\text{Inventories}}$$

$$= \frac{\$7,036}{\$1,716} = 4.10x.$$

	1999	1998	1997	Ind.
Inv. T.	4.1x	4.5x	4.8x	6.1x

Comments on Inventory Turnover

- Inventory turnover is below industry average.
- Firm might have old inventory, or its control might be poor.
- No improvement is currently forecasted.

DSO is the average number of days after making a sale before receiving cash.

$$DSO = \frac{Receivables}{Average\ sales\ per\ day}$$

$$= \frac{Receivables}{Sales/360} = \frac{\$878}{\$7,036/360}$$

$$= 44.9\ days.$$

Appraisal of DSO

	1999	1998	1997	Ind.
DSO	44.9	39.0	36.8	32.0

- Firm collects too slowly, and situation is getting worse.
- Poor credit policy.

Fixed Assets and Total Assets Turnover Ratios

$$\frac{Fixed\ assets}{turnover} = \frac{Sales}{Net\ fixed\ assets}$$

$$= \frac{\$7,036}{\$817} = 8.61x.$$

$$\frac{Total\ assets}{turnover} = \frac{Sales}{Total\ assets}$$

$$= \frac{\$7,036}{\$3,497} = 2.01x.$$

(More...)

	1999	1998	1997	Ind.
FA TO	8.6x	6.2x	10.0x	7.0x
TA TO	2.0x	2.0x	2.3x	2.6x

- FA turnover is expected to exceed industry average. Good.

- TA turnover not up to industry average. Caused by excessive current assets (A/R and inventory).

Calculate the forecasted operating capital requirement ratio (OCR).

$$\text{Operating capital} = \text{Net operating working capital} + \text{Net fixed assets}$$

Net operating working capital = ($14,000 + $878,000 + $1,716,480) - ($436,800 + $408,000) = $1,763,680.

Operating capital = $1,763,680 + $817,040 = $2,580,720.

(More...)

OCR = Operating capital/Sales
= $2,580,720/$7,035,600
= 36.7%.

	1999	1998	1997	Ind.
OCR	36.7%	31.8%	33.2%	29.5%

- The OCR is not improving.
- It is worse than the industry average.

Calculate the debt, TIE, and fixed charge coverage ratios.

$$\text{Debt ratio} = \frac{\text{Total debt}}{\text{Total assets}}$$

$$= \frac{\$1,445 + \$500}{\$3,497} = 55.6\%.$$

$$\text{TIE} = \frac{\text{EBIT}}{\text{Int. expense}}$$

$$= \frac{\$510.6}{\$88} = 5.8x.$$

(More...)

$$\text{Fixed charge coverage} = \text{FCC}$$

$$= \frac{\text{EBIT} + \text{Lease payments}}{\text{Interest expense} + \text{Lease pmt.} + \frac{\text{Sinking fund pmt.}}{(1 - T)}}$$

$$= \frac{\$510.6 + \$40}{\$88 + \$40 + \$0} = 4.3x.$$

All three ratios reflect use of debt, but focus on different aspects.

How do the debt management ratios compare with industry averages?

	1999	1998	1997	Ind.
D/A	55.6%	95.4%	54.8%	50.0%
TIE	5.8x	-3.9x	3.3x	6.2x
FCC	4.3x	-3.0x	2.4x	5.1x

Too much debt, but projected to improve.

---

3 - 22

After-tax operating profit margin (ATOPM)

$$\text{ATOPM} = \frac{\text{EBIT}(1 - T)}{\text{Sales}} = \frac{\$510,640(1 - 0.4)}{\$7,035,600}$$

$$= 4.4\%.$$

	1999	1998	1997	Ind.
ATOPM	4.4%	-7.1%	3.7%	4.3%

Very bad in 1998, but projected to exceed industry average in 1999.

---

3 - 23

Profit Margin (PM)

$$\text{PM} = \frac{\text{NI}}{\text{Sales}} = \frac{\$253.6}{\$7,036} = 3.6\%.$$

	1999	1998	1997	Ind.
PM	3.6%	-8.9%	2.6%	3.5%

Very bad in 1998, but projected to exceed industry average in 1999. Looking good.

---

3 - 24

Basic Earning Power (BEP)

$$\text{BEP} = \frac{\text{EBIT}}{\text{Total assets}}$$

$$= \frac{\$510.6}{\$3,497} = 14.6\%.$$

(More...)

	1999	1998	1997	Ind.
BEP	14.6%	-24.1%	14.2%	19.1%

- BEP removes effect of taxes and financial leverage. Useful for comparison.
- Projected to be below average.
- Room for improvement.

Return on Assets (ROA) and Return on Equity (ROE)

$$ROA = \frac{Net\ income}{Total\ assets}$$

$$= \frac{\$253.6}{\$3,497} = 7.3\%.$$

(More...)

$$ROE = \frac{Net\ income}{Common\ equity}$$

$$= \frac{\$253.6}{\$1,552} = 16.3\%.$$

	1999	1998	1997	Ind.
ROA	7.3%	-18.1%	6.0%	9.1%
ROE	16.3%	-391.0%	13.3%	18.2%

Both below average but improving.

Effects of Debt on ROA and ROE

- ROA is lowered by debt--interest expense lowers net income, which also lowers ROA.

- However, the use of debt lowers equity, and if equity is lowered more than net income, ROE would increase.

Calculate and appraise the P/E and M/B ratios.

Price = $12.17.

$$EPS = \frac{NI}{Shares\ out.} = \frac{\$253.6}{250} = \$1.01.$$

$$P/E = \frac{Price\ per\ share}{EPS} = \frac{\$12.17}{\$1.01} = 12x.$$

(More...)

$$BVPS = \frac{Com.\ equity}{Shares\ out.}$$

$$= \frac{\$1,552}{250} = \$6.21.$$

$$M/B = \frac{Mkt.\ price\ per\ share}{Book\ value\ per\ share}$$

$$= \frac{\$12.17}{\$6.21} = 1.96x.$$

(More...)

	1999	1998	1997	Ind.
P/E	12.0x	-0.4x	9.7x	14.2x
M/B	1.96x	1.7x	1.3x	2.4x

■ P/E: How much investors will pay for $1 of earnings. High is good.

■ M/B: How much paid for $1 of book value. Higher is good.

■ P/E and M/B are high if ROE is high, risk is low.

Explain the Du Pont System

$$\left(\begin{array}{c}\text{Profit}\\\text{margin}\end{array}\right)\left(\begin{array}{c}\text{TA}\\\text{turnover}\end{array}\right)\left(\begin{array}{c}\text{Equity}\\\text{multiplier}\end{array}\right) = \text{ROE}$$

$$\frac{\text{NI}}{\text{Sales}} \times \frac{\text{Sales}}{\text{TA}} \times \frac{\text{TA}}{\text{CE}} = \text{ROE}.$$

Year	PM		TATO		EM		ROE
1997	2.6%	x	2.3	x	2.2	=	13.2%
1998	-8.9%	x	2.0	x	21.6	=	-391.0%
1999	3.6%	x	2.0	x	2.3	=	16.3%
Ind.	3.5%	x	2.6	x	2.0	=	18.2%

The Du Pont system focuses on:

■ Expense control (PM)

■ Asset utilization (TATO)

■ Debt utilization (EM)

It shows how these factors combine to determine the ROE.

Simplified Firm Data

A/R	$ 878	Debt	$1,945
Other CA	1,802	Equity	1,552
Net FA	817		
Total assets	$3,497	L&E	$3,497

$$\frac{\text{Sales}}{\text{day}} = \frac{\$7,035,600}{360} = \$19,543.$$

Q. How would reducing DSO to 32 days affect the company?

Effect of reducing DSO from 44.9 days to 32 days:

Old A/R = $19,543 x 44.9= $878,000

New A/R = $19,543 x 32.0= 625,376

Cash freed up: $252,624

Initially shows up as additional cash.

New Balance Sheet

Added cash	$ 253	Debt	$1,945
A/R	625	Equity	1,552
Other CA	1,802		
Net FA	817		
Total assets	$3,497	Total L&E	$3,497

What could be done with the new cash? Effect on stock price and risk?

3 - 37

Potential use of freed up cash

- Repurchase stock. Higher ROE, higher EPS.
- Expand business. Higher profits.
- Reduce debt. Better debt ratio; lower interest, hence higher NI.

(More...)

3 - 38

- Inventories are also too high. Could analyze the effect of an inventory reduction on freeing up cash and increasing the quick ratio and asset management ratios. Such an analysis would be similar to what was done with DSO in previous slides.
- All these actions would likely improve stock price.

3 - 39

Would you lend money to this company?

- Maybe. The situation could improve, and the loan, with a high interest rate to reflect the risk, could be a good investment.
- However, company should not have relied so heavily on debt financing in the past.

3 - 40

What are some potential problems and limitations of financial ratio analysis?

- Comparison with industry averages is difficult if the firm operates many different divisions.
- "Average" performance is not necessarily good.
- Seasonal factors can distort ratios.

(More...)

---

3 - 41

- Window dressing techniques can make statements and ratios look better.
- Different accounting and operating practices can distort comparisons.
- Sometimes it is difficult to tell if a ratio value is "good" or "bad."
- Often, different ratios give different signals, so it is difficult to tell, on balance, whether a company is in a strong or weak financial condition.

---

3 - 42

What are some qualitative factors analysts should consider when evaluating a company's likely future financial performance?

- Are the company's revenues tied to a single customer?
- To what extent are the company's revenues tied to a single product?
- To what extent does the company rely on a single supplier?

(More...)

- What percentage of the company's business is generated overseas?
- What is the competitive situation?
- What does the future have in store?
- What is the company's legal and regulatory environment?
- And so on.

Assume that you recently graduated with a degree in finance and have just reported to work as an investment advisor at the brokerage firm of Balik and Kiefer Inc. Your first assignment is to explain the nature of the U.S. financial markets to Michelle DellaTorre, a professional tennis player who has just come to the United States from Chile. DellaTorre is a highly ranked tennis player who expects to invest substantial amounts of money through Balik and Kiefer. She is also very bright, and, therefore, she would like to understand in general terms what will happen to her money. Your boss has developed the following set of questions which you must ask and answer to explain the U.S. financial system to DellaTorre.

a. What is a market? How are physical asset markets differentiated from financial markets?

b. Differentiate between money markets and capital markets.

c. Differentiate between a primary market and a secondary market. If Apple Computer decided to issue additional common stock, and DellaTorre purchased 100 shares of this stock from Merrill Lynch, the underwriter, would this transaction be a primary market transaction or a secondary market transaction? Would it make a difference if DellaTorre purchased previously outstanding Apple stock in the over-the-counter market?

d. Describe the three primary ways in which capital is transferred between savers and borrowers.

e. Securities can be traded on organized exchanges or in the over-the-counter market. Define each of these markets, and describe how stocks are traded in each of them.

f. What do we call the price that a borrower must pay for debt capital? What is the price of equity capital? What are the four most fundamental factors that affect the cost of money, or the general level of interest rates, in the economy?

g. What is the real risk-free rate of interest (k^*) and the nominal risk-free rate (k_{RF})? How are these two rates measured?

---

h. Define the terms inflation premium (IP), default risk premium (DRP), liquidity premium (LP), and maturity risk premium (MRP). Which of these premiums is included when determining the interest rate on (1) short-term U.S. Treasury securities, (2) long-term U.S. Treasury securities, (3) short-term corporate securities, and (4) long-term corporate securities? Explain how the premiums would vary over time and among the different securities listed above.

i. DellaTorre is also interested in investing in countries other than the United States. Describe the various types of risks that arise when investing overseas.

j. What is the term structure of interest rates? What is a yield curve? At any given time, how would the yield curve facing an AAA-rated company compare with the yield curve for U.S. Treasury securities? At any given time, how would the yield curve facing a BB-rated company compare with the yield curve for U.S. Treasury securities? Draw a graph to illustrate your answer.

k. Two main theories have been advanced to explain the shape of the yield curve: (1) the expectations theory and (2) the liquidity preference theory. Briefly describe each of these theories. Do economists regard one as being "true"?

l. Suppose most investors expect the inflation rate to be 5 percent next year, 6 percent the following year, and 8 percent thereafter. The real risk-free rate is 3 percent. The maturity risk premium is zero for bonds that mature in 1 year or less, 0.1 percent for 2-year bonds, and then the MRP increases by 0.1 percent per year thereafter for 20 years, after which it is stable. What is the interest rate on 1-year, 10-year, and 20-year Treasury bonds? Draw a yield curve with these data. Is your yield curve consistent with the expectations theory or with the liquidity preference theory?

CHAPTER 4
The Financial Environment: Markets, Institutions, and Interest Rates

- Financial markets
- Types of financial institutions
- Determinants of interest rates
- Yield curves

Define these markets

- Markets in general
- Markets for physical assets
- Markets for financial assets
- Money versus capital markets
- Primary versus secondary markets
- Spot versus future markets

Three Primary Ways Capital Is Transferred Between Savers and Borrowers

- Direct transfer
- Through an investment banking house
- Through a financial intermediary

Organized Exchanges versus Over-the-Counter Market

■ Auction markets versus dealer markets (exchanges versus the OTC market)

■ NYSE versus NASDAQ system

■ Differences are narrowing

■ What do we call the price, or cost, of debt capital?

The interest rate

■ What do we call the price, or cost, of equity capital?

$$\text{Required return} = \text{Dividend yield} + \text{Capital gain} .$$

What four factors affect the cost of money?

■ Production opportunities

■ Time preferences for consumption

■ Risk

■ Expected inflation

Real versus Nominal Rates

k^* = Real risk-free rate.
T-bond rate if no inflation;
1% to 4%.

k = Any nominal rate.

k_{RF} = Rate on Treasury securities.

$$k = k^* + IP + DRP + LP + MRP.$$

Here:

k = Required rate of return on a debt security.

k^* = Real risk-free rate.

IP = Inflation premium.

DRP = Default risk premium.

LP = Liquidity premium.

MRP = Maturity risk premium.

Premiums Added to k* for Different Types of Debt

■ ST Treasury: only IP for ST inflation

■ LT Treasury: IP for LT inflation, MRP

■ ST corporate: ST IP, DRP, LP

■ LT corporate: IP, DRP, MRP, LP

---

4 - 10

What various types of risks arise when investing overseas?

Country risk: Arises from investing or doing business in a particular country. It depends on the country's economic, political, and social environment.

Exchange rate risk: If investment is denominated in a currency other than the dollar, the investment's value will depend on what happens to exchange rate.

---

4 - 11

Two Factors Lead to Exchange Rate Fluctuations

- Changes in relative inflation will lead to changes in exchange rates.

- An increase in country risk will also cause that country's currency to fall.

---

4 - 12

What is the "term structure of interest rates"? What is a "yield curve"?

- Term structure: the relationship between interest rates (or yields) and maturities.

- A graph of the term structure is called the yield curve.

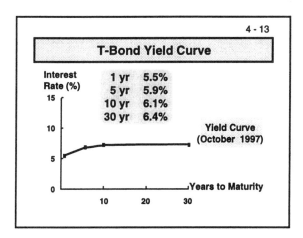

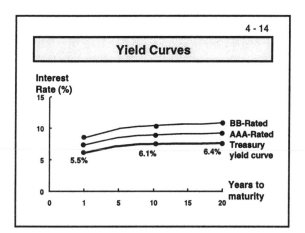

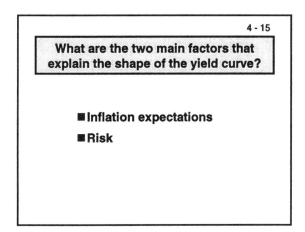

Expectations Theory

- Shape of the yield curve depends on the investors' expectations about future interest rates.

- If interest rates are expected to increase, long-term rates will be higher than short-term rates, and vice versa. Thus, the yield curve can slope up or down.

The Pure Expectations Hypothesis (PEH)

- MRP = 0.

- Long-term rates are an average of current and expected future short-term rates.

- If PEH is correct, you can use the yield curve to back out expected future interest rates.

Example

- Assume that 1-year securities yield 6% today, and the market expects that 1-year securities will yield 7% in 1 year, and that 1-year securities will yield 8% in 2 years.

- If the PEH is correct, the 2-year rate today should be (6% + 7%)/2 = 6.5%.

- If the PEH is correct, the 3-year rate today should be (6% + 7% + 8%)/3 = 7%.

Risk

- Some argue that the PEH isn't correct, because securities of different maturities have different risk.
- General view (supported by most evidence) is that lenders prefer short-term securities because they view long-term securities as riskier.
- Thus, investors demand a MRP to buy long-term securities (i.e., MRP > 0).

Combining Risk and Expectations

- Inflation for Yr 1 is 5%.
- Inflation for Yr 2 is 6%.
- Inflation for Yr 3 and beyond is 8%.
- $k^* = 3\%$.
- $MRP_t = 0.1\%(t - 1)$.

(More...)

Yield Curve Construction

Step 1: Find the average expected inflation rate over years 1 to n:

$$IP_n = \frac{\sum_{t=1}^{n} INFL_t}{n}.$$

IP_1 = 5%/1.0 = 5.00%.

IP_{10} = [5 + 6 + 8(8)]/10 = 7.5%.

IP_{20} = [5 + 6 + 8(18)]/20 = 7.75%.

Must earn these IPs to break even versus inflation; that is, these IPs would permit you to earn k* (before taxes).

Step 2: Find MRP based on this equation:

$$MRP_t = 0.1\%(t - 1).$$

MRP_1 = 0.1% x 0 = 0.0%.

MRP_{10} = 0.1% x 9 = 0.9%.

MRP_{20} = 0.1% x 19 = 1.9%.

Step 3: Add the IPs and MRPs to k*:

$$k_{RFt} = k^* + IP_t + MRP_t.$$

k_{RF} = Quoted market interest rate on treasury securities.

Assume k* = 3%:

k_{RF1} = 3% + 5% + 0.0% = 8.0%.

k_{RF10} = 3% + 7.5% + 0.9% = 11.4%.

k_{RF20} = 3% + 7.75% + 1.9% = 12.7%.

BLUEPRINTS: CHAPTER 5
RISK AND RETURN: THE BASICS

Assume that you recently graduated with a major in finance, and you just landed a job as a financial planner with Merrill Finch Inc., a large financial services corporation. Your first assignment is to invest $100,000 for a client. Because the funds are to be invested in a business at the end of one year, you have been instructed to plan for a one-year holding period. Further, your boss has restricted you to the following investment alternatives, shown with their probabilities and associated outcomes. (Disregard for now the items at the bottom of the data; you will fill in the blanks later.)

State of the Economy	Prob.	T-Bills	High Tech	Collec-tions	U.S. Rubber	Market Portfolio	2-stock Portfolio
				Returns on Alternative Investments			
				Estimated Rate of Return			
Recession	0.1	8.0%	-22.0%	28.0%	10.0%*	-13.0%	3.0%
Below avg	0.2	8.0	-2.0	14.7	-10.0	1.0	
Average	0.4	8.0	20.0	0.0	7.0	15.0	10.0%
Above avg	0.2	8.0	35.0	-10.0	45.0	29.0	
Boom	0.1	8.0	50.0	-20.0	30.0	43.0	15.0
k-Hat ($\hat{k}$)				1.7%	13.8%	15.0%	
Std dev (σ)		0.0		13.4	18.8	15.3	
Coef of var (CV)				7.9	1.4	1.0	
Beta (b)				-0.86	0.68		

* Note that the estimated returns of U.S. Rubber do not always move in the same direction as the overall economy. For example, when the economy is below average, consumers purchase fewer tires than they would if the economy was stronger. However, if the economy is in a flat-out recession, a large number of consumers who were planning to purchase a new car may choose to wait and instead purchase new tires for the car they currently own. Under these circumstances, we would expect U.S. Rubber's stock price to be higher if there is a recession than if the economy was just below average.

Merrill Finch's economic forecasting staff has developed probability estimates for the state of the economy, and its security analysts have developed a sophisticated computer program which was used to estimate the rate of return on each alternative under each state of the economy. High Tech Inc. is an electronics firm; Collections Inc. collects past-due debts; and U.S. Rubber manufactures tires and various other rubber and plastics products. Merrill Finch also maintains an "index fund" which owns a market-weighted fraction of all publicly traded stocks; you can invest in that fund, and thus obtain average stock market results. Given the situation as described, answer the following questions.

a. What are investment returns? What is the return on an investment that costs $1,000 and is sold after one year for $1,100?

---

b. (1) Why is the T-bill's return independent of the state of the economy? Do T-bills promise a completely risk-free return?

(2) Why are High Tech's returns expected to move with the economy whereas Collections' are expected to move counter to the economy?

c. Calculate the expected rate of return on each alternative and fill in the blanks on the row for $\hat{k}$ in the table above.

d. You should recognize that basing a decision solely on expected returns is only appropriate for risk-neutral individuals. Since your client, like virtually everyone, is risk averse, the riskiness of each alternative is an important aspect of the decision. One possible measure of risk is the standard deviation of returns.

(1) Calculate this value for each alternative, and fill in the blank on the row for σ in the table above.

(2) What type of risk is measured by the standard deviation?

(3) Draw a graph which shows *roughly* the shape of the probability distributions for High Tech, U.S. Rubber, and T-bills.

e. Suppose you suddenly remembered that the coefficient of variation (CV) is generally regarded as being a better measure of stand-alone risk than the standard deviation when the alternatives being considered have widely differing expected returns. Calculate the missing CVs and fill in the blanks on the row for CV in the table above. Does the CV produce the same risk rankings as the standard deviation?

f. Suppose you created a 2-stock portfolio by investing $50,000 in High Tech and $50,000 in Collections.

(1) Calculate the expected return $\left(\hat{k}_p\right)$, the standard deviation (σ_p), and the coefficient of variation (CV$_p$) for this portfolio and fill in the appropriate blanks in the table above.

(2) How does the riskiness of this 2-stock portfolio compare with the riskiness of the individual stocks if they were held in isolation?

g. Suppose an investor starts with a portfolio consisting of one randomly selected stock. What would happen (1) to the riskiness and (2) to the expected return of the portfolio as more and more randomly selected stocks were added to the portfolio? What is the implication for investors? Draw a graph of the two portfolios to illustrate your answer.

h. (1) Should portfolio effects impact the way investors think about the riskiness of individual stocks?

(2) If you decided to hold a 1-stock portfolio, and consequently were exposed to more risk than diversified investors, could you expect to be compensated for all of your risk; that is, could you earn a risk premium on that part of your risk that you could have eliminated by diversifying?

i. The expected rates of return and the beta coefficients of the alternatives as supplied by Merrill Finch's computer program are as follows:

Security	Return ($\hat{k}$)	Risk (Beta)
High Tech	17.4%	1.29
Market	15.0	1.00
U.S. Rubber	13.8	0.68
T-bills	8.0	0.00
Collections	1.7	(0.86)

(1) What is a beta coefficient, and how are betas used in risk analysis?

(2) Do the expected returns appear to be related to each alternative's market risk?

(3) Is it possible to choose among the alternatives on the basis of the information developed thus far? Use the data given at the start of the problem to construct a graph which shows how the T-bill's, High Tech's, and Collections' beta coefficients are calculated. Then discuss what betas measure and how they are used in risk analysis.

j. (1) Write out the Security Market Line (SML) equation, use it to calculate the required rate of return on each alternative, and then graph the relationship between the expected and required rates of return.

(2) How do the expected rates of return compare with the required rates of return?

(3) Does the fact that Collections has an expected return which is less than the T-bill rate make any sense?

(4) What would be the market risk and the required return of a 50-50 portfolio of High Tech and Collections? Of High Tech and U.S. Rubber?

k. (1) Suppose investors raised their inflation expectations by 3 percentage points over current estimates as reflected in the 8 percent T-bill rate. What effect would higher inflation have on the SML and on the returns required on high- and low-risk securities?

(2) Suppose instead that investors' risk aversion increased enough to cause the market risk premium to increase by 3 percentage points. (Inflation remains constant.) What effect would this have on the SML and on returns of high- and low-risk securities?

CHAPTER 5
Risk and Return: The Basics

- Basic return concepts
- Basic risk concepts
- Stand-alone risk
- Portfolio (market) risk
- Risk and return: CAPM/SML

What are investment returns?

- Investment returns measure the financial results of an investment.
- Returns may be historical or prospective (anticipated).
- Returns can be expressed in:
  - Dollar terms.
  - Percentage terms.

What is the return on an investment that costs $1,000 and is sold after 1 year for $1,100?

- Dollar return:

  $ Received - $ Invested
  $1,100   - $1,000   = $100.

- Percentage return:

  $ Return/$ Invested
  $100/$1,000   = 0.10 = 10%.

What is investment risk?

- Typically, investment returns are not known with certainty.
- Investment risk pertains to the probability of earning a return less than that expected.
- The greater the chance of a return far below the expected return, the greater the risk.

Probability distribution

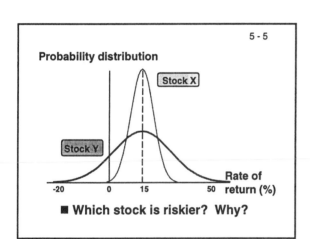

Stock X

Stock Y

Rate of return (%)

-20   0   15   50

- Which stock is riskier? Why?

Assume the Following Investment Alternatives

Economy	Prob.	T-Bill	HT	Coll	USR	MP
Recession	0.10	8.0%	-22.0%	28.0%	10.0%	-13.0%
Below avg.	0.20	8.0	-2.0	14.7	-10.0	1.0
Average	0.40	8.0	20.0	0.0	7.0	15.0
Above avg.	0.20	8.0	35.0	-10.0	45.0	29.0
Boom	0.10	8.0	50.0	-20.0	30.0	43.0
	1.00					

What is unique about the T-bill return?

- The T-bill will return 8% regardless of the state of the economy.
- Is the T-bill riskless? Explain.

Do the returns of HT and Collections move with or counter to the economy?

- HT moves with the economy, so it is positively correlated with the economy. This is the typical situation.
- Collections moves counter to the economy. Such negative correlation is unusual.

Calculate the expected rate of return on each alternative.

$\hat{k}$ = expected rate of return.

$$\hat{k} = \sum_{i=1}^{n} k_i P_i.$$

$\hat{k}_{HT}$ = 0.10(-22%) + 0.20(-2%)
      + 0.40(20%) + 0.20(35%)
      + 0.10(50%) = 17.4%.

	$\hat{k}$
HT	17.4%
Market	15.0
USR	13.8
T-bill	8.0
Collections	1.7

■ HT has the highest rate of return.
■ Does that make it best?

What is the standard deviation of returns for each alternative?

σ = Standard deviation

$$\sigma = \sqrt{\text{Variance}} = \sqrt{\sigma^2}$$
$$= \sqrt{\sum_{i=1}^{n}\left(k_i - \hat{k}\right)^2 P_i}.$$

$$\sigma = \sqrt{\sum_{i=1}^{n}\left(k_i - \hat{k}\right)^2 P_i}.$$

HT:
$$\sigma = ((-22 - 17.4)^2 0.10 + (-2 - 17.4)^2 0.20$$
$$+ (20 - 17.4)^2 0.40 + (35 - 17.4)^2 0.20$$
$$+ (50 - 17.4)^2 0.10)^{1/2} = 20.0\%.$$

$\sigma_{\text{T-bills}} = 0.0\%.$ $\sigma_{\text{Coll}} = 13.4\%.$
$\sigma_{\text{HT}} = 20.0\%.$ $\sigma_{\text{USR}} = 18.8\%.$
$\sigma_{\text{M}} = 15.3\%.$

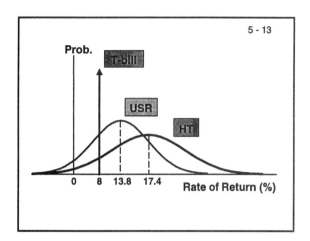

Prob.

T-bill

USR

HT

0   8   13.8   17.4   Rate of Return (%)

- Standard deviation measures the stand-alone risk of an investment.

- The larger the standard deviation, the higher the probability that returns will be far below the expected return.

- Coefficient of variation is an alternative measure of stand-alone risk.

Expected Return versus Risk

Security	Expected return	Risk, σ
HT	17.4%	20.0%
Market	15.0	15.3
USR	13.8	18.8
T-bills	8.0	0.0
Collections	1.7	13.4

- Which alternative is best?

Portfolio Risk and Return

Assume a two-stock portfolio with $50,000 in HT and $50,000 in Collections.

Calculate $\hat{k}_p$ and σ_p.

Portfolio Return, $\hat{k}_p$

$\hat{k}_p$ **is a weighted average:**

$$\hat{k}_p = \sum_{i=1}^{n} w_i \hat{k}_i.$$

$\hat{k}_p = 0.5(17.4\%) + 0.5(1.7\%) = 9.6\%.$

$\hat{k}_p$ is between $\hat{k}_{HT}$ and $\hat{k}_{Coll}.$

Alternative Method

		Estimated Return		
Economy	Prob.	HT	Coll.	Port.
Recession	0.10	-22.0%	28.0%	3.0%
Below avg.	0.20	-2.0	14.7	6.4
Average	0.40	20.0	0.0	10.0
Above avg.	0.20	35.0	-10.0	12.5
Boom	0.10	50.0	-20.0	15.0

$\hat{k}_p = (3.0\%)0.10 + (6.4\%)0.20 + (10.0\%)0.40$
$+ (12.5\%)0.20 + (15.0\%)0.10 = 9.6\%.$

(More...)

- $\sigma_p = ((3.0 - 9.6)^2 0.10 + (6.4 - 9.6)^2 0.20 + (10.0 - 9.6)^2 0.40 + (12.5 - 9.6)^2 0.20 + (15.0 - 9.6)^2 0.10)^{1/2} = 3.3\%$.

- σ_p is much lower than:
  - either stock (20% and 13.4%).
  - average of HT and Coll (16.7%).

- The portfolio provides average return but much lower risk. The key here is negative correlation.

Two-Stock Portfolios

- Two stocks can be combined to form a riskless portfolio if r = -1.0.

- Risk is not reduced at all if the two stocks have r = +1.0.

- In general, stocks have r ≈ 0.65, so risk is lowered but not eliminated.

- Investors typically hold many stocks.

- What happens when r = 0?

What would happen to the riskiness of an average 1-stock portfolio as more randomly selected stocks were added?

- σ_p would decrease because the added stocks would not be perfectly correlated, but $\hat{k}_p$ would remain relatively constant.

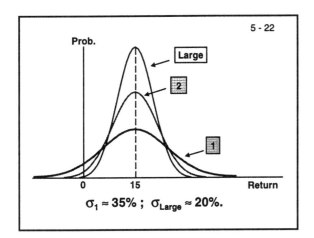

Prob.

Large

2

1

$\sigma_1 \approx 35\%$; $\sigma_{Large} \approx 20\%$.

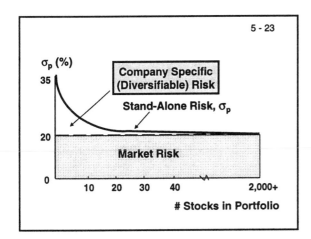

σ_p (%)

35

Company Specific (Diversifiable) Risk

Stand-Alone Risk, σ_p

20

Market Risk

0

10   20   30   40   2,000+

Stocks in Portfolio

| Stand-alone risk | = | Market risk | + | Diversifiable risk | . |

Market risk is that part of a security's stand-alone risk that *cannot* be eliminated by diversification.

Firm-specific, or diversifiable, risk is that part of a security's stand-alone risk that *can* be eliminated by diversification.

Conclusions

■ As more stocks are added, each new stock has a smaller risk-reducing impact on the portfolio.

■ σ_p falls very slowly after about 40 stocks are included. The lower limit for σ_p is about 20% = σ_M .

■ By forming well-diversified portfolios, investors can eliminate about half the riskiness of owning a single stock.

Can an investor holding one stock earn a return commensurate with its risk?

■ No. Rational investors will minimize risk by holding portfolios.

■ They bear only market risk, so prices and returns reflect this lower risk.

■ The one-stock investor bears higher (stand-alone) risk, so the return is less than that required by the risk.

How is market risk measured for individual securities?

■ Market risk, which is relevant for stocks held in well-diversified portfolios, is defined as the contribution of a security to the overall riskiness of the portfolio.

■ It is measured by a stock's beta coefficient, which measures the stock's volatility relative to the market.

■ What is the relevant risk for a stock held in isolation?

How are betas calculated?

■ Run a regression with returns on the stock in question plotted on the Y axis and returns on the market portfolio plotted on the X axis.

■ The slope of the regression line, which measures relative volatility, is defined as the stock's beta coefficient, or b.

Beta Illustration

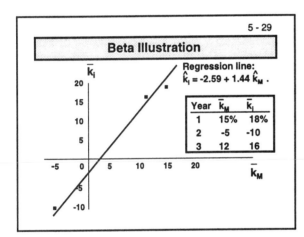

Regression line:
$\hat{k}_I = -2.59 + 1.44\, \hat{k}_M$.

Year	$\bar{k}_M$	$\bar{k}_I$
1	15%	18%
2	-5	-10
3	12	16

How is beta calculated?

■ The regression line, and hence beta, can be found using a calculator with a regression function or a spreadsheet program. In this example, b = 1.44.

■ Analysts typically use five years' of monthly returns to establish the regression line.

How is beta interpreted?

- If b = 1.0, stock has average risk.

- If b > 1.0, stock is riskier than average.

- If b < 1.0, stock is less risky than average.

- Most stocks have betas in the range of 0.5 to 1.5.

- Can a stock have a negative beta?

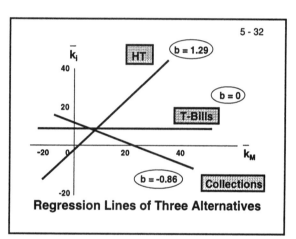

Regression Lines of Three Alternatives

Expected Return versus Market Risk

Security	Expected return	Risk, b
HT	17.4%	1.29
Market	15.0	1.00
USR	13.8	0.68
T-bills	8.0	0.00
Collections	1.7	-0.86

- Which of the alternatives is best?

Use the SML to calculate each alternative's required return.

- The Security Market Line (SML) is part of the Capital Asset Pricing Model (CAPM).
- SML: $k_i = k_{RF} + (k_M - k_{RF})b_i$.
- Assume $k_{RF} = 8\%$; $\hat{k}_M = k_M = 15\%$.
- $RP_M = k_M - k_{RF} = 15\% - 8\% = 7\%$.

Required Rates of Return

$$
\begin{aligned}
k_{HT} &= 8.0\% + (15.0\% - 8.0\%)(1.29) \\
&= 8.0\% + (7\%)(1.29) \\
&= 8.0\% + 9.0\% & = 17.0\%. \\
k_M &= 8.0\% + (7\%)(1.00) & = 15.0\%. \\
k_{USR} &= 8.0\% + (7\%)(0.68) & = 12.8\%. \\
k_{T\text{-}bill} &= 8.0\% + (7\%)(0.00) & = 8.0\%. \\
k_{Coll} &= 8.0\% + (7\%)(-0.86) & = 2.0\%.
\end{aligned}
$$

Expected versus Required Returns

	$\hat{k}$	k	
HT	17.4%	17.0%	Undervalued
Market	15.0	15.0	Fairly valued
USR	13.8	12.8	Undervalued
T-bills	8.0	8.0	Fairly valued
Coll	1.7	2.0	Overvalued

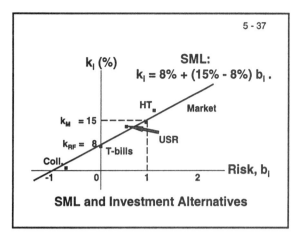

k_I (%)

SML:
$$k_I = 8\% + (15\% - 8\%) \, b_I \, .$$

HT

Market

$k_M = 15$

$k_{RF} = 8$

T-bills

USR

Coll.

Risk, b_I

-1   0   1   2

SML and Investment Alternatives

Calculate beta for a portfolio with 50% HT and 50% Collections

b_p = Weighted average
= $0.5(b_{HT}) + 0.5(b_{Coll})$
= $0.5(1.29) + 0.5(-0.86)$
= 0.22.

What is the required rate of return on the HT/Collections portfolio?

k_p = Weighted average k
= $0.5(17\%) + 0.5(2\%)$ = 9.5%.

Or use SML:

$k_p = k_{RF} + (k_M - k_{RF}) \, b_p$
= $8.0\% + (15.0\% - 8.0\%)(0.22)$
= $8.0\% + 7\%(0.22) = 9.5\%$.

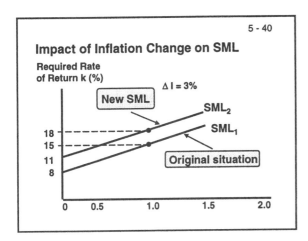

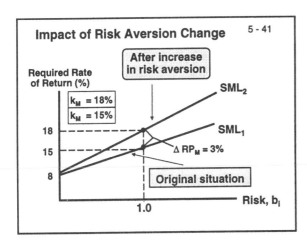

5 - 42

Has the CAPM been verified through empirical tests?

- ■ No. The statistical tests have problems that make empirical verification virtually impossible.

- ■ Investors may be concerned about both stand-alone risk and market risk.

- ■ Furthermore, investors' required returns are based on future risk, but betas are based on historical data.

To begin, briefly review the Chapter 5 Mini Case. Then, extend your knowledge or risk and return by answering the following questions.

a. What is the Capital Asset Pricing Model (CAPM)? What are the assumptions that underlie the model?

b. Construct a reasonable, but hypothetical, graph which shows risk, as measured by portfolio standard deviation, on the X axis and expected rate of return on the Y axis. Now add an illustrative feasible (or attainable) set of portfolios, and show what portion of the feasible set is efficient. What makes a particular portfolio efficient? Don't worry about specific values when constructing the graph--merely illustrate how things look with "reasonable" data.

c. Now add a set of indifference curves to the graph created for Part b. What do these curves represent? What is the optimal portfolio for this investor? Finally, add a second set of indifference curves which leads to the selection of a different optimal portfolio. Why do the two investors choose different portfolios?

d. Now add the risk-free asset. What impact does this have on the efficient frontier?

e. Write out the equation for the Capital Market Line (CML) and draw it on the graph. Interpret the CML. Now add a set of indifference curves, and illustrate how an investor's optimal portfolio is some combination of the risky portfolio and the risk-free asset. What is the composition of the risky portfolio?

f. What is a characteristic line? How is this line used to estimate a stock's beta coefficient? Write out and explain the formula that relates total risk, market risk, and diversifiable risk.

g. What are two potential tests that can be conducted to verify the CAPM? What are the results of such tests? What is Roll's critique of CAPM tests?

h. Briefly explain the difference between the CAPM and the Arbitrage Pricing Theory (APT).

i. What is the current status of the APT?

CHAPTER 6
Risk and Return: Extensions

- ■ Capital Asset Pricing Model (CAPM)
  - ● Efficient frontier
  - ● Capital Market Line (CML)
  - ● Security Market Line (SML)
  - ● Beta calculation
- ■ Arbitrage pricing theory

What is the CAPM?

- ■ The CAPM is an equilibrium model that specifies the relationship between risk and required rate of return for assets held in well-diversified portfolios.
- ■ It is based on the premise that only one factor affects risk.
- ■ What is that factor?

What are the assumptions of the CAPM?

- ■ Investors all think in terms of a single holding period.
- ■ All investors have identical expectations.
- ■ Investors can borrow or lend unlimited amounts at the risk-free rate.
  (More...)

- All assets are perfectly divisible.
- There are no taxes and no transactions costs.
- All investors are price takers, that is, investors' buying and selling won't influence stock prices.
- Quantities of all assets are given and fixed.

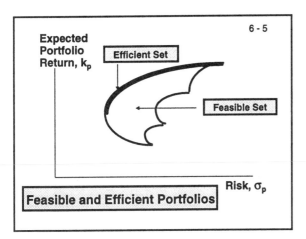

Feasible and Efficient Portfolios

- The feasible set of portfolios represents all portfolios that can be constructed from a given set of stocks.
- An efficient portfolio is one that offers:
  - the most return for a given amount of risk, or
  - the least risk for a give amount of return.
- The collection of efficient portfolios is called the efficient set or efficient frontier.

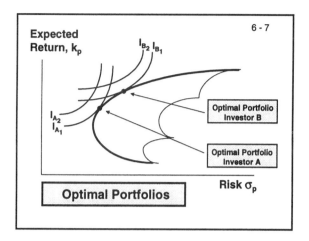

Expected Return, k_p

I_{B_2} I_{B_1}

I_{A_2}
I_{A_1}

Optimal Portfolio Investor B

Optimal Portfolio Investor A

Risk σ_p

Optimal Portfolios

- Indifference curves reflect an investor's attitude toward risk as reflected in his or her risk/return tradeoff function. They differ among investors because of differences in risk aversion.

- An investor's optimal portfolio is defined by the tangency point between the efficient set and the investor's indifference curve.

What impact does k_{RF} have on the efficient frontier?

- When a risk-free asset is added to the feasible set, investors can create portfolios that combine this asset with a portfolio of risky assets.

- The straight line connecting k_{RF} with M, the tangency point between the line and the old efficient set, becomes the new efficient frontier.

Efficient Set with a Risk-Free Asset

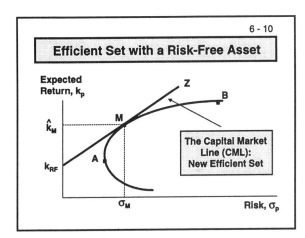

What is the Capital Market Line?

- The Capital Market Line (CML) is all linear combinations of the risk-free asset and Portfolio M.
- Portfolios below the CML are inferior.
  - The CML defines the new efficient set.
  - All investors will choose a portfolio on the CML.

The CML Equation

$$\hat{k}_p = k_{RF} + \left[\frac{\hat{k}_M - k_{RF}}{\sigma_M} \right] \sigma_{p}.$$

Intercept   Slope   Risk measure

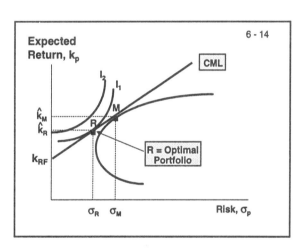

What does the CML tell us?

- The expected rate of return on any efficient portfolio is equal to the risk-free rate plus a risk premium.
- The optimal portfolio for any investor is the point of tangency between the CML and the investor's indifference curves.

Expected Return, k_p

CML

$\hat{k}_M$
$\hat{k}_R$

M

R

k_{RF}

R = Optimal Portfolio

σ_R σ_M Risk, σ_p

What is the Security Market Line (SML)?

- The CML gives the risk/return relationship for efficient portfolios.
- The Security Market Line (SML), also part of the CAPM, gives the risk/return relationship for individual stocks.
  - The SML was discussed in Chapter 5.
  - The measure of risk used in the SML is the beta coefficient, b.

How are betas calculated?

- Run a regression line of past returns on Stock i versus returns on the market.
- The regression line is called the characteristic line.
- The slope coefficient of the characteristic line is defined as the beta coefficient.

Illustration of beta calculation

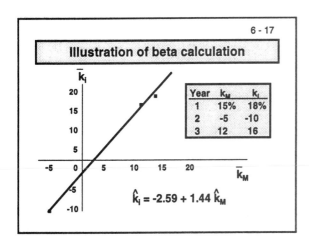

Year	k_M	k_i
1	15%	18%
2	-5	-10
3	12	16

$$\hat{k}_i = -2.59 + 1.44\ \hat{k}_M$$

How do you find beta?

- "By Eye": Plot points, draw in regression line; slope is rise/run. The rise is the difference in k_i, the run is the difference in k_M.
- Calculator: Enter the data points and use the "least squares regression" function:

$$k_i = a + bk_M = -2.59 + 1.44\ k_M.$$

(More...)

■ **Computer:** In the real world, analysts use a computer with statistical or spreadsheet software to perform the regression.

- At least a year's worth of weekly or monthly returns are used.

- Most analysts use 5 years of monthly returns.

(More...)

■ If beta = 1.0, stock is average risk.

■ If beta > 1.0, stock is riskier than average.

■ If beta < 1.0, stock is less risky than average.

■ Most stocks have betas in the range of 0.5 to 1.5.

What is the relationship between stand-alone, market, and diversifiable risk.

$$\sigma_j^2 = b_j^2 \, \sigma_M^2 + \sigma_{e_j}^2.$$

σ_j^2 = variance
= stand-alone risk of Stock j.

$b_j^2 \, \sigma_M^2$ = market risk of Stock j.

$\sigma_{e_j}^2$ = variance of error term
= diversifiable risk of Stock j.

What are two potential tests that can be conducted to verify the CAPM?

- Beta stability tests
- Tests based on the slope of the SML

Tests of the SML indicate:

- A more-or-less linear relationship between realized returns and market risk.

- Slope is less than predicted.

- Irrelevance of diversifiable risk specified in the CAPM model can be questioned.

(More...)

- Betas of individual securities are not good estimators of future risk.

- Betas of portfolios of 10 or more randomly selected stocks are reasonably stable.

- Past portfolio betas are good estimates of future portfolio volatility.

Are there problems with the CAPM tests?

- **Yes.**
  - Richard Roll questioned whether it was even conceptually possible to test the CAPM.
  - Roll showed that it is virtually impossible to prove investors behave in accordance with CAPM theory.

What are our conclusions regarding the CAPM?

- **It is impossible to verify.**
- **Recent studies have questioned its validity.**
- **Investors seem to be concerned with both market risk and stand-alone risk. Therefore, the SML may not produce a correct estimate of k_i.** (More...)

- **CAPM/SML concepts are based on expectations, yet betas are calculated using historical data. A company's historical data may not reflect investors' expectations about future riskiness.**
- **Other models are being developed that will one day replace the CAPM, but it still provides a good framework for thinking about risk and return.**

What is the difference between the CAPM and the Arbitrage Pricing Theory (APT)?

- The CAPM is a single factor model.

- The APT proposes that the relationship between risk and return is more complex and may be due to multiple factors such as GDP growth, expected inflation, tax rate changes, and dividend yield.

Required Return for Stock i under the APT

$$k_i = k_{RF} + (k_1 - k_{RF})b_1 + (k_2 - k_{RF})b_2 + ... + (k_j - k_{RF})b_j.$$

k_j = required rate of return on a portfolio sensitive only to economic Factor j.

b_j = sensitivity of Stock i to economic Factor j.

What is the status of the APT?

- The APT is being used for some real world applications.

- Its acceptance has been slow because the model does not specify what factors influence stock returns.

- More research on risk and return models is needed to find a model that is theoretically sound, empirically verified, and easy to use.

BLUEPRINTS: CHAPTER 7
TIME VALUE OF MONEY

Assume that you are nearing graduation and that you have applied for a job with a local bank. As part of the bank's evaluation process, you have been asked to take an examination which covers several financial analysis techniques. The first section of the test addresses discounted cash flow analysis. See how you would do by answering the following questions.

a. Draw time lines for (1) a $100 lump sum cash flow at the end of year 2, (2) an ordinary annuity of $100 per year for 3 years, and (3) an uneven cash flow stream of -$50, $100, $75, and $50 at the end of Years 0 through 3.

b. (1) What is the future value of an initial $100 after 3 years if it is invested in an account paying 10 percent annual interest?

   (2) What is the present value of $100 to be received in 3 years if the appropriate interest rate is 10 percent?

c. We sometimes need to find how long it will take a sum of money (or anything else) to grow to some specified amount. For example, if a company's sales are growing at a rate of 20 percent per year, how long will it take sales to double?

d. What is the difference between an ordinary annuity and an annuity due? What type of annuity is shown below? How would you change it to the other type of annuity?

e. (1) What is the future value of a 3-year ordinary annuity of $100 if the appropriate interest rate is 10 percent?

   (2) What is the present value of the annuity?

   (3) What would the future and present values be if the annuity were an annuity due?

f. What is the present value of the following uneven cash flow stream? The appropriate interest rate is 10 percent, compounded annually.

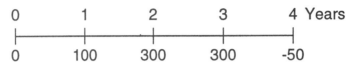

0	1	2	3	4 Years
0	100	300	300	-50

g. What annual interest rate will cause $100 to grow to $125.97 in 3 years?

h. (1) Will the future value be larger or smaller if we compound an initial amount more often than annually, for example, every 6 months, or *semiannually*, holding the stated interest rate constant? Why?

    (2) Define (a) the stated, or quoted, or nominal, rate (i_{Nom}), (b) the periodic rate (i_{Per}), and (c) the effective annual rate (EAR).

    (3) What is the effective annual rate for a nominal rate of 10 percent, compounded semiannually? Compounded quarterly? Compounded daily?

    (4) What is the future value of $100 after 3 years under 10 percent semiannual compounding? Quarterly compounding?

i. Will the effective annual rate ever be equal to the nominal (quoted) rate?

j. (1) What is the value at the end of Year 3 of the following cash flow stream if the quoted interest rate is 10 percent, compounded semiannually?

0	1	2	3 Years
0	100	100	100

    (2) What is the PV of the same stream?

    (3) Is the stream an annuity?

    (4) An important rule is that you should *never* show a nominal rate on a time line or use it in calculations unless what condition holds? (Hint: Think of annual compounding, when i_{Nom} = EAR = i_{Per}.) What would be wrong with your answer to questions j(1) and j(2) if you used the nominal rate (10 %) rather than the periodic rate ($i_{Nom}/2$ = 10%/2 = 5%)?

k. (1) Construct an amortization schedule for a $1,000, 10 percent annual rate loan with 3 equal installments.

    (2) What is the annual interest expense for the borrower, and the annual interest income for the lender, during Year 2?

l. Suppose on January 1, 1999, you deposit $100 in an account that pays a nominal, or quoted, interest rate of 11.33463 percent, with interest added (compounded) daily. How much will you have in your account on October 1, or after 9 months?

m. Now, suppose you leave your money in the bank for 21 months. Thus, on January 1, 1999, you deposit $100 in an account that pays a 12 percent effective annual interest rate. How much will be in your account on October 1, 2000?

n. Suppose someone offered to sell you a note calling for the payment of $1,000 15 months from today. They offer to sell it to you for $850. You have $850 in a bank time deposit which pays a 6.76649 percent nominal rate with daily compounding, which is a 7 percent effective annual interest rate, and you plan to leave the money in the bank unless you buy the note. The note is not risky—you are sure it will be paid on schedule. Should you buy the note? Check the decision in three ways: (1) by comparing your future value if you buy the note versus leaving your money in the bank, (2) by comparing the PV of the note with your current bank account, and (3) by comparing the EAR on the note versus that of the bank account.

o. Suppose the note discussed in Part n had a cost of $850, but called for 5 quarterly payments of $190 each, with the first payment due in 3 months rather than $1,000 at the end of 15 months. Would it be a good investment for you?

CHAPTER 7
Time Value of Money

- Future value
- Present value
- Rates of return
- Amortization

Time lines show timing of cash flows.

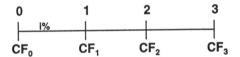

```
0        1        2        3
|---i%---|--------|--------|
CF₀     CF₁      CF₂      CF₃
```

$$0 \quad 1 \quad 2 \quad 3$$
$$CF_0 \quad CF_1 \quad CF_2 \quad CF_3$$

Tick marks at ends of periods, so Time 0 is today; Time 1 is the end of Period 1; or the beginning of Period 2.

Time line for a $100 lump sum due at the end of Year 2.

```
0      i%      1        2  Year
|--------------|--------|
                       100
```

Time line for an ordinary annuity of $100 for 3 years.

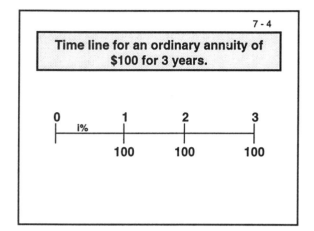

Time line for uneven CFs: -$50 at t = 0 and $100, $75, and $50 at the end of Years 1 through 3.

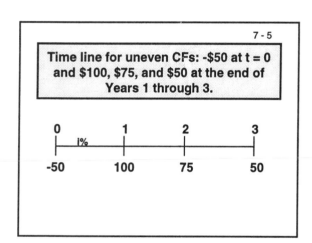

What's the FV of an initial $100 after 3 years if i = 10%?

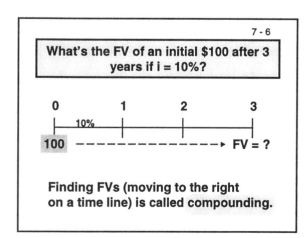

Finding FVs (moving to the right on a time line) is called compounding.

After 1 year:

$$FV_1 = PV + INT_1 = PV + PV(i)$$
$$= PV(1 + i)$$
$$= \$100(1.10)$$
$$= \$110.00.$$

After 2 years:

$$FV_2 = PV(1 + i)^2$$
$$= \$100(1.10)^2$$
$$= \$121.00.$$

After 3 years:

$$FV_3 = PV(1 + i)^3$$
$$= \$100(1.10)^3$$
$$= \$133.10.$$

In general,

$$FV_n = PV(1 + i)^n.$$

Four Ways to Find FVs

- Solve the equation with a regular calculator.
- Use tables.
- Use a financial calculator.
- Use a spreadsheet.

Financial Calculator Solution

Financial calculators solve this equation:

$$FV_n = PV(1 + I)^n.$$

There are 4 variables. If 3 are known, the calculator will solve for the 4th.

Here's the setup to find FV:

INPUTS	3	10	-100	0	
	N	I/YR	PV	PMT	FV
OUTPUT					133.10

Clearing automatically sets everything to 0, but for safety enter PMT = 0.

Set: P/YR = 1, END.

What's the PV of $100 due in 3 years if i = 10%?

Finding PVs is discounting, and it's the reverse of compounding.

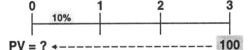

PV = ?

Solve $FV_n = PV(1 + i)^n$ for PV:

$$PV = \frac{FV_n}{(1+i)^n} = FV_n\left(\frac{1}{1+i}\right)^n$$

$$PV = \$100\left(\frac{1}{1.10}\right)^3$$
$$= \$100\,(0.7513) = \$75.13.$$

Financial Calculator Solution

INPUTS	3	10		0	100
	N	I/YR	PV	PMT	FV
OUTPUT			-75.13		

Either PV or FV must be negative. Here PV = -75.13. Put in $75.13 today, take out $100 after 3 years.

Finding the Time to Double

```
0        1        2        ?
|--------|--------|--------|
   20%
-1                         2
```

$$FV = PV(1 + i)^n$$
$$\$2 = \$1(1 + 0.20)^n$$
$$(1.2)^n = \$2/\$1 = 2$$
$$n\,LN(1.2) = LN(2)$$
$$n = LN(2)/LN(1.2)$$
$$n = 0.693/0.182 = 3.8.$$

Financial Calculator

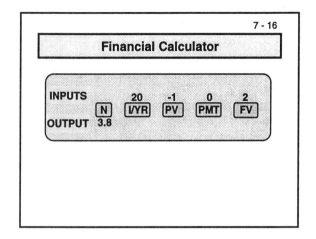

INPUTS

N	I/YR	PV	PMT	FV
	20	-1	0	2

OUTPUT 3.8

What's the difference between an ordinary annuity and an annuity due?

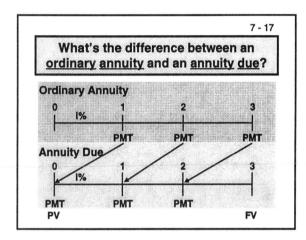

Ordinary Annuity

```
0        1        2        3
    i%
        PMT      PMT      PMT
```

Annuity Due

```
0        1        2        3
    i%
PMT      PMT      PMT
PV                         FV
```

What's the FV of a 3-year ordinary annuity of $100 at 10%?

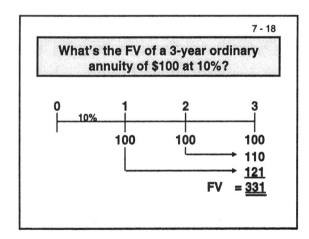

```
0        1        2        3
    10%
        100      100      100
                          110
                          121
              FV  = 331
```

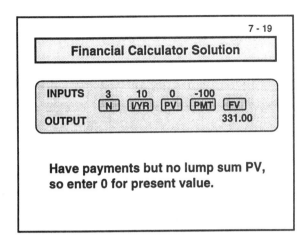

7 - 19

Financial Calculator Solution

INPUTS	3	10	0	-100	
	N	I/YR	PV	PMT	FV
OUTPUT					331.00

Have payments but no lump sum PV, so enter 0 for present value.

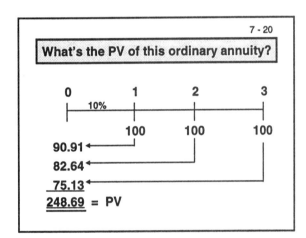

7 - 20

What's the PV of this ordinary annuity?

```
   0          1          2          3
      10%
   |          |          |          |
             100        100        100
 90.91 ◄──────┘          |          |
 82.64 ◄─────────────────┘          |
 75.13 ◄────────────────────────────┘
248.69 = PV
```

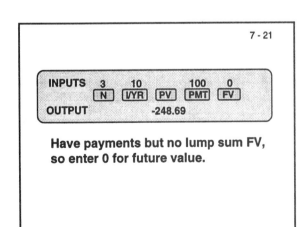

7 - 21

INPUTS	3	10		100	0
	N	I/YR	PV	PMT	FV
OUTPUT			-248.69		

Have payments but no lump sum FV, so enter 0 for future value.

Spreadsheet Solution

	A	B	C	D
1	0	1	2	3
2		100	100	100
3	248.69			

Excel Formula in cell A3:

=NPV(10%,B2:D2)

Special Function for Annuities

For ordinary annuities, this formula in cell A3 gives 248.96:

=PV(10%,3,-100)

A similar function gives the future value of 331.00:

=FV(10%,3,-100)

Find the FV and PV if the annuity were an annuity due.

Switch from "End" to "Begin".
Then enter variables to find PVA_3 =
$273.55.

INPUTS	3	10		100	0
	N	I/YR	PV	PMT	FV
OUTPUT			-273.55		

Then enter PV = 0 and press FV to find
FV = $364.10.

Excel Function for Annuities Due

Change the formula to:

=PV(10%,3,-100,0,1)

The fourth term, 0, tells the function
there are no other cash flows. The
fifth term tells the function that it is an
annuity due. A similar function gives
the future value of an annuity due:

=FV(10%,3,-100,0,1)

What is the PV of this uneven cash flow stream?

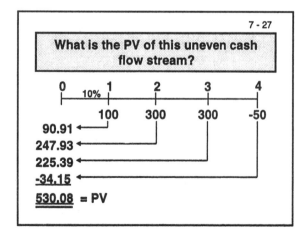

```
 0    10%  1      2      3      4
 |---------|------|------|------|
           100    300    300    -50
 90.91 ←
247.93 ←
225.39 ←
-34.15 ←
530.08  = PV
```

■ Input in "CFLO" register:

CF_0 =   0

CF_1 = 100

CF_2 = 300

CF_3 = 300

CF_4 = -50

■ Enter I = 10%, then press NPV button to get NPV = 530.09. (Here NPV = PV.)

Spreadsheet Solution

	A	B	C	D	E
1	0	1	2	3	4
2		100	300	300	-50
3	530.09				

Excel Formula in cell A3:

=NPV(10%,B2:E2)

What interest rate would cause $100 to grow to $125.97 in 3 years?

$100(1 + i)^3 = \$125.97.$

$(1 + i)^3 = \$125.97/\$100 = 1.2597$

$1 + i = (1.2597)^{1/3} = 1.08$

$i = 8\%.$

INPUTS	3		-100	0	125.97
	N	I/YR	PV	PMT	FV
OUTPUT		8%			

Will the FV of a lump sum be larger or smaller if we compound more often, holding the stated I% constant? Why?

LARGER! If compounding is more frequent than once a year--for example, semiannually, quarterly, or daily--interest is earned on interest more often.

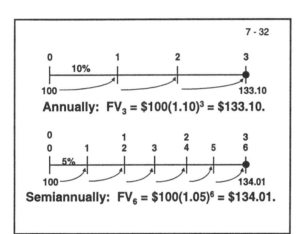

Annually: $FV_3 = \$100(1.10)^3 = \$133.10$.

Semiannually: $FV_6 = \$100(1.05)^6 = \$134.01$.

We will deal with 3 different rates:

i_{Nom} = nominal, or stated, or quoted, rate per year.

i_{Per} = periodic rate.

EAR = EFF% = effective annual rate .

- i_{Nom} is stated in contracts. Periods per year (m) must also be given.
- Examples:
  - 8%; Quarterly
  - 8%, Daily interest (365 days)

- Periodic rate = $i_{Per} = i_{Nom}/m$, where m is number of compounding periods per year. m = 4 for quarterly, 12 for monthly, and 360 or 365 for daily compounding.
- Examples:

8% quarterly: $i_{Per} = 8\%/4 = 2\%$.

8% daily (365): $i_{Per} = 8\%/365 = 0.021918\%$.

- Effective Annual Rate (EAR = EFF%): The annual rate which causes PV to grow to the same FV as under multi-period compounding.

Example: EFF% for 10%, semiannual:

$$FV = (1 + i_{Nom}/m)^m$$
$$= (1.05)^2 = 1.1025.$$

EFF% = 10.25% because

$$(1.1025)^1 = 1.1025.$$

Any PV would grow to same FV at 10.25% annually or 10% semiannually.

- An investment with monthly payments is different from one with quarterly payments. Must put on EFF% basis to compare rates of return. Use EFF% only for comparisons.

- Banks say "interest paid daily." Same as compounded daily.

How do we find EFF% for a nominal rate of 10%, compounded semiannually?

$$\text{EFF\%} = \left(1 + \frac{i_{Nom}}{m}\right)^m - 1$$

$$= \left(1 + \frac{0.10}{2}\right)^2 - 1.0$$

$$= (1.05)^2 - 1.0$$

$$= 0.1025 = 10.25\%.$$

Or use a financial calculator.

EAR = EFF% of 10%

EAR_{Annual} $\qquad = \boxed{10\%.}$

$\text{EAR}_Q \qquad = (1 + 0.10/4)^4 - 1 \qquad = \boxed{10.38\%.}$

$\text{EAR}_M \qquad = (1 + 0.10/12)^{12} - 1 \qquad = \boxed{10.47\%.}$

$\text{EAR}_{D(360)} \quad = (1 + 0.10/360)^{360} - 1 = \boxed{10.52\%.}$

FV of \$100 after 3 years under 10% semiannual compounding? Quarterly?

$$FV_n = PV\left(1 + \frac{i_{Nom}}{m}\right)^{mn}.$$

$$FV_{3S} = \$100\left(1 + \frac{0.10}{2}\right)^{2 \times 3}$$

$$= \$100(1.05)^6 = \$134.01.$$

$$FV_{3Q} = \$100(1.025)^{12} = \$134.49.$$

Can the effective rate ever be equal to the nominal rate?

- Yes, but only if annual compounding is used, i.e., if $m = 1$.

- If $m > 1$, EFF% will always be greater than the nominal rate.

When is each rate used?

i_{Nom}: Written into contracts, quoted by banks and brokers. <u>Not</u> used in calculations or shown on time lines.

i_{Per}: Used in calculations, shown on time lines.

If i_{Nom} has annual compounding, then $i_{Per} = i_{Nom}/1 = i_{Nom}$.

EAR = EFF%: Used to compare returns on investments with different payments per year.

(Used for calculations if and only if dealing with annuities where payments don't match interest compounding periods.)

What's the value at the end of Year 3 of the following CF stream if the quoted interest rate is 10%, compounded semiannually?

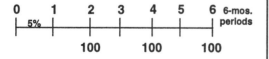

■ Payments occur annually, but compounding occurs each 6 months.

■ So we can't use normal annuity valuation techniques.

1st Method: Compound Each CF

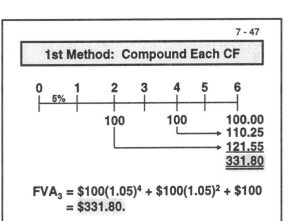

$FVA_3 = \$100(1.05)^4 + \$100(1.05)^2 + \$100$
$= \$331.80.$

2nd Method: Treat as an Annuity

Could you find the FV with a financial calculator?

Yes, by following these steps:

a. Find the EAR for the quoted rate:

$$EAR = \left(1 + \frac{0.10}{2}\right)^2 - 1 = 10.25\%.$$

---

b. Use EAR = 10.25% as the annual rate in your calculator:

```
INPUTS     3      10.25    0      -100
          [N]    [I/YR]   [PV]   [PMT]   [FV]
OUTPUT                                   331.80
```

What's the PV of this stream?

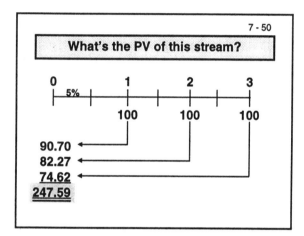

```
0          1          2          3
   5%
          100        100        100

90.70 ◄
82.27 ◄
74.62 ◄
247.59
```

Amortization

Construct an amortization schedule for a $1,000, 10% annual rate loan with 3 equal payments.

Step 1: Find the required payments.

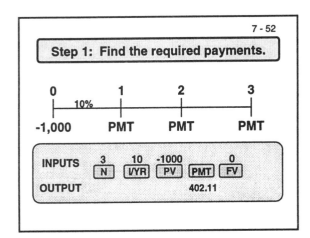

INPUTS

| $\frac{3}{N}$ | $\frac{10}{I/YR}$ | $\frac{-1000}{PV}$ | PMT | $\frac{0}{FV}$ |

OUTPUT   402.11

Step 2: Find interest charge for Year 1.

$$INT_t = Beg\ bal_t\ (i)$$
$$INT_1 = \$1,000(0.10) = \boxed{\$100.}$$

Step 3: Find repayment of principal in Year 1.

$$Repmt = PMT - INT$$
$$= \$402.11 - \$100$$
$$= \boxed{\$302.11.}$$

Step 4: Find ending balance after Year 1.

$$End\ bal\ = Beg\ bal - Repmt$$
$$= \$1,000 - \$302.11 = \$697.89.$$

Repeat these steps for Years 2 and 3 to complete the amortization table.

---

7 - 55

YR	BEG BAL	PMT	INT	PRIN PMT	END BAL
1	$1,000	$402	$100	$302	$698
2	698	402	70	332	366
3	366	402	37	366	0
TOT		1,206.34	206.34	1,000	

Interest declines. Tax implications.

---

7 - 56

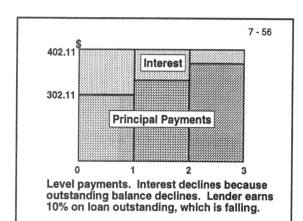

Level payments. Interest declines because outstanding balance declines. Lender earns 10% on loan outstanding, which is falling.

---

7 - 57

- Amortization tables are widely used--for home mortgages, auto loans, business loans, retirement plans, and so on. They are very important!

- Financial calculators (and spreadsheets) are great for setting up amortization tables.

On January 1 you deposit $100 in an account that pays a nominal interest rate of 11.33463%, with daily compounding (365 days).

How much will you have on October 1, or after 9 months (273 days)? (Days given.)

---

i_{Per} = 11.33463%/365
     = 0.031054% per day.

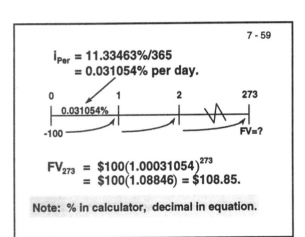

FV_{273} = $100(1.00031054)^{273}$
        = $100(1.08846) = $108.85.

Note: % in calculator, decimal in equation.

---

i_{Per} = i_{Nom}/m
     = 11.33463/365
     = 0.031054% per day.

INPUTS	273		-100	0	
	N	I/YR	PV	PMT	FV
OUTPUT					108.85

Enter i in one step.
Leave data in calculator.

Now suppose you leave your money in the bank for 21 months, which is 1.75 years or 273 + 365 = 638 days.

How much will be in your account at maturity?

Answer: Override N = 273 with N = 638. FV = $121.91.

---

i_{Per} = 0.031054% per day.

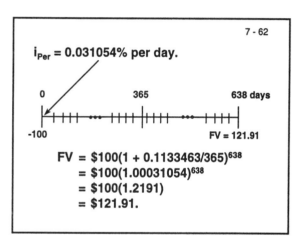

$$FV = \$100(1 + 0.1133463/365)^{638}$$
$$= \$100(1.00031054)^{638}$$
$$= \$100(1.2191)$$
$$= \$121.91.$$

You are offered a note which pays $1,000 in 15 months (or 456 days) for $850. You have $850 in a bank which pays a 6.76649% nominal rate, with 365 daily compounding, which is a daily rate of 0.018538% and an EAR of 7.0%. You plan to leave the money in the bank if you don't buy the note. The note is riskless.

Should you buy it?

$i_{Per} = 0.018538\%$ per day.

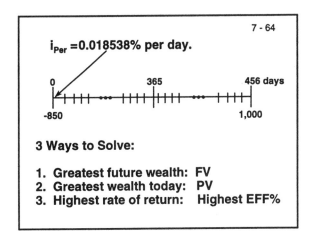

```
        0            365           456 days
        |             |             |
      -850                        1,000
```

3 Ways to Solve:

1. Greatest future wealth: FV
2. Greatest wealth today: PV
3. Highest rate of return: Highest EFF%

---

1. Greatest Future Wealth

Find FV of $850 left in bank for 15 months and compare with note's FV = $1,000.

$FV_{Bank} = \$850(1.00018538)^{456}$
$= \$924.97$ in bank.

Buy the note: $1,000 > $924.97.

Calculator Solution to FV:

$i_{Per} = i_{Nom}/m$
$= 6.76649\%/365$
$= 0.018538\%$ per day.

INPUTS	456	↓	-850	0	
	N	I/YR	PV	PMT	FV
OUTPUT					924.97

Enter i_{Per} in one step.

---

2. Greatest Present Wealth

Find PV of note, and compare with its $850 cost:

$$PV = \$1,000/(1.00018538)^{456}$$
$$= \$918.95.$$

INPUTS	6.76649/365 =				
	456	.018538		0	1000
	N	I/YR	PV	PMT	FV
OUTPUT			-918.95		

PV of note is greater than its $850 cost, so buy the note. Raises your wealth.

---

3. Rate of Return

Find the EFF% on note and compare with 7.0% bank pays, which is your opportunity cost of capital:

$$FV_n = PV(1 + i)^n$$
$$\$1,000 = \$850(1 + i)^{456}$$

Now we must solve for i.

INPUTS	456		-850	0	1000
	N	I/YR	PV	PMT	FV
OUTPUT	0.035646% per day				

Convert % to decimal:

Decimal = 0.035646/100 = 0.00035646.

$$EAR = EFF\% = (1.00035646)^{365} - 1$$
$$= 13.89\%.$$

Using interest conversion:

  P/YR = 365
NOM% = 0.035646(365) = 13.01
 EFF% = 13.89

Since 13.89% > 7.0% opportunity cost, buy the note.

Robert Balik and Carol Kiefer are vice-presidents of Mutual of Chicago Insurance Company and codirectors of the company's pension fund management division. A major new client, the California League of Cities, has requested that Mutual of Chicago present an investment seminar to the mayors of the represented cities, and Balik and Kiefer, who will make the actual presentation, have asked you to help them by answering the following questions. Because the Walt Disney Company operates in one of the league's cities, you are to work Disney into the presentation. (See the vignette which opened the chapter for information on Disney.)

a. What are the key features of a bond?

b. What are call provisions and sinking fund provisions? Do these provisions make bonds more or less risky?

c. How is the value of any asset whose value is based on expected future cash flows determined?

d. How is the value of a bond determined? What is the value of a 10-year, $1,000 par value bond with a 10 percent annual coupon if its required rate of return is 10 percent?

e. (1) What would be the value of the bond described in Part d if, just after it had been issued, the expected inflation rate rose by 3 percentage points, causing investors to require a 13 percent return? Would we now have a discount or a premium bond? (If you do not have a financial calculator, $PVIF_{13\%,10} = 0.2946$; $PVIFA_{13\%,10} = 5.4262$.)

(2) What would happen to the bonds' value if inflation fell, and k_d declined to 7 percent? Would we now have a premium or a discount bond?

(3) What would happen to the value of the 10-year bond over time if the required rate of return remained at 13 percent, or if it remained at 7 percent? (Hint: With a financial calculator, enter N, I, PMT, and FV, and then change (override) N to see what happens to the PV as the bond approaches maturity.)

f. (1) What is the yield to maturity on a 10-year, 9 percent annual coupon, $1,000 par value bond that sells for $887.00? That sells for $1,134.20? What does the fact that a bond sells at a discount or at a premium tell you about the relationship between k_d and the bond's coupon rate?

---

(2) What are the total return, the current yield, and the capital gains yield for the discount bond? (Assume the bond is held to maturity and the company does not default on the bond.)

g. What is *interest rate (or price) risk*? Which bond has more interest rate risk, an annual payment 1-year bond or a 10-year bond? Why?

h. What is *reinvestment rate risk*? Which has more reinvestment rate risk, a 1-year bond or a 10-year bond?

i. How does the equation for valuing a bond change if semiannual payments are made? Find the value of a 10-year, semiannual payment, 10 percent coupon bond if nominal $k_d = 13\%$. (Hint: $PVIF_{6.5\%,20} = 0.2838$ and $PVIFA_{6.5\%,20} = 11.0185$.)

j. Suppose you could buy, for $1,000, either a 10 percent, 10-year, annual payment bond or a 10 percent, 10-year, semiannual payment bond. They are equally risky. Which would you prefer? If $1,000 is the proper price for the semiannual bond, what is the equilibrium price for the annual payment bond?

k. Suppose a 10-year, 10 percent, semiannual coupon bond with a par value of $1,000 is currently selling for $1,135.90, producing a nominal yield to maturity of 8 percent. However, the bond can be called after 5 years for a price of $1,050.

(1) What is the bond's *nominal yield to call (YTC)*?

(2) If you bought this bond, do you think you would be more likely to earn the YTM or the YTC? Why?

l. Disney's bonds were issued with a yield to maturity of 7.5 percent. Does the yield to maturity represent the promised or expected return on the bond?

m. Disney's bonds were rated AA- by S&P. Would you consider these bonds investment grade or junk bonds?

n. What factors determine a company's bond rating?

CHAPTER 8
Bonds and Their Valuation

- Key features of bonds
- Bond valuation
- Measuring yield
- Assessing risk

Key Features of a Bond

1. **Par value:** Face amount; paid at maturity. Assume $1,000.

2. **Coupon interest rate:** Stated interest rate. Multiply by par value to get dollars of interest. Generally fixed.

(More...)

3. **Maturity:** Years until bond must be repaid. Declines.

4. **Issue date:** Date when bond was issued.

5. **Default risk:** Risk that issuer will not make interest or principal payments.

How does adding a call provision affect a bond?

- Issuer can refund if rates decline. That helps the issuer but hurts the investor.
- Therefore, borrowers are willing to pay more, and lenders require more, on callable bonds.
- Most bonds have a deferred call and a declining call premium.

What's a sinking fund?

- Provision to pay off a loan over its life rather than all at maturity.
- Similar to amortization on a term loan.
- Reduces risk to investor, shortens average maturity.
- But not good for investors if rates decline after issuance.

Sinking funds are generally handled in 2 ways

1. Call x% at par per year for sinking fund purposes.
2. Buy bonds on open market.

Company would call if k_d is below the coupon rate and bond sells at a premium. Use open market purchase if k_d is above coupon rate and bond sells at a discount.

Financial Asset Valuation

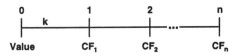

$$PV = \frac{CF_1}{(1+k)^1} + \frac{CF_2}{(1+k)^2} + \ldots + \frac{CF_n}{(1+k)^n}.$$

■ The discount rate (k_I) is the <u>opportunity cost of capital</u>, i.e., the rate that could be earned on alternative investments of equal risk.

$$k_i = k^* + IP + LP + MRP + DRP$$

for debt securities.

What's the value of a 10-year, 10% coupon bond if $k_d = 10\%$?

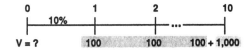

$$V_B = \frac{\$100}{(1+k_d)^1} + \ldots + \frac{\$100}{(1+k_d)^{10}} + \frac{\$1,000}{(1+k_d)^{10}}$$

$$= \$90.91 + \ldots + \$38.55 + \$385.54$$
$$= \$1,000.$$

The bond consists of a 10-year, 10% annuity of $100/year plus a $1,000 lump sum at t = 10:

PV annuity = $ 614.46
PV maturity value = 385.54
Value of bond = $1,000.00

INPUTS

	10	10		100	1000
	N	I/YR	PV	PMT	FV

OUTPUT -1,000

What would happen if expected inflation rose by 3%, causing k = 13%?

INPUTS

	10	13		100	1000
	N	I/YR	PV	PMT	FV

OUTPUT -837.21

When k_d rises, <u>above</u> the coupon rate, the bond's value falls <u>below</u> par, so it sells at a discount.

What would happen if inflation fell, and k_d declined to 7%?

INPUTS

	10	7		100	1000
	N	I/YR	PV	PMT	FV

OUTPUT -1,210.71

If coupon rate > k_d, price rises above par, and bond sells at a premium.

Suppose the bond was issued 20 years ago and now has 10 years to maturity. What would happen to its value over time if the required rate of return remained at 10%, or at 13%, or at 7%?

Bond Value ($)

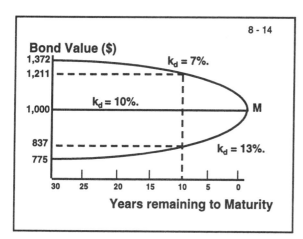

$k_d = 7\%.$

$k_d = 10\%.$

$k_d = 13\%.$

1,372
1,211
1,000
837
775

M

30   25   20   15   10   5   0

Years remaining to Maturity

- At maturity, the value of any bond must equal its par value.
- The value of a premium bond would decrease to $1,000.
- The value of a discount bond would increase to $1,000.
- A par bond stays at $1,000 if k_d remains constant.

What's "yield to maturity"?

- YTM is the rate of return earned on a bond held to maturity. Also called "promised yield."

What's the YTM on a 10-year, 9% annual coupon, $1,000 par value bond that sells for $887?

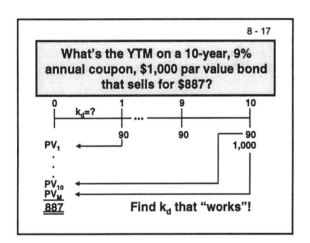

Find k_d that "works"!

Find k_d

$$V_B = \frac{INT}{(1 + k_d)^1} + \cdots + \frac{INT}{(1 + k_d)^N} + \frac{M}{(1 + k_d)^N}$$

$$887 = \frac{90}{(1 + k_d)^1} + \cdots + \frac{90}{(1 + k_d)^{10}} + \frac{1,000}{(1 + k_d)^{10}}$$

INPUTS	10		-887	90	1000
	N	I/YR	PV	PMT	FV
OUTPUT		10.91			

■ If coupon rate < k_d, bond sells at a discount.

■ If coupon rate = k_d, bond sells at its par value.

■ If coupon rate > k_d, bond sells at a premium.

■ If k_d rises, price falls.

■ Price = par at maturity.

Find YTM if price were $1,134.20.

INPUTS	10		-1134.2	90	1000
	N	I/YR	PV	PMT	FV
OUTPUT		7.08			

Sells at a premium. Because coupon = 9% > k_d = 7.08%, bond's value > par.

Definitions

Current yield = $\dfrac{\text{Annual coupon pmt}}{\text{Current price}}$

Capital gains yield = $\dfrac{\text{Change in price}}{\text{Beginning price}}$

Exp total return = YTM = Exp Curr yld + Exp cap gains yld

Find current yield and capital gains yield for a 9%, 10-year bond when the bond sells for $887 and YTM = 10.91%.

Current yield $= \dfrac{\$90}{\$887}$

$= 0.1015 = \boxed{10.15\%.}$

YTM = Current yield + Capital gains yield.

Cap gains yield = YTM - Current yield
$= 10.91\% - 10.15\%$
$= \boxed{0.76\%.}$

Could also find values in Years 1 and 2, get difference, and divide by value in Year 1. Same answer.

What's interest rate (or price) risk? Does a 1-year or 10-year 10% bond have more risk?

Interest rate risk: Rising k_d causes bond's price to fall.

k_d	1-year	Change	10-year	Change
5%	$1,048		$1,386	
		4.8%		38.6%
10%	1,000		1,000	
		4.4%		25.1%
15%	956		749	

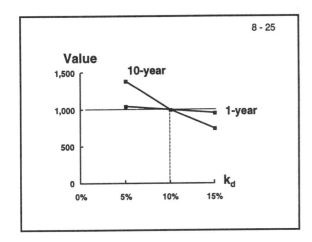

Value

What is reinvestment rate risk?

The risk that CFs will have to be reinvested in the future at lower rates, reducing income.

Illustration: Suppose you just won $500,000 playing the lottery. You'll invest the money and live off the interest. You buy a 1-year bond with a YTM of 10%.

Year 1 income = $50,000. At year-end get back $500,000 to reinvest.

If rates fall to 3%, income will drop from $50,000 to $15,000. Had you bought 30-year bonds, income would have remained constant.

- Long-term bonds: High interest rate risk, low reinvestment rate risk.
- Short-term bonds: Low interest rate risk, high reinvestment rate risk.
- Nothing is riskless!

True or False: "All 10-year bonds have the same price and reinvestment rate risk."

False! Low coupon bonds have less reinvestment rate risk but more price risk than high coupon bonds.

Semiannual Bonds

1. Multiply years by 2 to get periods = 2n.
2. Divide nominal rate by 2 to get periodic rate = $k_d/2$.
3. Divide annual INT by 2 to get PMT = INT/2.

INPUTS	2n	$k_d/2$	OK	INT/2	OK
	N	I/YR	PV	PMT	FV
OUTPUT					

Find the value of 10-year, 10% coupon, semiannual bond if k_d = 13%.

	2(10)	13/2		100/2	
INPUTS	20	6.5		50	1000
	N	I/YR	PV	PMT	FV
OUTPUT			-834.72		

You could buy, for $1,000, either a 10%, 10-year, annual payment bond or an equally risky 10%, 10-year semiannual bond. Which would you prefer?

The semiannual bond's EFF% is:

$$EFF\% = \left(1 + \frac{i_{Nom}}{m}\right)^m - 1 = \left(1 + \frac{0.10}{2}\right)^2 - 1 = 10.25\% .$$

10.25% > 10% EFF% on annual bond, so buy semiannual bond.

If $1,000 is the proper price for the semiannual bond, what is the proper price for the annual payment bond?

■ Semiannual bond has k_{Nom} = 10%, with EFF% = 10.25%. Should earn same EFF% on annual payment bond, so:

	10	10.25		100	1000
INPUTS					
	N	I/YR	PV	PMT	FV
OUTPUT			-984.80		

■ At a price of $984.80, the annual and semiannual bonds would be in equilibrium, because investors would earn EFF% = 10.25% on either bond.

A 10-year, 10% semiannual coupon, $1,000 par value bond is selling for $1,135.90 with an 8% yield to maturity. It can be called after 5 years at $1,050.

What's the bond's nominal yield to call (YTC)?

INPUTS	10		-1135.9	50	1050
	N	I/YR	PV	PMT	FV
OUTPUT		3.765 x 2 = 7.53%			

k_{Nom} = 7.53% is the rate brokers would quote. Could also calculate EFF% to call:

EFF% = $(1.03765)^2 - 1$ = 7.672%.

This rate could be compared to monthly mortgages, and so on.

If you bought bonds, would you be more likely to earn YTM or YTC?

- Coupon rate = 10% vs. YTC = k_d = 7.53%. Could raise money by selling new bonds which pay 7.53%.
- Could thus replace bonds which pay $100/year with bonds that pay only $75.30/year.
- Investors should expect a call, hence YTC = 7.5%, not YTM = 8%.

- In general, if a bond sells at a premium, then (1) coupon > k_d, so (2) a call is likely.
- So, expect to earn:
  - YTC on premium bonds.
  - YTM on par & discount bonds.

- Disney recently issued 100-year bonds with a YTM of 7.5%--this represents the promised return. The expected return was less than 7.5% when the bonds were issued.
- If issuer defaults, investors receive less than the promised return. Therefore, the expected return on corporate and municipal bonds is less than the promised return.

Bond Ratings Provide One Measure of Default Risk

	Investment Grade				Junk Bonds			
Moody's	Aaa	Aa	A	Baa	Ba	B	Caa	C
S&P	AAA	AA	A	BBB	BB	B	CCC	D

What factors affect default risk and bond ratings?

- ■ Financial performance
  - ● Debt ratio
  - ● TIE, FCC ratios
  - ● Current ratios

(More...)

- ■ Provisions in the bond contract
  - ● Secured versus unsecured debt
  - ● Senior versus subordinated debt
  - ● Guarantee provisions
  - ● Sinking fund provisions
  - ● Debt maturity

(More...)

- ■ **Other factors**
  - ● **Earnings stability**
  - ● **Regulatory environment**
  - ● **Potential product liability**
  - ● **Accounting policies**

_____

_____

_____

_____

_____

_____

_____

Robert Balik and Carol Kiefer are senior vice-presidents of the Mutual of Chicago Insurance Company. They are co-directors of the company's pension fund management division, with Balik having responsibility for fixed income securities (primarily bonds) and Kiefer being responsible for equity investments. A major new client, the California League of Cities, has requested that Mutual of Chicago present an investment seminar to the mayors of the represented cities, and Balik and Kiefer, who will make the actual presentation, have asked you to help them.

To illustrate the common stock valuation process, Balik and Kiefer have asked you to analyze the Bon Temps Company, an employment agency that supplies word processor operators and computer programmers to businesses with temporarily heavy workloads. You are to answer the following questions.

a. Describe briefly the legal rights and privileges of common stockholders.

b. (1) Write out a formula that can be used to value any stock, regardless of its dividend pattern.

 (2) What is a constant growth stock? How are constant growth stocks valued?

 (3) What happens if a company has a constant g which exceeds k_s? Will many stocks have expected $g > k_s$ in the short run (i.e., for the next few years)? In the long run (i.e., forever)?

c. Assume that Bon Temps has a beta coefficient of 1.2, that the risk-free rate (the yield on T-bonds) is 7 percent, and that the required rate of return on the market is 12 percent. What is the required rate of return on the firm's stock?

d. Assume that Bon Temps is a constant growth company whose last dividend (D_0, which was paid yesterday) was $2.00, and whose dividend is expected to grow indefinitely at a 6 percent rate.

 (1) What is the firm's expected dividend stream over the next 3 years?

 (2) What is the firm's current stock price?

 (3) What is the stock's expected value 1 year from now?

 (4) What are the expected dividend yield, the capital gains yield, and the total return during the first year?

e. Now assume that the stock is currently selling at $30.29. What is the expected rate of return on the stock?

f. What would the stock price be if its dividends were expected to have zero growth?

g. Now assume that Bon Temps is expected to experience supernormal growth of 30 percent for the next 3 years, then to return to its long-run constant growth rate of 6 percent. What is the stock's value under these conditions? What is its expected dividend yield and capital gains yield in Year 1? In Year 4?

h. Is the stock price based more on long-term or short-term expectations? Answer this by finding the percentage of Bon Temps current stock price based on dividends expected more than 3 years in the future.

i. Suppose Bon Temps is expected to experience zero growth during the first 3 years and then to resume its steady-state growth of 6 percent in the fourth year. What is the stock's value now? What is its expected dividend yield and its capital gains yield in Year 1? In Year 4?

j. Finally, assume that Bon Temps' earnings and dividends are expected to decline by a constant 6 percent per year, that is, $g = -6\%$. Why would anyone be willing to buy such a stock and at what price should it sell? What would be the dividend yield and capital gains yield in each year?

k. Bon Temps embarks on an aggressive expansion that requires additional capital. Management decides to finance the expansion by borrowing $40 million and by halting dividend payments to increase retained earnings. The projected free cash flows for the next three years are -$5 million, $10 million, and $20 million. After the third year, free cash flow is projected to grow at a constant 6 percent. The overall cost of capital is $k_c = 10\%$. What is the value of bon Temps' operations? If it has 10 million shares of stock, what is the price per share?

l. What does market equilibrium mean?

m. If equilibrium does not exist, how will it be established?

n. What is the Efficient Markets Hypothesis, what are its three forms, and what are its implications?

o. Phyfe Company recently issued preferred stock. It pays an annual dividend of $5, and the issue price was $50 per share. What is the expected return to an investor on this preferred stock?

9 - 1

CHAPTER 9
Stocks and Their Valuation

- Features of common stock
- Determining common stock values
- Efficient markets
- Preferred stock

---

9 - 2

Facts about Common Stock

- Represents ownership.
- Ownership implies control.
- Stockholders elect directors.
- Directors elect management.
- Management's goal: Maximize stock price.

---

9 - 3

What's classified stock? How might classified stock be used?

- Classified stock has special provisions.
- Could classify existing stock as founders' shares, with voting rights but dividend restrictions.
- New shares might be called "Class A" shares, with voting restrictions but full dividend rights.

When is a stock sale an initial public offering (IPO)?

- A firm "goes public" through an IPO when the stock is first offered to the public.

- Prior to an IPO, shares are typically owned by the firm's managers, key employees, and, in many situations, venture capital providers.

Stock Value = PV of Dividends

$$\hat{P}_0 = \frac{D_1}{(1+k_s)^1} + \frac{D_2}{(1+k_s)^2} + \frac{D_3}{(1+k_s)^3} + \ldots + \frac{D_\infty}{(1+k_s)^\infty}$$

What is a constant growth stock?

One whose dividends are expected to grow forever at a constant rate, g.

For a constant growth stock,

$$D_1 = D_0(1+g)^1$$
$$D_2 = D_0(1+g)^2$$
$$D_t = D_t(1+g)^t$$

If g is constant, then:

$$\hat{P}_0 = \frac{D_0(1+g)}{k_s - g} = \frac{D_1}{k_s - g}$$

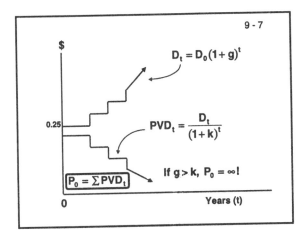

$$D_t = D_0(1+g)^t$$

$$PVD_t = \frac{D_t}{(1+k)^t}$$

If $g > k$, $P_0 = \infty$!

$$P_0 = \sum PVD_t$$

0.25

$

0   Years (t)

---

9 - 8

What happens if $g > k_s$?

$$\hat{P}_0 = \frac{D_1}{k_s - g} \quad \text{requires} \quad k_s > g.$$

- If $k_s < g$, get negative stock price, which is nonsense.

- We can't use model unless (1) $g < k_s$ and (2) g is expected to be constant forever. Because g must be a long-term growth rate, it cannot be $> k_s$.

---

9 - 9

Assume beta = 1.2, k_{RF} = 7%, and k_M = 12%. What is the required rate of return on the firm's stock?

Use the SML to calculate k_s:

$$\begin{aligned} k_s &= k_{RF} + (k_M - k_{RF})b_{Firm} \\ &= 7\% + (12\% - 7\%)\,(1.2) \\ &= 13\%. \end{aligned}$$

D_0 was $2.00 and g is a constant 6%. Find the expected dividends for the next 3 years, and their PVs. k_s = 13%.

```
      0   g=6%   1        2        3        4
      |----------|--------|--------|--------|
  D_0=2.00     2.12    2.2472   2.3820
  1.8761  13%
  1.7599  ←
  1.6508  ←
```

What's the stock's market value? D_0 = 2.00, k_s = 13%, g = 6%.

Constant growth model:

$$\hat{P}_0 = \frac{D_0(1+g)}{k_s - g} = \frac{D_1}{k_s - g}$$

$$= \frac{\$2.12}{0.13 - 0.06} = \frac{\$2.12}{0.07}\ \$30.29.$$

What is the stock's market value one year from now, $\hat{P}_1$?

- D_1 will have been paid, so expected dividends are D_2, D_3, D_4 and so on. Thus,

$$\hat{P}_1 = \frac{D_2}{k_s - g}$$

$$= \frac{\$2.2472}{0.07} = \$32.10.$$

Find the expected dividend yield and capital gains yield during the first year.

$$\text{Dividend yield} = \frac{D_1}{P_0} = \frac{\$2.12}{\$30.29} = 7.0\%.$$

$$\text{CG Yield} = \frac{\hat{P}_1 - P_0}{P_0} = \frac{\$32.10 - \$30.29}{\$30.29}$$
$$= 6.0\%.$$

Find the total return during the first year.

- Total return = Dividend yield + Capital gains yield.
- Total return = 7% + 6% = 13%.
- Total return = 13% = k_s.
- For constant growth stock:
    Capital gains yield = 6% = g.

Rearrange model to rate of return form:

$$\hat{P}_0 = \frac{D_1}{k_s - g} \text{ to } \hat{k}_s = \frac{D_1}{P_0} + g.$$

Then, $\hat{k}_s$ = $2.12/$30.29 + 0.06
        = 0.07 + 0.06 = 13%.

What would P_0 be if g = 0?

The dividend stream would be a perpetuity.

```
0    k_s=13%   1        2        3
|─────────────|────────|────────|────────────►
              2.00     2.00     2.00
```

$$\hat{P}_0 = \frac{PMT}{k} = \frac{\$2.00}{0.13} = \$15.38.$$

If we have supernormal growth of 30% for 3 years, then a long-run constant g = 6%, what is $\hat{P}_0$? k is still 13%.

- Can no longer use constant growth model.
- However, growth becomes constant after 3 years.

Nonconstant growth followed by constant growth:

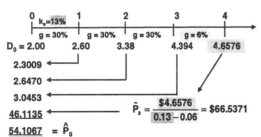

```
        0  k_s=13%   1          2          3          4
        |───────────|──────────|──────────|──────────|────►
           g = 30%    g = 30%    g = 30%     g = 6%
D_0 = 2.00    2.60       3.38       4.394      4.6576
   2.3009 ◄────┘
   2.6470 ◄──────────────┘
   3.0453 ◄─────────────────────────┘
  46.1135 ◄─────────────── $\hat{P}_3 = \frac{\$4.6576}{0.13 - 0.06} = \$66.5371$
  54.1067  = $\hat{P}_0$
```

What is the expected dividend yield and capital gains yield at t = 0? At t = 4?

At t = 0:

$$\text{Dividend yield} = \frac{D_1}{P_0} = \frac{\$2.60}{\$54.11} = 4.8\%.$$

CG Yield = 13.0% - 4.8% = 8.2%.

(More...)

■ During nonconstant growth, dividend yield and capital gains yield are not constant.

■ If current growth is greater than g, current capital gains yield is greater than g.

■ After t = 3, g = constant = 6%, so the t t = 4 capital gains gains yield = 6%.

■ Because k_s = 13%, the t = 4 dividend yield = 13% - 6% = 7%.

Is the stock price based on short-term growth?

■ The current stock price is $54.11.

■ The PV of dividends beyond year 3 is $46.11 ($R_3$ discounted back to t = 0).

■ The percentage of stock price due to "long-term" dividends is:

$$\frac{\$46.11}{\$54.11} = 85.2\%.$$

If most of a stock's value is due to long-term cash flows, why do so many managers focus on quarterly earnings?

- Sometimes changes in quarterly earnings are a signal of future changes in cash flows. This would affect the current stock price.

- Sometimes managers have bonuses tied to quarterly earnings.

Suppose g = 0 for t = 1 to 3, and then g is a constant 6%. What is $\hat{P}_0$?

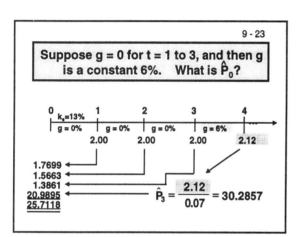

$$\hat{P}_3 = \frac{2.12}{0.07} = 30.2857$$

What is dividend yield and capital gains yield at t = 0 and at t = 3?

t = 0: $\dfrac{D_1}{P_0} = \dfrac{2.00}{\$25.72} = 7.8\%$.

CGY = 13.0% - 7.8% = 5.2%.

t = 3: Now have constant growth with g = capital gains yield = 6% and dividend yield = 7%.

If g = -6%, would anyone buy the stock? If so, at what price?

Firm still has earnings and still pays dividends, so $\hat{P}_0 > 0$:

$$\hat{P}_0 = \frac{D_0(1+g)}{k_s - g} = \frac{D_1}{k_s - g}$$

$$= \frac{\$2.00(0.94)}{0.13 - (-0.06)} = \frac{\$1.88}{0.19} = \$9.89.$$

What are the annual dividend and capital gains yield?

Capital gains yield = g = -6.0%.

Dividend yield = 13.0% - (-6.0%)
= 19.0%.

Both yields are constant over time, with the high dividend yield (19%) offsetting the negative capital gains yield.

Expansion Plan

■ Finance expansion by borrowing $40 million and halting dividends.
■ Projected free cash flows (FCF):
 ● Year 1 FCF = -$5 million.
 ● Year 2 FCF = $10 million.
 ● Year 3 FCF = $20 million.
 ● FCF grows at constant rate of 6% after year 3. (More...)

- The corporate cost of capital, k_c, is 10%.

- The company has 10 million shares of stock.

Find the value of operations by discounting the free cash flows at the cost of capital.

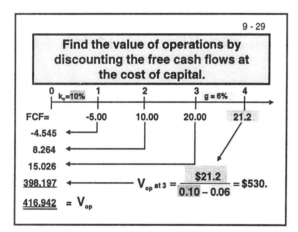

$$V_{op \, at \, 3} = \frac{\$21.2}{0.10 - 0.06} = \$530.$$

Find the price per share of common stock.

Value of equity = Value of operations
- Value of debt

= $416.94 - $40

= $376.94 million.

Price per share = $376.94/10 = $37.69.

What is market equilibrium?

In equilibrium, stock prices are stable. There is no general tendency for people to buy versus to sell.

The expected price, $\hat{P}$, must equal the actual price, P. In other words, the fundamental value must be the same as the price.

(More...)

In equilibrium, expected returns must equal required returns:

$$\hat{k}_s = D_1/P_0 + g = k_s = k_{RF} + (k_M - k_{RF})b.$$

How is equilibrium established?

If $\hat{k}_s = \dfrac{\hat{D}_1}{P_0} + g > k_s$, then P_0 is "too low."

If the price is lower than the fundamental value, then the stock is a "bargain."

Buy orders will exceed sell orders, the price will be bid up, and D_1/P_0 falls until

$$D_1/P_0 + g = \hat{k}_s = k_s.$$

Why do stock prices change?

$$\hat{P}_0 = \frac{D_1}{k_i - g}$$

- $k_i = k_{RF} + (k_M - k_{RF})b_i$ could change.
  - Inflation expectations
  - Risk aversion
  - Company risk

- g could change.

What's the Efficient Market Hypothesis (EMH)?

Securities are normally in equilibrium and are "fairly priced." One cannot "beat the market" except through good luck or inside information.

(More...)

1. **Weak-form EMH:**
   Can't profit by looking at past trends. A recent decline is no reason to think stocks will go up (or down) in the future.
   Evidence supports weak-form EMH, but "technical analysis" is still used.

2. Semistrong-form EMH:
All publicly available information is reflected in stock prices, so it doesn't pay to pore over annual reports looking for undervalued stocks. Largely true.

3. Strong-form EMH:
All information, even inside information, is embedded in stock prices. Not true--insiders can gain by trading on the basis of insider information, but that's illegal.

Markets are generally efficient because:

1. 100,000 or so trained analysts--MBAs, CFAs, and PhDs--work for firms like Fidelity, Merrill, Morgan, and Prudential.

2. These analysts have similar access to data and megabucks to invest.

3. Thus, news is reflected in P_0 almost instantaneously.

Preferred Stock

- Hybrid security.
- Similar to bonds in that preferred stockholders receive a fixed dividend which must be paid before dividends can be paid on common stock.
- However, unlike bonds, preferred stock dividends can be omitted without fear of pushing the firm into bankruptcy.

What's the expected return on preferred stock with $V_{ps} = \$50$ and annual dividend = \$5?

$$V_{ps} = \$50 = \frac{\$5}{\hat{k}_{ps}}$$

$$\hat{k}_{ps} = \frac{\$5}{\$50} = 0.10 = 10.0\%.$$

During the last few years, Cox Technologies has been too constrained by the high cost of capital to make many capital investments. Recently, though, capital costs have been declining, and the company has decided to look seriously at a major expansion program that had been proposed by the marketing department. Assume that you are an assistant to Jerry Lee, the financial vice-president. Your first task is to estimate Cox's cost of capital. Lee has provided you with the following data, which he believes may be relevant to your task:

1. The firm's tax rate is 40 percent.

2. The current price of Cox's 12 percent coupon, semiannual payment, noncallable bonds with 15 years remaining to maturity is $1,153.72. Cox does not use short-term interest-bearing debt on a permanent basis. New bonds would be privately placed with no flotation cost.

3. The current price of the firm's 10 percent, $100 par value, quarterly dividend, perpetual preferred stock is $113.10. Cox would incur flotation costs of $2.00 per share on a new issue.

4. Cox's common stock is currently selling at $50 per share. Its last dividend (D_0) was $4.19, and dividends are expected to grow at a constant rate of 5 percent in the foreseeable future. Cox's beta is 1.2, the yield on T-bonds is 7 percent, and the market risk premium is estimated to be 6 percent. For the bond-yield-plus-risk-premium approach, the firm uses a 4 percentage point risk premium.

5. Cox's target capital structure is 30 percent long-term debt, 10 percent preferred stock, and 60 percent common equity.

To structure the task somewhat, Lee has asked you to answer the following questions.

a. (1) What sources of capital should be included when you estimate Cox's weighted average cost of capital (WACC)?

(2) Should the component costs be figured on a before-tax or an after-tax basis?

(3) Should the costs be historical (embedded) costs or new (marginal) costs?

b. What is the market interest rate on Cox's debt and its component cost of debt?

c. (1) What is the firm's cost of preferred stock?

(2) Cox's preferred stock is riskier to investors than its debt, yet the preferred's yield to investors is lower than the yield to maturity on the debt. Does this suggest that you have made a mistake? (Hint: Think about taxes.)

d. (1) What are the two primary ways companies raise common equity?

   (2) Why is there a cost associated with reinvested earnings?

   (3) Cox doesn't plan to issue new shares of common stock. Using the CAPM approach, what is Cox's estimated cost of equity?

e. (1) What is the estimated cost of equity using the discounted cash flow (DCF) approach?

   (2) Suppose the firm has historically earned 15 percent on equity (ROE) and retained 35 percent of earnings, and investors expect this situation to continue in the future. How could you use this information to estimate the future dividend growth rate, and what growth rate would you get? Is this consistent with the 5 percent growth rate given earlier?

   (3) Could the DCF method be applied if the growth rate was not constant? How?

f. What is the cost of equity based on the bond-yield-plus-risk-premium method?

g. What is your final estimate for the cost of equity, k_s?

h. What is Cox's weighted average cost of capital (WACC)?

i. What are four common mistakes in estimating the WACC that Cox should avoid?

j. What are the three types of risk, and which is most relevant for estimating the cost of capital?

k. What are two ways to estimate divisional betas?

l. Should Cox use the same cost of capital for all projects? How might it adjust the cost of capital for different projects?

CHAPTER 10
The Cost of Capital

- Cost of Capital Components
  - Debt
  - Preferred
  - Common Equity
- WACC

What types of long-term capital do firms use?

- Long-term debt
- Preferred stock
- Common equity

Should we focus on before-tax or after-tax capital costs?

- Tax effects associated with financing can be incorporated either in capital budgeting cash flows or in cost of capital.
- Most firms incorporate tax effects in the cost of capital. Therefore, focus on after-tax costs.
- Only cost of debt is affected.

Should we focus on historical (embedded) costs or new (marginal) costs?

The cost of capital is used primarily to make decisions which involve raising and investing new capital. So, we should focus on marginal costs.

A 15-year, 12% semiannual bond sells for $1,153.72. What's k_d?

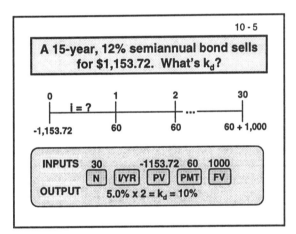

Component Cost of Debt

- Interest is tax deductible, so

$$k_{d\ AT} = k_{d\ BT}(1 - T)$$
$$= 10\%(1 - 0.40) = 6\%.$$

- Use nominal rate.
- Flotation costs small, so ignore.

What's the cost of preferred stock?
$P_P = \$113.10$; 10%Q; Par = $100; F = \$2.

Use this formula:

$$k_{ps} = \frac{D_{ps}}{P_n} = \frac{0.1(\$100)}{\$113.10 - \$2.00}$$

$$= \frac{\$10}{\$111.10} = 0.090 = 9.0\%.$$

Picture of Preferred

```
    0   k_ps = ?   1        2              ∞
    |──────────────|────────|────  ...  ───|
  -111.1         2.50     2.50           2.50
```

$$\$111.10 = \frac{D_Q}{k_{Per}} = \frac{\$2.50}{k_{Per}}.$$

$$k_{Per} = \frac{\$2.50}{\$111.10} = 2.25\%; \; k_{ps(Nom)} = 2.25\%(4) = 9\%.$$

Note:

- Flotation costs for preferred are significant, so are reflected. Use net price.
- Preferred dividends are not deductible, so no tax adjustment. Just k_{ps}.
- Nominal k_{ps} is used.

Is preferred stock more or less risky to investors than debt?

- More risky; company not required to pay preferred dividend.

- However, firms want to pay preferred dividend. Otherwise, (1) cannot pay common dividend, (2) difficult to raise additional funds, and (3) preferred stockholders may gain control of firm.

Why is yield on preferred lower than k_d?

- Corporations own most preferred stock, because 70% of preferred dividends are nontaxable to corporations.
- Therefore, preferred often has a lower B-T yield than the B-T yield on debt.
- The A-T yield to investors and A-T cost to the issuer are higher on preferred than on debt, which is consistent with the higher risk of preferred.

Example:

$k_{ps} = 9\%$ $k_d = 10\%$ $T = 40\%$

$k_{ps, AT} = k_{ps} - k_{ps} (1 - 0.7)(T)$

$\qquad = 9\% - 9\%(0.3)(0.4) \qquad = 7.92\%$

$k_{d, AT} = 10\% - 10\%(0.4) \qquad = \underline{6.00}\%$

A-T Risk Premium on Preferred $= \underline{1.92}\%$

What are the two ways that companies can raise common equity?

- Companies can issue new shares of common stock.
- Companies can reinvest earnings.

Why is there a cost for reinvested earnings?

- Earnings can be reinvested or paid out as dividends.
- Investors could buy other securities, earn a return.
- Thus, there is an opportunity cost if earnings are reinvested.

- Opportunity cost: The return stockholders could earn on alternative investments of equal risk.
- They could buy similar stocks and earn k_s, or company could repurchase its own stock and earn k_s. So, k_s, is the cost of reinvested earnings and it is the cost of equity.

Three ways to determine the cost of equity, k_s:

1. CAPM: $k_s = k_{RF} + (k_M - k_{RF})b$
$= k_{RF} + (RP_M)b$.

2. DCF: $k_s = D_1/P_0 + g$.

3. Own-Bond-Yield-Plus-Risk Premium:

$$k_s = k_d + RP.$$

What's the cost of equity based on the CAPM?
$k_{RF} = 7\%$, $RP_M = 6\%$, b = 1.2.

$k_s = k_{RF} + (k_M - k_{RF})b$.

$= 7.0\% + (6.0\%)1.2 = \boxed{14.2\%}$.

What's the DCF cost of equity, k_s?
Given: $D_0 = \$4.19$; $P_0 = \$50$; g = 5%.

$$k_s = \frac{D_1}{P_0} + g = \frac{D_0(1+g)}{P_0} + g$$

$$= \frac{\$4.19(1.05)}{\$50} + 0.05$$

$$= 0.088 + 0.05$$

$$= \boxed{13.8\%}.$$

Suppose the company has been earning 15% on equity (ROE = 15%) and retaining 35% (dividend payout = 65%), and this situation is expected to continue.

What's the expected future g?

Retention growth rate:

g = b(ROE) = 0.35(15%) = 5.25%.

Here b = Fraction retained.

Close to g = 5% given earlier. Think of bank account paying 10% with b = 0, b = 1.0, and b = 0.5. What's g?

Could DCF methodology be applied if g is not constant?

- YES, nonconstant g stocks are expected to have constant g at some point, generally in 5 to 10 years.
- But calculations get complicated.

Find k_s using the own-bond-yield-plus-risk-premium method.
$(k_d = 10\%, RP = 4\%.)$

$k_s = k_d + RP$

$= 10.0\% + 4.0\% = 14.0\%$

■ This RP $\neq$ CAPM RP_M.
■ Produces ballpark estimate of k_s. Useful check.

What's a reasonable final estimate of k_s?

Method	Estimate
CAPM	14.2%
DCF	13.8%
$k_d + RP$	14.0%
Average	14.0%

What's the WACC?

$WACC = w_d k_d (1 - T) + w_{ps} k_{ps} + w_{ce} k_s$

$= 0.3(10\%)(0.6) + 0.1(9\%) + 0.6(14\%)$

$= 1.8\% + 0.9\% + 8.4\% = 11.1\%.$

Four Mistakes to Avoid

1. When estimating the cost of debt, use the current interest rate on new debt, not the coupon rate on existing debt.

2. When estimating the risk premium for the CAPM approach, don't subtract the *current* long-term T-bond rate from the *historical* average return on common stocks.

(More ...)

For example, if the historical k_M has been about 12.7% and inflation drives the current k_{RF} up to 10%, the current market risk premium is not 12.7% - 10% = 2.7%!

(More ...)

3. Use the target capital structure to determine the weights.

If you don't know the target weights, then use the current market value of equity, and never the book value of equity.

If you don't know the market value of debt, then the book value of debt often is a reasonable approximation, especially for short-term debt.

(More...)

4. Capital components are sources of funding that come from investors.

Accounts payable, accruals, and deferred taxes are not sources of funding that come from investors, so they are not included in the calculation of the WACC.

We do adjust for these items when calculating the cash flows of the project, but not when calculating the WACC.

Three Types of Risk

- Stand-alone risk
- Corporate risk
- Market risk

Market, or beta, risk is most relevant for estimating the WACC.

Methods for estimating a division's or a project's beta

- Pure play. Find several publicly traded companies exclusively in project's business. Use average of their betas as proxy for project's beta.

Hard to find such companies.

■ Accounting beta. Run regression between project's ROA and S&P index ROA.

Accounting betas are correlated (0.5-0.6) with market betas.

But normally can't get data on new projects' ROAs before the capital budgeting decision has been made.

Should Cox use the same WACC for all projects?

No!

■ Cox should estimate divisional WACCs based on divisional betas and divisional debt capacities.

■ Cox might consider further adjustments to divisional WACCs for particularly risky or safe projects.

Assume that you recently went to work for Axis Components Company, a supplier of auto repair parts used in the after-market with products from Chrysler, Ford, and other auto makers. Your boss, the chief financial officer (CFO), has just handed you the estimated cash flows for two proposed projects. Project L involves adding a new item to the firm's ignition system line; it would take some time to build up the market for this product, so the cash inflows would increase over time. Project S involves an add-on to an existing line, and its cash flows would decrease over time. Both projects have 3-year lives, because Axis is planning to introduce entirely new models after 3 years.

Here are the projects' net cash flows (in thousands of dollars):

| | Expected Net Cash Flow | |
Year	Project L	Project S
0	($100)	($100)
1	10	70
2	60	50
3	80	20

Depreciation, salvage values, net working capital requirements, and tax effects are all included in these cash flows.

The CFO also made subjective risk assessments of each project, and he concluded that both projects have risk characteristics which are similar to the firm's average project. Axis's weighted average cost of capital is 10 percent. You must now determine whether one or both of the projects should be accepted.

a. What is capital budgeting? Are there any similarities between a firm's capital budgeting decisions and an individual's investment decisions?

b. What is the difference between independent and mutually exclusive projects? Between projects with normal and nonnormal cash flows?

c. (1) What is the payback period? Find the paybacks for Projects L and S.

   (2) What is the rationale for the payback method? According to the payback criterion, which project or projects should be accepted if the firm's maximum acceptable payback is 2 years, and if Projects L and S are independent? If they are mutually exclusive?

   (3) What is the difference between the regular and discounted payback periods?

---

(4) What is the main disadvantage of discounted payback? Is the payback method of any real usefulness in capital budgeting decisions?

d. (1) Define the term *net present value (NPV)*. What is each project's NPV?

(2) What is the rationale behind the NPV method? According to NPV, which project or projects should be accepted if they are independent? Mutually exclusive?

(3) Would the NPVs change if the cost of capital changed?

e. (1) Define the term *internal rate of return (IRR)*. What is each project's IRR?

(2) How is the IRR on a project related to the YTM on a bond?

(3) What is the logic behind the IRR method? According to IRR, which projects should be accepted if they are independent? Mutually exclusive?

(4) Would the projects' IRRs change if the cost of capital changed?

f. (1) Draw NPV profiles for Projects L and S. At what discount rate do the profiles cross?

(2) Look at your NPV profile graph without referring to the actual NPVs and IRRs. Which project or projects should be accepted if they are independent? Mutually exclusive? Explain. Are your answers correct at any cost of capital less than 23.6 percent?

g. (1) What is the underlying cause of ranking conflicts between NPV and IRR?

(2) What is the "reinvestment rate assumption," and how does it affect the NPV versus IRR conflict?

(3) Which method is the best? Why?

h. (1) Define the term *modified IRR (MIRR)*. Find the MIRRs for Projects L and S.

(2) What are the MIRR's advantages and disadvantages vis-a-vis the regular IRR? What are the MIRR's advantages and disadvantages vis-a-vis the NPV?

i. As a separate project (Project P), the firm is considering sponsoring a pavilion at the upcoming World's Fair. The pavilion would cost $800,000, and it is expected to result in $5 million of incremental cash inflows during its 1 year of operation. However, it would then take another year, and $5 million of costs, to demolish the site and return it to its original condition. Thus, Project P's expected net cash flows look like this (in millions of dollars):

Year	Net Cash Flows
0	($0.8)
1	5.0
2	(5.0)

The project is estimated to be of average risk, so its cost of capital is 10 percent.

(1) What is Project P's NPV? What is its IRR? Its MIRR?

(2) Draw Project P's NPV profile. Does Project P have normal or nonnormal cash flows? Should this project be accepted?

11 - 1

CHAPTER 11
The Basics of Capital Budgeting

Should we build this plant?

---

11 - 2

What is capital budgeting?

- Analysis of potential additions to fixed assets.
- Long-term decisions; involve large expenditures.
- Very important to firm's future.

---

11 - 3

Steps

1. Estimate CFs (inflows & outflows).
2. Assess riskiness of CFs.
3. Determine k = WACC for project.
4. Find NPV and/or IRR.
5. Accept if NPV > 0 and/or IRR > WACC.

An Example of Mutually Exclusive Projects

BRIDGE vs. **BOAT** to get products across a river.

Normal Cash Flow Project:

Cost (negative CF) followed by a series of positive cash inflows. <u>One</u> change of signs.

Nonnormal Cash Flow Project:

<u>Two</u> or more changes of signs. Most common: Cost (negative CF), then string of positive CFs, then cost to close project. Nuclear power plant, strip mine.

<u>Inflow (+) or Outflow (-) in Year</u>

0	1	2	3	4	5	N	NN
-	+	+	+	+	+	N	
-	+	+	+	+	-		NN
-	-	-	+	+	+	N	
+	+	+	-	-	-	N	
-	+	+	-	+	-		NN

What is the payback period?

The number of years required to recover a project's cost,

or how long does it take to get the business's money back?

Payback for Project L (Long: Most CFs in out years)

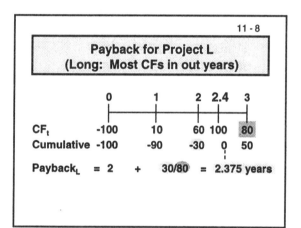

$$\text{Payback}_L = 2 + 30/80 = 2.375 \text{ years}$$

Project S (Short: CFs come quickly)

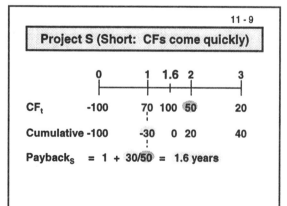

$$\text{Payback}_S = 1 + 30/50 = 1.6 \text{ years}$$

Strengths of Payback:

1. Provides an indication of a project's risk and liquidity.
2. Easy to calculate and understand.

Weaknesses of Payback:

1. Ignores the TVM.
2. Ignores CFs occurring after the payback period.

Discounted Payback: Uses discounted rather than raw CFs.

	0		1		2		3
		10%					
CF_t	-100		10		60		80
$PVCF_t$	-100		9.09		49.59		60.11
Cumulative	-100		-90.91		-41.32		18.79

Discounted payback $= 2 + 41.32/60.11 = 2.7$ yrs

Recover invest. + cap. costs in 2.7 yrs.

NPV: Sum of the PVs of inflows and outflows.

$$NPV = \sum_{t=0}^{n} \frac{CF_t}{(1+k)^t}.$$

Cost often is CF_0 and is negative.

$$NPV = \sum_{t=1}^{n} \frac{CF_t}{(1+k)^t} - CF_0.$$

What's Project L's NPV?

Project L:

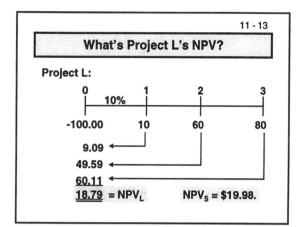

18.79 = NPV_L NPV_S = \$19.98.

Calculator Solution

Enter in CFLO for L:

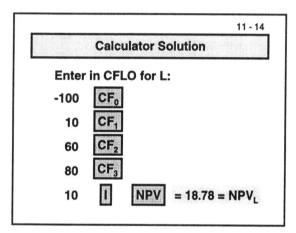

Rationale for the NPV Method

NPV = PV inflows - Cost
    = Net gain in wealth.

Accept project if NPV > 0.

Choose between mutually exclusive projects on basis of higher NPV. Adds most value.

Using NPV method, which project(s) should be accepted?

- ■ If Projects S and L are mutually exclusive, accept S because $NPV_s > NPV_L$.

- ■ If S & L are independent, accept both; NPV > 0.

Internal Rate of Return: IRR

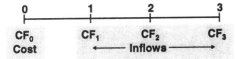

IRR is the discount rate that forces PV inflows = cost. This is the same as forcing NPV = 0.

NPV: Enter k, solve for NPV.

$$\sum_{t=0}^{n} \frac{CF_t}{(1+k)^t} = NPV.$$

IRR: Enter NPV = 0, solve for IRR.

$$\sum_{t=0}^{n} \frac{CF_t}{(1+IRR)^t} = 0.$$

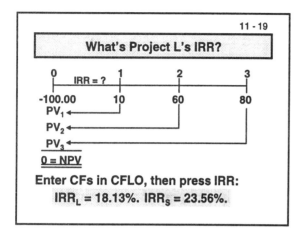

11 - 19

What's Project L's IRR?

Enter CFs in CFLO, then press IRR:
$IRR_L = 18.13\%$. $IRR_S = 23.56\%$.

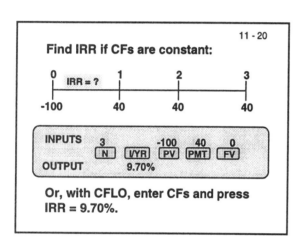

11 - 20

Find IRR if CFs are constant:

Or, with CFLO, enter CFs and press
IRR = 9.70%.

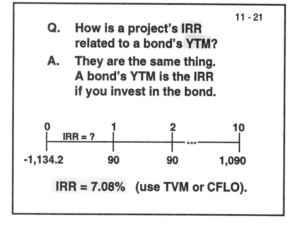

11 - 21

Q. How is a project's IRR
related to a bond's YTM?

A. They are the same thing.
A bond's YTM is the IRR
if you invest in the bond.

IRR = 7.08% (use TVM or CFLO).

Rationale for the IRR Method

If IRR > WACC, then the project's rate of return is greater than its cost-- some return is left over to boost stockholders' returns.

<u>Example</u>: WACC = 10%, IRR = 15%.
               Profitable.

IRR Acceptance Criteria

- If IRR > k, accept project.

- If IRR < k, reject project.

Decisions on Projects S and L per IRR

- If S and L are independent, accept both. IRRs > k = 10%.

- If S and L are mutually exclusive, accept S because $IRR_S > IRR_L$.

Construct NPV Profiles

Enter CFs in CFLO and find NPV_L and NPV_S at different discount rates:

k	NPV_L	NPV_S
0	50	40
5	33	29
10	19	20
15	7	12
20	(4)	5

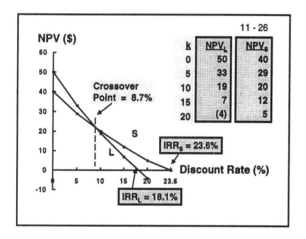

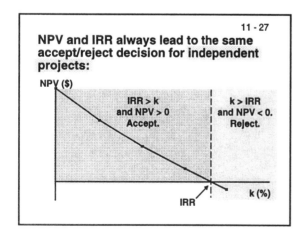

NPV and IRR always lead to the same accept/reject decision for independent projects:

Mutually Exclusive Projects

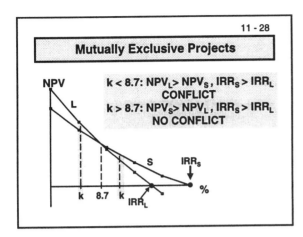

$k < 8.7$: $NPV_L > NPV_S$, $IRR_S > IRR_L$
CONFLICT
$k > 8.7$: $NPV_S > NPV_L$, $IRR_S > IRR_L$
NO CONFLICT

To Find the Crossover Rate

1. Find cash flow differences between the projects. See data at beginning of the case.
2. Enter these differences in CFLO register, then press IRR. Crossover rate = 8.68%, rounded to 8.7%.
3. Can subtract S from L or vice versa, but better to have first CF negative.
4. If profiles don't cross, one project dominates the other.

Two Reasons NPV Profiles Cross

1. **Size (scale) differences.** Smaller project frees up funds at $t = 0$ for investment. The higher the opportunity cost, the more valuable these funds, so high k favors small projects.

2. **Timing differences.** Project with faster payback provides more CF in early years for reinvestment. If k is high, early CF especially good, $NPV_S > NPV_L$.

Reinvestment Rate Assumptions

- NPV assumes reinvest at k (opportunity cost of capital).

- IRR assumes reinvest at IRR.

- Reinvest at opportunity cost, k, is more realistic, so NPV method is best. NPV should be used to choose between mutually exclusive projects.

Managers like rates--prefer IRR to NPV comparisons. Can we give them a better IRR?

Yes, MIRR is the discount rate which causes the PV of a project's terminal value (TV) to equal the PV of costs. TV is found by compounding inflows at WACC.

Thus, MIRR assumes cash inflows are reinvested at WACC.

MIRR for Project L (k = 10%)

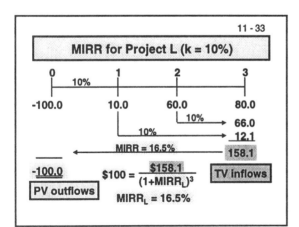

$$\$100 = \frac{\$158.1}{(1+MIRR_L)^3}$$

$MIRR_L = 16.5\%$

To find TV with 10B, enter in CFLO:

$CF_0 = 0$, $CF_1 = 10$, $CF_2 = 60$, $CF_3 = 80$
$I = 10$
NPV = 118.78 = PV of inflows.
Enter PV = -118.78, N = 3, I = 10, PMT = 0.
Press FV = 158.10 = FV of inflows.
Enter FV = 158.10, PV = -100, PMT = 0,
N = 3.
Press I = 16.50% = MIRR.

Why use MIRR versus IRR?

MIRR correctly assumes reinvestment at opportunity cost = WACC. MIRR also avoids the problem of multiple IRRs.

Managers like rate of return comparisons, and MIRR is better for this than IRR.

Pavilion Project: NPV and IRR?

```
   0          1          2
   |  k = 10% |          |
 -800       5,000     -5,000
```

Enter CFs in CFLO, enter I = 10.
NPV = -386.78
IRR = ERROR. Why?

We got IRR = ERROR because there are 2 IRRs. Nonnormal CFs--two sign changes. Here's a picture:

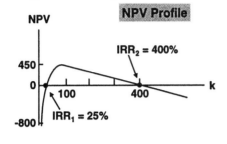

NPV Profile

Logic of Multiple IRRs

1. At very low discount rates, the PV of CF_2 is large & negative, so NPV < 0.

2. At very high discount rates, the PV of both CF_1 and CF_2 are low, so CF_0 dominates and again NPV < 0.

3. In between, the discount rate hits CF_2 harder than CF_1, so NPV > 0.

4. Result: 2 IRRs.

Could find IRR with calculator:

1. Enter CFs as before.

2. Enter a "guess" as to IRR by storing the guess. Try 10%:

   10 ▆▆▆ STO

   ▆▆▆ IRR = 25% = lower IRR

   Now guess large IRR, say, 200:

   200 ▆▆▆ STO

   ▆▆▆ IRR = 400% = upper IRR

When there are nonnormal CFs and more than one IRR, use MIRR:

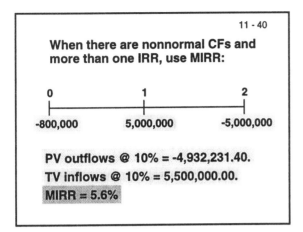

```
0              1              2
├──────────────┼──────────────┤
-800,000    5,000,000    -5,000,000
```

PV outflows @ 10% = -4,932,231.40.
TV inflows @ 10% = 5,500,000.00.
MIRR = 5.6%

Accept Project P?

NO. Reject because MIRR = 5.6% < k = 10%.

Also, if MIRR < k, NPV will be negative: NPV = -$386,777.

BLUEPRINTS: CHAPTER 12
CASH FLOW ESTIMATION
AND OTHER TOPICS IN CAPITAL BUDGETING

John Crockett Furniture Company is considering adding a new line to its product mix, and the capital budgeting analysis is being conducted by Joan Samuels, a recently graduated finance MBA. The production line would be set up in unused space in Crockett's main plant. The machinery's invoice price would be approximately $200,000; another $10,000 in shipping charges would be required; and it would cost an additional $30,000 to install the equipment. Further, the firm's inventories would have to be increased by $25,000 to handle the new line, but its accounts payable would rise by $5,000. The machinery has an economic life of 4 years, and Crockett has obtained a special tax ruling which places the equipment in the MACRS 3-year class. The machinery is expected to have a salvage value of $25,000 after 4 years of use.

The new line would generate $125,000 in incremental net revenues (before taxes and excluding depreciation) in each of the next 4 years. The firm's tax rate is 40 percent, and its overall weighted average cost of capital is 10 percent.

a. Set up, without numbers, a time line for the project's cash flows.

b. (1) Construct incremental operating cash flow statements for the project's 4 years of operations.

   (2) Does your cash flow statement include any financial flows such as interest expense or dividends? Why or why not?

c. (1) Suppose the firm had spent $100,000 last year to rehabilitate the production line site. Should this be included in the analysis? Explain.

   (2) Now assume that the plant space could be leased out to another firm at $25,000 a year. Should this be included in the analysis? If so, how?

   (3) Finally, assume that the new product line is expected to decrease sales of the firm's other lines by $50,000 per year. Should this be considered in the analysis? If so, how?

d. Disregard the assumptions in Part c. What is Crockett's net investment outlay on this project? What is the net nonoperating cash flow at the time the project is terminated? Based on these cash flows, what are the project's NPV, IRR, MIRR, and payback? Do these indicators suggest that the project should be undertaken?

---

e. Assume now that the project is a replacement project rather than a new, or expansion, project. Describe how the analysis would differ for a replacement project.

f. Explain what is meant by cash flow estimation bias. What are some steps that Crockett's management could take to eliminate the incentives for bias in the decision process?

g. Do you think it likely that the project being considered here might have option value over and above the indicated NPV? If so, how might this be handled?

h. Assume that inflation is expected to average 5 percent over the next 4 years. Does it appear that Crockett's cash flow estimates are real or nominal? That is, are all the cash flows stated in the Time 0 dollars or have the cash flows been increased to account for expected inflation? Further, would it appear that the 10 percent cost of capital is a nominal or real interest rate? Does it appear that the current NPV is biased because of inflation effects? If so, in what direction, and how could any bias be removed?

i. In an unrelated analysis, Joan was asked to choose between the following two mutually exclusive projects:

	Expected Net Cash Flow	
Year	Project S	Project L
0	($100,000)	($100,000)
1	60,000	33,500
2	60,000	33,500
3	--	33,500
4	--	33,500

The projects provide a necessary service, so whichever one is selected is expected to be repeated into the foreseeable future. Both projects have a 10 percent cost of capital.

(1) What is each project's initial NPV without replication?

(2) Now apply the replacement chain approach to determine the projects' extended NPVs. Which project should be chosen?

(3) Repeat the analysis using the equivalent annual annuity approach.

(4) Now assume that the cost to replicate Project S in 2 years will increase to $105,000 because of inflationary pressures. How should the analysis be handled now, and which project should be chosen?

j. Crockett is also considering another project which has a physical life of 3 years; that is, the machinery will be totally worn out after 3 years. However, if the project were abandoned prior to the end of 3 years, the machinery would have a positive salvage (or abandonment) value. Here are the project's estimated cash flows:

Year	Initial Investment and Operating Cash Flows	End-of-Year Net Abandonment Value
0	($5,000)	$5,000
1	2,100	3,100
2	2,000	2,000
3	1,750	0

Using the 10 percent cost of capital, what is the project's NPV if it is operated for the full 3 years? Would the NPV change if the company planned to abandon the project at the end of Year 2? At the end of Year 1? What is the project's optimal (economic) life?

CHAPTER 12
Project Cash Flow Analysis

■ Relevant cash flows
■ Working capital treatment
■ Unequal project lives
■ Abandonment value
■ Inflation

Proposed Project

■ Cost: $200,000 + $10,000 shipping + $30,000 installation.
■ Depreciable cost $240,000.
■ Inventories will rise by $25,000 and payables will rise by $5,000.
■ Economic life = 4 years.
■ Salvage value = $25,000.
■ MACRS 3-year class.

■ Incremental gross sales = $250,000.
■ Incremental cash operating costs = $125,000.
■ Tax rate = 40%.
■ Overall cost of capital = 10%.

Set up without numbers a time line for the project CFs.

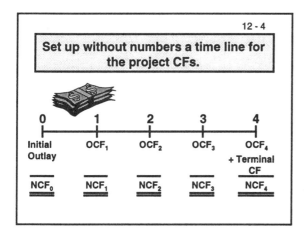

0	1	2	3	4
Initial Outlay	OCF_1	OCF_2	OCF_3	OCF_4 + Terminal CF
NCF_0	NCF_1	NCF_2	NCF_3	NCF_4

Incremental Cash Flow

= Corporate cash flow
<u>with</u> project

minus

Corporate cash flow
<u>without</u> project

Should CFs include interest expense? Dividends?

- NO. The costs of capital are already incorporated in the analysis since we use them in discounting.

- If we included them as cash flows, we would be double counting capital costs.

Suppose $100,000 had been spent last year to improve the production line site. Should this cost be included in the analysis?

- NO. This is a <u>sunk cost</u>. Focus on incremental investment and operating cash flows.

Suppose the plant space could be leased out for $25,000 a year. Would this affect the analysis?

- Yes. Accepting the project means we will not receive the $25,000. This is an <u>opportunity cost</u> and it should be charged to the project.
- A.T. opportunity cost = $25,000 (1 - T) = $15,000 annual cost.

If the new product line would decrease sales of the firm's other products by $50,000 per year, would this affect the analysis?

- Yes. The effects on the other projects' CFs are "externalities".
- Net CF loss per year on other lines would be a cost to this project.
- Externalities will be positive if new projects are complements to existing assets, negative if substitutes.

Net Investment Outlay at t = 0 (000s)

Equipment	($200)
Freight + Inst.	(40)
Change in NWC	(20)
Net CF$_0$	($260)

ΔNWC = $25,000 - $5,000
= $20,000.

Depreciation Basics

Basis = Cost
+ Shipping
+ Installation
$240,000

Annual Depreciation Expense (000s)

Year	%	x Basis =	Depr.
1	0.33	$240	$ 79
2	0.45		108
3	0.15		36
4	0.07		17

Year 1 Operating Cash Flows (000s)

	Year 1
Net revenue	$125
Depreciation	(79)
Before-tax income	$ 46
Taxes (40%)	(18)
Net income	$ 28
Depreciation	79
Net operating CF	$107

Year 4 Operating Cash Flows (000s)

	Year 1	Year 4
Net revenue	$125	$125
Depreciation	(79)	(17)
Before-tax income	$ 46	$108
Taxes (40%)	(18)	(43)
Net income	$ 28	$ 65
Depreciation	79	17
Net operating CF	$107	$ 82

Net Terminal Cash Flow at t = 4 (000s)

Salvage value	$25
Tax on SV	(10)
Recovery on NWC	20
Net terminal CF	$35

12 - 16

What if you terminate a project before the asset is fully depreciated?

Cash flow from sale = Sale proceeds
- taxes paid.

Taxes are based on difference between sales price and tax basis, where:

Basis = Original basis - Accum. deprec.

---

12 - 17

Example: If Sold After 3 Years (000s)

- Original basis = $240.
- After 3 years = $17 remaining.
- Sales price = $25.
- Tax on sale = 0.4($25-$17)
  = $3.2.
- Cash flow = $25-$3.2=$21.7.

---

12 - 18

Project Net CFs on a Time Line

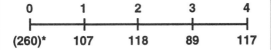

0	1	2	3	4
(260)*	107	118	89	117

Enter CFs in CFLO register and I = 10.
NPV = $81,573.
IRR = 23.8%.

*In thousands.

What is the project's MIRR? (000s)

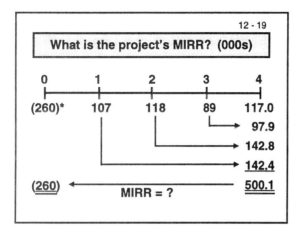

0	1	2	3	4
(260)*	107	118	89	117.0

97.9

142.8

142.4

(260) ← MIRR = ? 500.1

Calculator Solution

1. Enter positive CFs in CFLO:
   I = 10; Solve for NPV = $341.60.
2. Use TVM keys: PV = 341.60, N = 4
   I = 10; PMT = 0; Solve for FV = 500.10.
   (TV of inflows)
3. Use TVM keys: N = 4; FV = 500.10;
   PV = -260; PMT= 0; Solve for I = 17.8.

MIRR = 17.8%.

What is the project's payback? (000s)

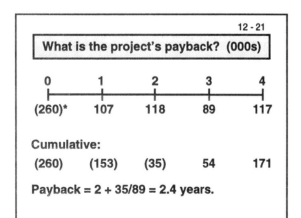

0	1	2	3	4
(260)*	107	118	89	117

Cumulative:

(260)	(153)	(35)	54	171

Payback = 2 + 35/89 = 2.4 years.

12 - 22

If this were a replacement rather than a new project, would the analysis change?

Yes. The old equipment would be sold and the incremental CFs would be the changes from the old to the new situation.

---

12 - 23

- Revenues.
- Costs.
- The relevant depreciation would be the change with the new equipment.
- Also, if the firm sold the old machine now, it would not receive the salvage value at the end of the machine's life.

---

12 - 24

What is the role of the financial staff in the cash flow estimation process?

- Coordination with other departments
- Maintaining consistency of assumptions
- Elimination of biases in the forecasts

What is cash flow estimation bias?

- CF's are estimated for many future periods.

- If company has many projects and errors are random and unbiased, errors will cancel out (aggregate NPV estimate will be OK).

- Studies show that forecasts often are biased (overly optimistic revenues, underestimated costs).

What steps can management take to eliminate the incentives for cash flow estimation bias?

- Routinely compare CF estimates with those actually realized and reward managers who are forecasting well, penalize those who are not.

- When evidence of bias exists, the project's CF estimates should be lowered or the cost of capital raised to offset the bias.

What is option value?

- Investment in a project may lead to other valuable opportunities.

- Investment now may extinguish opportunity to undertake same project in the future.

- True project NPV = NPV + value of options.

If 5% inflation is expected over the next 5 years, are the firm's cash flow estimates accurate?

- No. Net revenues are assumed to be constant over the 4-year project life, so inflation effects have <u>not</u> been incorporated into the cash flows.

Real vs. Nominal Cash flows

- In DCF analysis, k includes an estimate of inflation.
- If cash flow estimates are not adjusted for inflation (i.e., are in today's dollars), this will bias the NPV downward.
- This bias may offset the optimistic bias of management.

S and L are mutually exclusive and will be repeated. k = 10%. Which is better? (000s)

```
0        1        2        3        4
|--------|--------|--------|--------|
```

Project S:
(100)   60   60

Project L:
(100)   33.5   33.5   33.5   33.5

	S	L
CF_0	-100,000	-100,000
CF_1	60,000	33,500
N_j	2	4
I	10	10
NPV	4,132	6,190

$NPV_L > NPV_S$. But is L better? Can't say yet. Need to perform common life analysis.

■ Note that Project S could be repeated after 2 years to generate additional profits.

■ Can use either <u>replacement chain</u> or <u>equivalent annual annuity</u> analysis to make decision.

Replacement Chain Approach (000s)

Project S with Replication:

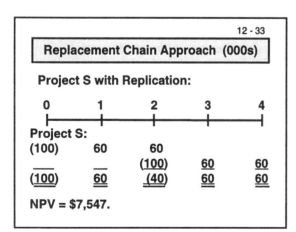

```
    0       1       2       3       4
    ├───────┼───────┼───────┼───────┤

Project S:
(100)      60      60
                  (100)      60      60
   ───      ──    ────      ──      ──
(100)      60    (40)       60      60
```

NPV = $7,547.

Or, use NPVs:

```
  0        1         2        3         4
  ├────────┼─────────┼────────┼─────────┤
4,132              4,132
3,415  ◄──── 10% ────┘
7,547
```

Compare to Project L NPV = $6,190.

Equivalent Annual Annuity (EAA) Approach

Finds the constant annuity payment whose PV is equal to the project's raw NPV over its original life.

EAA Calculator Solution

- Project S
  - PV = Raw NPV = $4,132.
  - n = Original project life = 2.
  - k = 10%.
  - Solve for PMT = EAA_S = $2,381.
- Project L
  - PV = $6,190; n = 4; k = 10%.
  - Solve for PMT = EAA_L = $1,953.

- The project, in effect, provides an annuity of EAA.

- $EAA_S > EAA_L$ so pick S.

- Replacement chains and EAA always lead to the same decision if cash flows are expected to stay the same.

If the cost to repeat S in two years rises to $105,000, which is best? (000s)

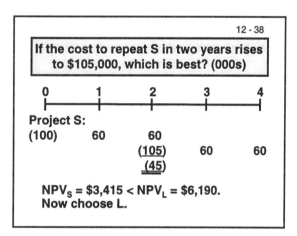

Project S:

0	1	2	3	4
(100)	60	60		
		(105)	60	60
		(45)		

$NPV_S = \$3,415 < NPV_L = \$6,190.$
Now choose L.

Types of Abandonment

- Sale to another party who can obtain greater cash flows, e.g., IBM sold typewriter division.

- Abandon because losing money, e.g., smokeless cigarette.

Consider another project with a 3-year life. If abandoned prior to Year 3, the machinery will have positive abandonment value.

Year	CF	Abandonment Value
0	($5,000)	$5,000
1	2,100	3,100
2	2,000	2,000
3	1,750	0

CFs Under Each Alternative (000s)

	0	1	2	3
1. No abandonment	(5)	2.1	2	1.75
2. Abandon 2 years	(5)	2.1	4	
3. Abandon 1 year	(5)	5.2		

Assuming a 10% cost of capital, what is the project's optimal life?

$NPV_{(no)}$ = -$123.

$NPV_{(2)}$ = $215.

$NPV_{(1)}$ = -$273.

Conclusions

- The project is acceptable only if operated for 2 years.
- A project's engineering life does not always equal its economic life.
- The ability to abandon a project may make an otherwise unattractive project acceptable.
- Abandonment possibilities will be very important when we get to risk.

BLUEPRINTS: CHAPTER 13
RISK ANALYSIS AND REAL OPTIONS

The Chapter 12 Mini Case contains the details of a new-project capital budgeting evaluation being conducted by Joan Samuels at the John Crockett Furniture Company. However, in the initial analysis the riskiness of the project was not considered. The base case, or expected, cash flow estimates as they were estimated in Chapter 12 (in thousands of dollars) are given next. Crockett's corporate cost of capital (WACC) is 10 percent.

As Joan's assistant, you have been directed to answer the following questions:

a. What does the term "risk" mean in the context of capital budgeting, to what extent can risk be quantified, and when risk is quantified, is the quantification based primarily on statistical analysis of historical data or on subjective, judgmental estimates?

b. (1) What are the three types of risk that are relevant in capital budgeting?

   (2) How is each of these risk types measured, and how do they relate to one another?

   (3) How is each type of risk used in the capital budgeting process?

c. (1) What is sensitivity analysis?

   (2) Perform a sensitivity analysis on the unit sales, salvage value, and cost of capital for the project. Assume that each of these variables can vary from its base case, or expected, value by plus and minus 10, 20, and 30 percent. Include a sensitivity diagram, and discuss the results.

   (3) What is the primary weakness of sensitivity analysis? What is its primary usefulness?

d. Assume that Joan Samuels is confident of her estimates of all the variables that affect the project's cash flows except unit sales: If product acceptance is poor, unit sales would be only 900 units a year, while a strong consumer response would produce sales of 1,600 units. In either case, cash costs would still amount to 50 percent of revenues. Joan believes that there is a 25 percent chance of poor acceptance, a 25 percent chance of excellent acceptance, and a 50 percent chance of average acceptance (the base case).

	Year				
	0	1	2	3	4
Investment in:					
Fixed assets	($240)				
Net working capital	(20)				
Unit sales		1,250	1,250	1,250	1,250
Sales price (dollars)		$200	$200	$200	$200
Gross revenue		$250	$250	$250	$250
Cash operating costs (50%)		125	125	125	125
Operating profit		$125	$125	$125	$125
Depreciation		79	108	36	17
EBIT		$ 46	$ 17	$ 89	$108
Taxes (40%)		18	7	36	43
Net operating income		$ 28	$ 10	$ 53	$ 65
Add back depreciation		79	108	36	17
Net operating cash flow		$107	$118	$ 89	$ 82
Salvage value					25
Tax on salvage value (40%)					(10)
Recovery of NWC					20
Net cash flow	($260)	$107	$118	$ 89	$117

NPV at 10% cost of capital = $82.

IRR = 23.8%.

MIRR = 17.8%.

(1) What is the worst-case NPV? The best-case NPV?

(2) Use the worst-, most likely, and best-case NPVs and probabilities of occurrence to find the project's expected NPV, standard deviation, and coefficient of variation.

e. (1) Assume that Crockett's average project has a coefficient of variation in the range of 0.2 – 0.4. Would the new furniture line be classified as high risk, average risk, or low risk? What type of risk is being measured here?

(2) Based on common sense, how highly correlated do you think the project would be to the firm's other assets? (Give a correlation coefficient, or range of coefficients, based on your judgment.)

(3) How would this correlation coefficient and the previously calculated σ combine to affect the project's contribution to corporate, or within-firm, risk? Explain.

f. (1) Based on your judgment, what do you think the project's correlation coefficient would be with the general economy and thus with returns on "the market"?

(2) How would this correlation affect the project's market risk?

g. (1) Crockett typically adds or subtracts 3 percentage points to the overall cost of capital to adjust for risk. Should the new furniture line be accepted?

(2) Are there any subjective risk factors that should be considered before the final decision is made?

h. Define scenario analysis and simulation analysis, and discuss their principal advantages and disadvantages.

i. (1) Crockett's target capital structure is 50 percent debt and 50 percent common equity; its cost of debt is 12 percent; the risk-free rate is 10 percent; the market risk premium is 6 percent; and the firm's tax rate is 40 percent. If Joan's estimate of the new project's beta is 1.2, what is the project's market risk, and what is its cost of capital based on the CAPM?

(2) How does the project's market risk compare with the firm's overall market risk?

(3) How does the project's market risk compare with its stand-alone risk?

(4) Briefly describe a method that Joan could conceivably have used to estimate the project's market beta. How feasible do you think it would actually be in this case?

(5) What are the advantages and disadvantages of focusing on a project's market risk?

j. Crockett Furniture actually considers hundreds of potential projects each year, and it is not feasible for Joan to specify quantitatively a specific risk adjustment for each individual project. However, Joan has estimated divisional betas and divisional capital structures for each of Crockett's three divisions. The Heirloom Division produces handcrafted, luxury furniture, and its high beta and low debt capacity lead to a 14 percent divisional cost of capital. The Maple Division produces furniture targeted at middle-class consumers, and it has a 10 percent divisional cost of capital. The School Division produces cafeteria and office furniture for schools, and its stable demand gives it a low beta, a high debt capacity, and an 8 percent cost of capital. Joan classifies projects within each division as high, average, or low risk. She adds 2 percent to the divisional cost of capital for high-risk projects, she makes no adjustment for average-risk projects, and she subtracts 1 percent for low-risk projects.

(1) Specify the different costs of capital that could be used for different projects.

(2) If the original project is a high-risk one in the Heirloom Division, should Joan approve it?

k. As a completely different project, Crockett is also evaluating two different production line systems for its overstuffed furniture line. Plan W requires more workers but less capital, while Plan C requires more capital but fewer workers. Both systems have estimated 3-year lives. Since the production line choice has no impact on revenues, Joan will base her decision on the relative costs of the two systems as set forth next:

| | Expected Net Costs | |
Year	Plan W	Plan C
0	($500)	($1,000)
1	(500)	(300)
2	(500)	(300)
3	(500)	(300)

(1) Assume initially that the two systems are both of average risk. Which one should be chosen?

(2) Now assume that the worker-intensive plan (W) is judged to be riskier than average, because future wage rates are very difficult to forecast. Under this condition, which system should be chosen?

(3) What is Plan W's IRR?

l. In a discussion with some of Crockett's engineers, Joan learns that the manufacturing facilities that are being added for the new Heirloom project could be converted to manufacture products for the School Division if demand is low for the new Heirloom product.

(1) How might this affect the value of the project?

(2) How might this affect the use of DCF methodology?

(3) Briefly describe some other types of real options.

(4) What factors increase the value of real options?

m. After examining all the potential projects, Joan discovers that there are many more projects this year with positive NPVs than in a normal year. What two problems might this extra large capital budget cause?

CHAPTER 13
Risk Analysis and Real Options

- Types of risk: stand-alone, corporate, and market
- Project risk and capital structure
- Risky outflows
- Effects of abandonment possibilities
- Real options
- Optimal capital budget

What does "risk" mean in capital budgeting?

- Uncertainty about a project's future profitability.
- Measured by σ_{NPV}, σ_{IRR}, beta.
- Will taking on the project increase the firm's and stockholders' risk?

Is risk analysis based on historical data or subjective judgment?

- Can sometimes use historical data, but generally cannot.
- So risk analysis in capital budgeting is usually based on subjective judgments.

13 - 4

What three types of risk are relevant in capital budgeting?

- Stand-alone risk
- Corporate risk
- Market (or beta) risk

---

13 - 5

How is each type of risk measured, and how do they relate to one another?

1. **Stand-Alone Risk:**
   - The project's risk if it were the firm's only asset and there were no shareholders.
   - Ignores both firm and shareholder diversification.
   - Measured by the σ or CV of NPV, IRR, or MIRR.

---

13 - 6

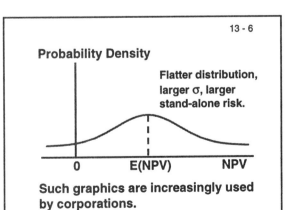

Probability Density

Flatter distribution, larger σ, larger stand-alone risk.

0   E(NPV)   NPV

Such graphics are increasingly used by corporations.

---

2. Corporate Risk:

- Reflects the project's effect on corporate earnings stability.
- Considers firm's other assets (diversification within firm).
- Depends on:
  - project's σ, and
  - its correlation with returns on firm's other assets.
- Measured by the project's corporate beta.

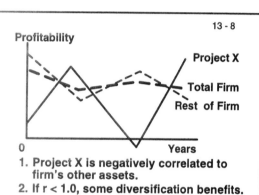

Profitability

Project X

Total Firm

Rest of Firm

0   Years

1. Project X is negatively correlated to firm's other assets.
2. If r < 1.0, some diversification benefits.
3. If r = 1.0, no diversification effects.

3. Market Risk:

- Reflects the project's effect on a well-diversified stock portfolio.
- Takes account of stockholders' other assets.
- Depends on project's σ and correlation with the stock market.
- Measured by the project's market beta.

How is each type of risk used?

- Market risk is theoretically best in most situations.
- However, creditors, customers, suppliers, and employees are more affected by corporate risk.
- Therefore, corporate risk is also relevant.

- Stand-alone risk is easiest to measure, more intuitive.
- Core projects are highly correlated with other assets, so stand-alone risk generally reflects corporate risk.
- If the project is highly correlated with the economy, stand-alone risk also reflects market risk.

What is sensitivity analysis?

- Shows how changes in a variable such as unit sales affect NPV or IRR.
- Each variable is fixed except one. Change this one variable to see the effect on NPV or IRR.
- Answers "what if" questions, e.g. "What if sales decline by 30%?"

Illustration

Change from	Resulting NPV (000s)		
Base Level	Unit Sales	Salvage	k
-30%	$ 10	$78	$105
-20	35	80	97
-10	58	81	89
0	82	82	82
+10	105	83	74
+20	129	84	67
+30	153	85	61

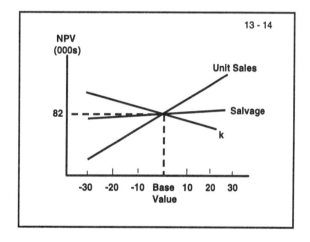

Results of Sensitivity Analysis

- Steeper sensitivity lines show greater risk. Small changes result in large declines in NPV.

- Unit sales line is steeper than salvage value or k, so for this project, should worry most about accuracy of sales forecast.

13 - 16
What are the weaknesses of sensitivity analysis?

- Does not reflect diversification.
- Says nothing about the likelihood of change in a variable, i.e. a steep sales line is not a problem if sales won't fall.
- Ignores relationships among variables.

13 - 17
Why is sensitivity analysis useful?

- Gives some idea of stand-alone risk.
- Identifies dangerous variables.
- Gives some breakeven information.

13 - 18
What is scenario analysis?

- Examines several possible situations, usually worst case, most likely case, and best case.
- Provides a range of possible outcomes.

Assume we know with certainty all variables except unit sales, which could range from 900 to 1,600.

Scenario	Probability	NPV(000)
Worst	0.25	$ 15
Base	0.50	82
Best	0.25	148

$$E(NPV) = \$ \ 82$$
$$\sigma(NPV) = 47$$
$$CV(NPV) = \sigma(NPV)/E(NPV) = 0.57$$

If the firm's average project has a CV of 0.2 to 0.4, is this a high-risk project? What type of risk is being measured?

- Since CV = 0.57 > 0.4, this project has high risk.

- CV measures a project's stand-alone risk. It does not reflect firm or stockholder diversification.

Would a project in a firm's core business likely be highly correlated with the firm's other assets?

- Yes. Economy and customer demand would affect all core products.

- But each product would be more or less successful, so correlation < +1.0.

- Core projects probably have correlations within a range of +0.5 to +0.9.

How do correlation and σ affect a project's contribution to corporate risk?

- If σ_P is relatively high, then project's corporate risk will be high unless diversification benefits are significant.

- If project cash flows are highly correlated with the firm's aggregate cash flows, then the project's corporate risk will be high if σ_P is high.

Would a core project in the furniture business be highly correlated with the general economy and thus with the "market"?

- Probably. Furniture is a deferrable luxury good, so sales are probably correlated with but more volatile than the general economy.

Would correlation with the economy affect market risk?

- Yes.
  - High correlation increases market risk (beta).
  - Low correlation lowers it.

With a 3% risk adjustment, should our project be accepted?

- Project k = 10% + 3% = 13%.
- That's 30% above base k.
- NPV = $60,541.
- Project remains acceptable after accounting for differential (higher) risk.

Should subjective risk factors be considered?

- Yes. A numerical analysis may not capture all of the risk factors inherent in the project.
- For example, if the project has the potential for bringing on harmful lawsuits, then it might be riskier than a standard analysis would indicate.

Are there any problems with scenario analysis?

- Only considers a few possible outcomes.
- Assumes that inputs are perfectly correlated--all "bad" values occur together and all "good" values occur together.
- Focuses on stand-alone risk, although subjective adjustments can be made.

What is a simulation analysis?

- A computerized version of scenario analysis which uses continuous probability distributions.

- Computer selects values for each variable based on given probability distributions.

(More...)

- NPV and IRR are calculated.

- Process is repeated many times (1,000 or more).

- End result: Probability distribution of NPV and IRR based on sample of simulated values.

- Generally shown graphically.

Probability Density

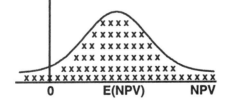

Also gives σ_{NPV}, CV_{NPV}, probability of NPV > 0.

What are the advantages of simulation analysis?

- Reflects the probability distributions of each input.
- Shows range of NPVs, the expected NPV, σ_{NPV}, and CV_{NPV}.
- Gives an intuitive graph of the risk situation.

What are the disadvantages of simulation?

- Difficult to specify probability distributions and correlations.
- If inputs are bad, output will be bad: "Garbage in, garbage out."
- May look more accurate than it really is. It is really a SWAG ("Scientific Wild A__ Guess").

(More...)

- Sensitivity, scenario, and simulation analyses do not provide a decision rule. They do not indicate whether a project's expected return is sufficient to compensate for its risk.
- Sensitivity, scenario, and simulation analyses all ignore diversification. Thus they measure only stand-alone risk, which may not be the most relevant risk in capital budgeting.

Find the project's market risk and cost of capital based on the CAPM.

- Target debt ratio = 50%.
- k_d = 12%.
- Tax rate = 40%.
- k_{RF} = 10%.
- beta $_{Project}$ = 1.2.
- Market risk premium = 6%.

- Beta = 1.2, so project has more market risk than average.
- Project's required return on equity:
  - $k_{sP} = k_{RF} + (k_M - k_{RF})b_P$
    $= 10\% + (6\%)1.2 = 17.2\%.$
  - $WACC_P = w_d k_d(1 - T) + w_e k_{sP}$
    $= 0.5(12\%)(0.6) + 0.5(17.2\%)$
    $= 12.2\%.$

How does the project's market risk compare with the firm's overall market risk?

- Project k = 12.2% versus company's k = 10%.
- Indicates that project's market risk is greater than firm's average project.

Is the project's relative market risk consistent with its stand-alone risk?

- Yes. Project CV = 0.57 versus 0.3 for an average project, which is consistent with project's higher market risk.

Methods for estimating a project's beta

- Pure play. Find several publicly traded companies exclusively in project's business. Use average of their betas as proxy for project's beta.

  Hard to find such companies.

- Accounting beta. Run regression between project's ROA and S&P index ROA.

  Accounting betas are correlated (0.5-0.6) with market betas.

  But normally can't get data on new projects' ROAs before the capital budgeting decision has been made.

Advantages and disadvantages of applying the CAPM in capital budgeting

■ **Advantages:**

- A project's market risk is the most relevant risk to stockholders, hence to determine the effect of the project on stock price.

- It results in a definite hurdle rate for use in evaluating the project.

■ **Disadvantages:**

- It is virtually impossible to estimate betas for many projects.

- People sometimes focus on market risk to the exclusion of corporate risk, and this may be a mistake.

Divisional Costs of Capital

Division	Beta	Debt Capacity	Cost of Capital
Heirloom	High	Low	14%
Maple	Avg.	Avg.	10%
School	Low	High	8%

Project Risk Adjustments

■ Crockett Furniture classifies each project within a division as high risk, average risk, and low risk. Crockett adjusts divisional costs of capital by:

● Adding 2% for high risk project

● No adjustment for average risk project

● Subtracting 1% for low risk project

What are the project costs of capital?

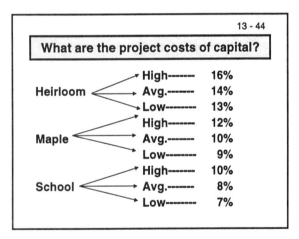

Heirloom	High-----	16%
	Avg.-----	14%
	Low-----	13%
Maple	High-----	12%
	Avg.-----	10%
	Low-----	9%
School	High-----	10%
	Avg.-----	8%
	Low-----	7%

Evaluating Our Project

■ Our project is a high risk project in the Heirloom division.

● Project cost of capital = 16%

● NPV = $42 thousand

Evaluating Risky Outflows

- Company is evaluating two alternative production processes. Plan W requires more workers but less capital. Plan C requires more capital but fewer workers.

- Both systems have 3-year lives.

- The choice will have no impact on revenues, so the decision will be based on relative costs.

Year	Plan W	Plan C
0	($500)	($1,000)
1	(500)	(300)
2	(500)	(300)
3	(500)	(300)

The two systems are of average risk, so k = 10%. Which to accept?

$PV_{COSTS-W}$ = -$1,743. $PV_{COSTS-C}$ = -$1,746.

W's costs are slightly lower so pick W.

Now suppose Plan W is riskier than Plan C because future wage rates are difficult to forecast. Would this affect the choice?

- If we add a 3% risk adjustment to the 10% to get k_W = 13%, new PV would be:

$$PV_{COSTS-W} = -\$1,681$$

which is < old $PV_{COSTS-W}$ = -$1,743.

- W now looks even better.

- Plan W now looks better, but since it is riskier, it should look worse!

- When costs are being discounted, we must use a lower discount rate to reflect higher risk. Thus, the appropriate discount rate would be 10% - 3% = 7%, making $PV_{COSTS-W}$ = -$1,812 > old -$1,743.

- With risk adjustment, $PV_{COSTS-W}$ > $PV_{COSTS-C}$, so now choose Plan C.

- Note that neither plan has an IRR.

- IRR is the discount rate that equates the PV (inflows) to the PV (outflows).

- Since there are only outflows, there can be no IRR (or MIRR).

- Similarly, a meaningful NPV can only be calculated if a project has both inflows and outflows.

- If CFs all have the same sign, the result is a PV, not an NPV.

Real Options

- Real options occur when managers have the opportunity to influence the cash flows of a project *after* the project has been implemented.

- Real options also are called:
  - Managerial options.
  - Strategic options.

13 - 52

How do real options increase the value of a project?

- Real options allow managers to avoid negative project cash flows or magnify positive project cash flows.
  - Increases size of expected cash flows.
  - Decreases risk of expected cash flows.

13 - 53

How is the DCF method affected?

(1) It's easy to quantify the increase in the size of the expected cash flows.

(2) It's very hard to quantify the decrease in the risk of the expected cash flows.

(3) The correct cost of capital cannot be identified, so the DCF method doesn't work very well.

13 - 54

Types of Real Options

- Flexibility options
- Abandonment options
- Options to contract or temporarily suspend operations
- Options to expand volume of product
- Options to expand into new geographic areas

(More...)

13 - 55

- Options to add complementary products
- Options to add successive generations of the same product
- Options to delay

---

13 - 56

What attributes increase the value of real options?

- All real options have a positive value.
- Even if it's not possible to determine a quantitative estimate of a real option's value, it's better to have a qualitative estimate than to ignore the real option.

(More...)

---

13 - 57

- Real options are more valuable if:
  - They have a long time until you must exercise them.
  - The underlying source of risk is very volatile.
  - Interest rates are high.

Choosing the Optimal Capital Budget

- Finance theory says to accept all positive NPV projects.
- Two problems can occur when there is not enough internally generated cash to fund all positive NPV projects:
  - An increasing marginal cost of capital.
  - Capital rationing

Increasing Marginal Cost of Capital

- Externally raised capital can have large flotation costs, which increase the cost of capital.
- Investors often perceive large capital budgets as being risky, which drives up the cost of capital.

(More...)

- If external funds will be raised, then the NPV of all projects should be estimated using this higher marginal cost of capital.

13 - 61

Capital Rationing

- Capital rationing occurs when a company chooses not to fund all positive NPV projects.

- The company typically sets an upper limit on the total amount of capital expenditures that it will make in the upcoming year.

(More...)

---

13 - 62

Reason: Companies want to avoid the direct costs (i.e., flotation costs) and the indirect costs of issuing new capital.

Solution: Increase the cost of capital by enough to reflect all of these costs, and then accept all projects that still have a positive NPV with the higher cost of capital.

(More...)

---

13 - 63

Reason: Companies don't have enough managerial, marketing, or engineering staff to implement all positive NPV projects.

Solution: Use linear programming to maximize NPV subject to not exceeding the constraints on staffing.

(More...)

Reason: Companies believe that the project's managers forecast unreasonably high cash flow estimates, so companies "filter" out the worst projects by limiting the total amount of projects that can be accepted.

Solution: Implement a post-audit process and tie the managers' compensation to the subsequent performance of the project.

EXTENSION

13E - 1

Chapter 13 Extension: The Optimal Capital Budget

- We've seen how to evaluate projects.

- We need cost of capital for evaluation.

- But corporate cost of capital depends on size of capital budget.

- Must combine WACC and capital budget analysis.

13E - 2

Blum Industries has 5 potential projects:

Project	Cost	CF	Life (N)	IRR
A	$400,000	$119,326	5	15%
B	200,000	56,863	5	13
B*	200,000	35,397	10	12
C	100,000	27,057	5	11
D	300,000	79,139	5	10

Projects B & B* are mutually exclusive, the others are independent. Neither B nor B* will be repeated.

13E - 3

Additional Information

Interest rate on new debt	8.0%
Tax rate	40.0%
Debt ratio	60.0%
Current stock price, P_0	$20.00
Last dividend, D_0	$2.00
Expected growth rate, g	6.0%
Flotation cost on CS, F	19.0%
Expected addition to RE	$200,000

(NI = $500,000, Payout = 60%.)

For differential project risk, add or subtract 2% to WACC.

Calculate WACC, then plot IOS and MCC schedules.

Step 1: Estimate the cost of equity

$$k_s = \frac{D_0(1 + g)}{P_0} + g = \frac{\$2(1.06)}{\$20} + 6\% = 16.6\%.$$

$$k_e = \frac{D_1}{P_0(1 - F)} + g = \frac{\$2(1.06)}{\$20(1 - 0.19)} + 6\%$$

$$= \frac{\$2.12}{\$16.2} + 6\% = 19.1\%.$$

Step 2: Estimate the WACCs

$$WACC_1 = w_d k_d(1 - T) + w_{ce} k_s$$
$$= (0.6)(8\%)(0.6) + 0.4(16.6\%) = 9.5\%.$$

$$WACC_2 = w_d k_d(1 - T) + w_{ce} k_e$$
$$= (0.6)(8\%)(0.6) + 0.4(19.1\%) = 10.5\%.$$

Step 3: Estimate the RE break point

$$BP_{RE} = \frac{Retained\ earnings}{Equity\ fraction}$$

$$= \frac{\$200,000}{0.4} = \$500,000.$$

Each dollar up to $500,000 has $0.40 of RE at cost of 16.6%, then WACC rises. Only 1 compensating cost increase, so only 1 break point.

FIGURE 1

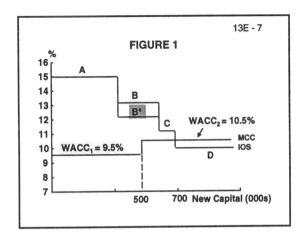

- The IOS schedule plots projects in descending order of IRR.
- Two potential IOS schedules--one with A, B, C, and D and another with A, B*, C, and D.
- The WACC has a break point at $500,000 of new capital.

What MCC do we use for capital budgeting, i.e., for calculating NPV?

- MCC: WACC that exists where IOS and MCC schedules intersect. In this case, MCC = 10.5%.

If all 5 projects are average risk, what's the optimal capital budget?

- MCC = 10.5%.

- IRR and NPV lead to same decisions for independent projects. Thus, all independent projects with IRRs above 10.5% should be accepted.

- Therefore, accept A and C, reject D, and accept B or B*.

- NPV and IRR can conflict for mutually exclusive projects.

- NPV method is better, so choose between B and B* based on NPV at WACC = 10.5%.

- NPV_{B*} = \$12,905 > NPV_B = \$12,830, so choose B* over B.

Suppose you aren't sure of WACC. At what WACC would B and B* have the same NPV?

Get differences:

CF_0 = 200,000 - 200,000 = 0

CF_{1-5} = 56,863 - 35,397 = 21,466

CF_{6-10} = 0 - 35,397 = -35,397

Indifference WACC = IRR = 10.52%.

The risk-adjusted rates are as follows:

WACC = 10.5% ± 2%

Project Risk	Risk-Adjusted Hurdle Rate
Low: C, D	8.5%
Average: B, B*	10.5
High: A	12.5

	IRR	Hurdle Rate	
A	15%	12.5%	Accept
B	13	10.5	Accept ⎤ one
B*	12	10.5	Accept ⎦
C	11	8.5	Accept
D	10	8.5	Accept

Now the optimal capital budget consists of A, B (or B*), C, and D, for a total of $1,000,000.

Corporate k is still = 10.5%, so NPV_{B*} still larger than NPV_B.

Sue Wilson, the new financial manager of Northwest Chemicals (NWC), an Oregon producer of specialized chemicals for use in fruit orchards, must prepare a financial forecast for 1999. NWC's 1998 sales were $2 billion, and the marketing department is forecasting a 25 percent increase for 1999. Wilson thinks the company was operating at full capacity in 1998, but she is not sure about this. The 1998 financial statements, plus some other data, are shown below.

A. 1998 Balance Sheet (millions of dollars)

		Percent of Sales				Percent of Sales
Cash & securities	$ 20	1%	Accounts payable and accruals	$ 100		5%
Accounts receivable	240	12%	Notes payable	100		
Inventory	240	12%	Total current liabilities	$ 200		
Total current assets	$ 500		Long-term debt	100		
Net fixed assets	500	25%	Common stock	500		
			Retained earnings	200		
Total assets	$1,000		Total liabilities and equity	$1,000		

B. 1998 Income Statement (millions of dollars)

		Percent of Sales
Sales	$2,000.00	
Variable costs	1,200.00	60%
Fixed costs	700.00	35%
Earnings before interest and taxes	$ 100.00	
Interest	16.00	
Earnings before taxes	$ 84.00	
Taxes (40%)	33.60	
Net income	$ 50.40	
Dividends (30%)	$ 15.12	
Addition to retained earnings	$ 35.28	

C. Key ratios

	NWC	Industry
Basic earning power	10.00%	20.00%
Profit margin	2.52	4.00
Return on equity	7.20	15.60
Days sales outstanding (360 days)	43.20 days	32.00 days
Inventory turnover	8.33×	11.00×
Fixed assets turnover	4.00	5.00
Total assets turnover	2.00	2.50
Debt/assets	30.00%	36.00%
Times interest earned	6.25×	9.40×
Current ratio	2.50	3.00
Payout ratio	30.00%	30.00%
Operating profit margin after taxes (NOPAT/Sales)	3.00%	5.00%
Operating capital requirement (Operating capital/Sales)	45.00	35.00
Return on invested capital (NOPAT/Operating capital)	6.67	14.00

Assume that you were recently hired as Wilson's assistant, and your first major task is to help her develop the forecast. She asked you to begin by answering the following set of questions.

a. Assume (1) that NWC was operating at full capacity in 1998 with respect to all assets, (2) that all assets must grow proportionally with sales, (3) that accounts payable and accruals will also grow in proportion to sales, and (4) that the 1998 profit margin and dividend payout will be maintained. Under these conditions, what will the company's financial requirements be for the coming year? Use the AFN equation to answer this question.

b. Now estimate the 1999 financial requirements using the percent of sales approach, making an initial forecast plus one additional "pass" to determine the effects of "financing feedbacks." Assume (1) that each type of asset, as well as payables, accruals, and fixed and variable costs, will be the same percent of sales in 1999 as in 1998; (2) that the payout ratio is held constant at 30 percent; (3) that external funds needed are financed 50 percent by notes payable and 50 percent by long-term debt (no new common stock will be issued); and (4) that all debt carries an interest rate of 8 percent.

c. Why do the two methods produce somewhat different AFN forecasts? Which method provides the more accurate forecast?

d. Calculate NWC's forecasted ratios, and compare them with the company's 1998 ratios and with the industry averages. How does NWC compare with the average firm in its industry, and is the company expected to improve during the coming year?

e. Calculate NWC's free cash flow for 1999.

f. Suppose NWC expects sales to grow 15 percent in 2000. In 2001 and all subsequent years, competition will cause NWC's sales to grow at a constant rate of 5 percent. If NWC's operations remain the same (i.e., the items that are a percent of sales will be the same percent of sales in years after 1998 and in 1998), the projected free cash flows for 2000 and 2001 are -$82.50 million and $25.88 million, respectively. After 2001, free cash flows are expected to grow at 5 percent per year. NWC's weighted average cost of capital is 9 percent. What is the value of NWC as of December 31, 1998? (Hint: Find the horizon value at 2001, and then find the present values of the horizon value and the free cash flows.)

g. Suppose you now learn that NWC's 1998 receivables and inventories were in line with required levels, given the firm's credit and inventory policies, but that excess capacity existed with regard to fixed assets. Specifically, fixed assets were operated at only 75 percent of capacity.

(1) What level of sales could have existed in 1998 with the available fixed assets? What would the fixed assets/sales ratio have been if NWC had been operating at full capacity?

(2) How would the existence of excess capacity in fixed assets affect the additional funds needed during 1999?

h. Without actually working out the numbers, how would you expect the ratios to change in the situation where excess capacity in fixed assets exists? Explain your reasoning.

i. Based on comparisons between NWC's days sales outstanding (DSO) and inventory turnover ratios with the industry average figures, does it appear that NWC is operating efficiently with respect to its inventory and accounts receivable? If the company were able to bring these ratios into line with the industry averages, what effect would this have on its AFN and its financial ratios? What effect would this have on free cash flow and the value of the company? (Note: Inventories and receivables will be discussed in detail in Chapter 21.)

j. The relationship between sales and the various types of assets is important in financial forecasting. The percent of sales approach, under the assumption that each asset item grows at the same rate as sales, leads to an AFN forecast that is reasonably close to the forecast using the AFN equation. Explain how each of the following factors would affect the accuracy of financial forecasts based on the AFN equation: (1) excess capacity, (2) base stocks of assets, such as shoes in a shoe store, (3) economies of scale in the use of assets, and (4) lumpy assets.

k. (1) How could regression analysis be used to detect the presence of the situations described above and then to improve the financial forecasts? Plot a graph of the following data, which is for a typical well-managed company in NWC's industry, to illustrate your answer.

	Sales	Inventories
1996	$1,280	$118
1997	1,600	138
1998	2,000	162
1999 (est.)	2,500	192

(2) On the same graph that plots the above data, draw a line which shows how the regression line must appear to justify the use of the AFN formula and the percent of sales forecasting procedure. As a part of your answer, show the growth rate in inventories that results from a 10 percent increase in sales from a sales level of (a) $200 and (b) $2,000 based on both the actual regression line and a *hypothetical* regression line which is linear and which goes through the origin.

l. How would changes in these items affect the AFN? (1) The dividend payout ratio, (2) the profit margin, (3) the capital intensity ratio, and (4) NWC begins buying from its suppliers on terms which permit it to pay after 60 days rather than after 30 days. (Consider each item separately and hold all other things constant.)

CHAPTER 14
Long-Term Financial Planning

- Plans: strategic, operating, and financial
- Pro forma financial statements
  - Sales forecasts
  - Percent of sales method
- Additional Funds Needed (AFN) formula

Pro Forma Financial Statements

- Three important uses:
  - Forecast the amount of external financing that will be required
  - Evaluate the impact that changes in the operating plan have on the value of the firm
  - Set appropriate targets for compensation plans

Steps in Financial Forecasting

- Forecast sales
- Project the assets needed to support sales
- Project internally generated funds
- Project outside funds needed
- Decide how to raise funds
- See effects of plan on ratios and stock price

1998 Balance Sheet
(Millions of $)

Cash & sec.	$ 20	Accts. pay. & accruals	$ 100
Accounts rec.	240	Notes payable	100
Inventories	240	Total CL	$ 200
Total CA	$ 500	L-T debt	100
		Common stk	500
Net fixed assets	500	Retained earnings	200
Total assets	$1,000	Total claims	$1,000

1998 Income Statement
(Millions of $)

Sales	$2,000.00
Less: Var. Costs (60%)	1,200.00
Fixed Costs	700.00
EBIT	$ 100.00
Interest	16.00
EBT	$ 84.00
Taxes (40%)	33.60
Net income	$ 50.40
Dividends (30%)	$15.12
Add'n to RE	$35.28

Key Ratios

	NWC	Industry	Condition
BEP	10.00%	20.00%	Poor
Profit Margin	2.52%	4.00%	"
ROE	7.20%	15.60%	"
DSO	43.20 days	32.00 days	"
Inv. turnover	8.33x	11.00x	"
F.A. turnover	4.00x	5.00x	"
T.A. turnover	2.00x	2.50x	"
Debt/ assets	30.00%	36.00%	Good
TIE	6.25x	9.40x	Poor
Current ratio	2.50x	3.00x	"
Payout ratio	30.00%	30.00%	O.K.

Key Ratios (Continued)

	NWC	Ind.	Cond.
Net oper. prof. margin after taxes (NOPAT/Sales)	3.00%	5.00%	Poor
Oper. capital requirement (Net oper. capital/Sales)	45.00%	35.00%	Poor
Return on invested capital (NOPAT/Net oper. capital)	6.67%	14.00%	Poor

---

14 - 8

AFN (Additional Funds Needed): Key Assumptions

- Operating at full capacity in 1998.
- Each type of asset grows proportionally with sales.
- Payables and accruals grow proportionally with sales.
- 1998 profit margin (2.52%) and payout (30%) will be maintained.
- Sales are expected to increase by $500 million. (%$\Delta$S = 25%)

---

14 - 9

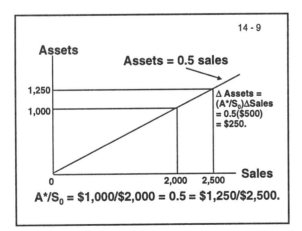

Assets

Assets = 0.5 sales

1,250

1,000

Δ Assets = (A*/S_0)ΔSales = 0.5($500) = $250.

Sales

0   2,000   2,500

$A*/S_0 = \$1,000/\$2,000 = 0.5 = \$1,250/\$2,500.$

Assets must increase by $250 million. What is the AFN, based on the AFN equation?

$$\text{AFN} = (A^*/S_0)\Delta S - (L^*/S_0)\Delta S - M(S_1)(1 - d)$$

$$= (\$1{,}000/\$2{,}000)(\$500)$$
$$- (\$100/\$2{,}000)(\$500)$$
$$- 0.0252(\$2{,}500)(1 - 0.3)$$

$$= \$180.9 \text{ million.}$$

Projecting Pro Forma Statements with the Percent of Sales Method

- Project sales based on forecasted growth rate in sales
- Forecast some items as a percent of the forecasted sales
  - Costs
  - Cash
  - Accounts receivable   (More...)

- Items as percent of sales (Continued...)
  - Inventories
  - Net fixed assets
  - Accounts payable and accruals
- Choose other items
  - Debt (which determines interest)
  - Dividends (which determines retained earnings)
  - Common stock

Percent of Sales: Inputs

	1998 Actual	1999 Proj.
Var. costs/Sales	60%	60%
Fix. costs/Sales	35%	35%
Cash/Sales	1%	1%
Acct. rec./Sales	12%	12%
Inv./Sales	12%	12%
Net FA/Sales	25%	25%
AP & accr./Sales	5%	5%

Other Inputs

Percent growth in sales	25%
Growth factor in sales (g)	1.25
Interest rate on debt	8%
Tax rate	40%
Dividend payout rate	30%

1999 1st Pass Income Statement

	1998	Factor	1999 1st Pass
Sales	$2,000	g=1.25	$2,500
Less: VC		Pct=60%	1,500
FC		Pct=35%	875
EBIT			$125
Interest	16	→	16
EBT			$109
Taxes (40%)			44
Net. income			$65
Div. (30%)			$19
Add. to RE			$46

Slide 14-16: 1999 1st Pass Balance Sheet (Assets)

Forecasted assets are a percent of forecasted sales.

1999 Sales = $2,500

	Factor	1999 1st Pass
Cash	Pct= 1%	$25
Accts. rec.	Pct=12%	300
Inventories	Pct=12%	300
Total CA		$625
Net FA	Pct=25%	625
Total assets		$1,250

Slide 14-17: 1999 1st Pass Balance Sheet (Claims)

1999 Sales = $2,500

	1998	Factor	1999 1st Pass
AP/accruals		Pct=5%	$125
Notes payable	100	→	100
Total CL			$225
L-T debt	100	→	100
Common stk.	500	→	500
Ret. earnings	200	+46*	246
Total claims			$1,071

*From 1st pass income statement.

Slide 14-18: What are the additional funds needed (AFN)?

- Forecasted total assets = $1,250
- Forecasted total claims = $1,071
- Forecast AFN = $ 179

NWC must have the assets to make forecasted sales. The balance sheets must balance. So, we must raise $179 externally.

Assumptions about How AFN Will Be Raised

- No new common stock will be issued.
- Any external funds needed will be raised as debt, 50% notes payable, and 50% L-T debt.

How will the AFN be financed?

Additional notes payable =
$$0.5 (\$179) = \$89.50 \approx \$90.$$

Additional L-T debt =
$$0.5 (\$179) = \$89.50 \approx \$89.$$

But this financing will add 0.08($179) = $14.32 to interest expense, which will lower NI and retained earnings.

1999 2nd Pass Income Statement

	1st Pass	Feedback	2nd Pass
Sales	$2,500	→	$2,500
Less: VC	1,500	→	1,500
FC	875	→	875
EBIT	$ 125	→	$ 125
Interest	16	+14	30
EBT	$ 109		$ 95
Taxes (40%)	44		38
Net income	$ 65		$ 57
Div. (30%)	$ 19		$ 17
Add. to RE	$ 46		$ 40

1999 2nd Pass Balance Sheet (Assets)

	1st Pass	AFN	2nd Pass
Cash	$25	→	$25
Accts. rec.	300	→	300
Inventories	300	→	300
Total CA	$625	→	$625
Net FA	625	→	625
Total assets	$1,250	→	$1,250

No change in asset requirements.

1999 2nd Pass Balance Sheet (Claims)

	1st Pass	Feedback	2nd Pass
AP/accruals	$ 125	→	$ 125
Notes payable	100	+90	190
Total CL	$ 225		$ 315
L-T debt	100	+89	189
Common stk.	500	→	500
Ret. earnings	246	-6	240
Total claims	$1,071		$1,244

Results After the Second Pass

- Forecasted assets = $1,250 (no change)
- Forecasted claims = $1,244 (higher)
- 2nd pass AFN = $ 6 (short)
- Cumulative AFN = $179 + $6 = $185.
- The $6 shortfall came from the $6 reduction in retained earnings. Additional passes could be made until assets exactly equal claims. $6(0.08) = $0.48 interest on 3rd pass.

Equation AFN = $181
vs.
Pro Forma AFN = $185.
Why are they different?

- Equation method assumes a constant profit margin.

- Pro forma method is more flexible. More important, it allows different items to grow at different rates.

Ratios After 2nd Pass

	1998	1999(E)	Industry	Cond.
BEP	10.00%	10.00%	20.00%	Poor
Profit Margin	2.52%	2.27%	4.00%	Poor
ROE	7.20%	7.68%	15.60%	Poor
DSO (days)	43.20	43.20	32.00	Poor
Inv. turnover	8.33x	8.33x	11.00x	Poor
FA turnover	4.00x	4.00x	5.00x	Poor
TA turnover	2.00x	2.00x	2.50x	Poor
D/A ratio	30.00%	40.34%	36.00%	Good
TIE	6.25x	4.12x	9.40x	Poor
Current ratio	2.50x	1.99x	3.00x	Poor
Payout ratio	30.00%	30.00%	30.00%	OK

Ratios after 2nd Pass (Continued)

	NWC	Ind.	Cond.
Net oper. prof. margin after taxes (NOPAT/Sales)	3.00%	5.00%	Poor
Oper. capital requirement (Net oper. capital/Sales)		45.00%	35.00% Poor
Return on invested capital (NOPAT/Net oper. capital)	6.67%	14.00%	Poor

Note: These are the same as in 1998 (see slide 14-7), because there have been no improvements in operations (i.e., all percent of sales items have same percentages in 1998 and 1999). Also, there are no differences between 1st pass and 2nd pass because changes in financing do not affect measures of operating performance.

What is the forecasted free cash flow for 1999?

	1998	1999(E)
Net operating WC (CA - AP & accruals)	$400	$500
Total operating capital (Net op. WC + net FA)	$900	$1,125
NOPAT (EBITx(1-T))	$60	$75
Less Inv. in op. capital		$225
Free cash flow		-$150

What is the value of NWC as of 12/31/98?

Assumptions:

	1999	2000	2001
(1) Growth in sales:	25%	15%	5%

(2) Constant annual growth rate in sales of 5% after 2001.

(3) All items that are based on percent of sales will be the same percent of sales for all years.

(4) WACC is 9%.

First, find horizon value: Value of free cash flows beyond 2001.

	1999(E)	2000(E)	2001(E)
Free cash flow	-$150	-$82.50	$25.88

$$\text{Horizon value} = \frac{FCF_{2002}}{WACC - g} = \frac{FCF_{2001}(1 + g)}{WACC - g}$$

$$= \frac{\$25.88(1.05)}{0.09 - 0.05}$$

Horizon value = $679.35.

14 - 31

Value of NWC is present value of all free cash flows and horizon value.

	1999	2000	2001
Free cash flow	-$150	-$82.50	$25.88
Horizon value			$679.35

Value of NWC = PV of horizon value and free cash flows at 9% WACC

Value of NWC = $337.51.

---

14 - 32

Suppose in 1998 fixed assets had been operated at only 75% of capacity.

$$\text{Capacity sales} = \frac{\text{Actual sales}}{\% \text{ of capacity}}$$

$$= \frac{\$2,000}{0.75} = \$2,667.$$

With the existing fixed assets, sales could be $2,667. Since sales are forecasted at only $2,500, no new fixed assets are needed.

---

14 - 33

How would the excess capacity situation affect the 1999 AFN?

■ The projected increase in fixed assets was $125, the AFN would decrease by $125.

■ Since no new fixed assets will be needed, AFN will fall by $125, to

$179 - $125 = $54.

Q. If sales went up to $3,000, not $2,500, what would the F.A. requirement be?

A. Target ratio = FA/Capacity sales
$$= \$500/\$2,667 = 18.75\%.$$

Have enough F.A. for sales up to $2,667, but need F.A. for another $333 of sales:

$$\Delta FA = 0.1875(\$333) = \$62.4.$$

How would excess capacity affect the forecasted ratios?

1. Sales wouldn't change but assets would be lower, so turnovers would be better.

2. Less new debt, hence lower interest, so higher profits, EPS, ROE (when financing feedbacks considered).

3. Debt ratio, TIE would improve.

1999 Forecasted Ratios: $S_{99} = \$2,500$

	% of 1998 Capacity		
	100%	75%	Industry
BEP	10.00%	11.11%	20.00%
Profit Margin	2.27%	2.51%	4.00%
ROE	7.68%	8.44%	15.60%
DSO (days)	43.20	43.20	32.00
Inv. turnover	8.33x	8.33x	11.00x
F.A. turnover	4.00x	5.00x	5.00x
T.A. turnover	2.00x	2.22x	2.50x
D/A ratio	40.34%	33.71%	36.00%
TIE	4.12x	6.15x	9.40x
Current ratio	1.99x	2.48x	3.00x

14 - 37

How is NWC performing with regard to its receivables and inventories?

- DSO is higher than the industry average, and inventory turnover is lower than the industry average.

- Improvements here would lower current assets, reduce capital requirements, and further improve profitability and other ratios.

_____

_____

_____

_____

_____

_____

_____

14 - 38

Improvements in Working Capital Management

	Before	After
DSO (days)	43.20	32.00
Accts. rec./Sales	12.00%	8.89%
Inventory turnover	8.33x	11.00x
Inventory/Sales	12.00%	9.09%

_____

_____

_____

_____

_____

_____

_____

14 - 39

Impact of Improvements in Working Capital Management

	Before	After
Free cash flow (1999)	-$150.0	$0.5
Free cash flow (2000)	-$82.5	-$59.9
Free cash flow (2001)	$25.9	$34.5
Value of company (12/31/98)	$337.5	$676.6

_____

_____

_____

_____

_____

_____

_____

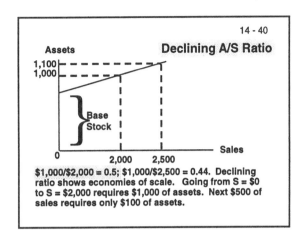

Declining A/S Ratio

$1,000/$2,000 = 0.5; $1,000/$2,500 = 0.44. Declining ratio shows economies of scale. Going from S = $0 to S = $2,000 requires $1,000 of assets. Next $500 of sales requires only $100 of assets.

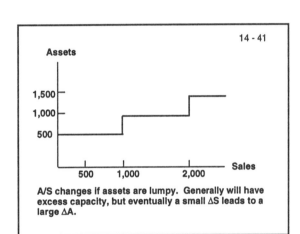

A/S changes if assets are lumpy. Generally will have excess capacity, but eventually a small ΔS leads to a large ΔA.

Summary: How different factors affect the AFN forecast.

■ **Excess capacity:**
  ● Existence lowers AFN.
■ **Base stocks of assets:**
  ● Leads to less-than-proportional asset increases.
■ **Economies of scale:**
  ● Also leads to less-than-proportional asset increases.
■ **Lumpy assets:**
  ● Leads to large periodic AFN requirements, recurring excess capacity.

Regression Analysis for Asset Forecasting

■ Get historical data on a good company, then fit a regression line to see how much a given sales increase will require in way of asset increase.

Example of Regression

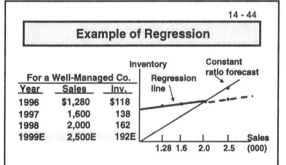

For a Well-Managed Co.		
Year	Sales	Inv.
1996	$1,280	$118
1997	1,600	138
1998	2,000	162
1999E	2,500E	192E

Constant ratio overestimates inventory required to go from $S_1 = \$2,000$ to $S_2 = \$2,500$.

Regression with 10B for Our Example

■ Same as finding beta coefficients.
■ Clear all

  1280 Input   118Σ+
  1600 Input   138Σ+
  2000 Input   162Σ+

  0 ■ ŷ, m → 40.0 = Inventory at sales = 0.
  ■ SWAP → 0.0611 = Slope coefficient.
  Inventory = 40.0 + 0.0611 Sales.
  LEAVE CALCULATOR ALONE!

Equation is now in the calculator. Let's use it by inputting new sales of $2,500 and getting forecasted inventory:

2500 ■■ $\hat{y}$, m ⟶ 192.66.

The constant ratio forecast was inventory = $300, so the regression forecast is lower by $107. This would free up $107 for use elsewhere, which would improve profitability and raise P_0.

How would increases in these items affect the AFN?

■ Higher dividend payout ratio?

   Increase AFN: Less retained earnings.

■ Higher profit margin?

   Decrease AFN: Higher profits, more retained earnings.

(More...)

■ Higher capital intensity ratio, A^*/S_0?

   Increase AFN: Need more assets for given sales increase.

■ Pay suppliers in 60 days rather than 30 days?

   Decrease AFN: Trade creditors supply more capital, i.e., L^*/S_0 increases.

BLUEPRINTS: CHAPTER 15
CAPITAL STRUCTURE DECISIONS: THE BASICS

Assume you have just been hired as business manager of PizzaPalace, a pizza restaurant located adjacent to campus. The company's EBIT was $500,000 last year, and since the university's enrollment is capped, EBIT is expected to remain constant (in real terms) over time. Since no expansion capital will be required, PizzaPalace plans to pay out all earnings as dividends. The management group owns about 50 percent of the stock, and the stock is traded in the over-the-counter market.

The firm is currently financed with all equity; it has 100,000 shares outstanding; and $P_0 = \$20$ per share. When you took your MBA corporate finance course, your instructor stated that most firms' owners would be financially better off if the firms used some debt. When you suggested this to your new boss, he encouraged you to pursue the idea. As a first step, assume that you obtained from the firm's investment banker the following estimated costs of debt and equity for the firm at different debt levels (in thousands of dollars):

Amount Borrowed	k_d	k_s
$ 0	--	15.0%
250	10.0%	15.5
500	11.0	16.5
750	13.0	18.0
1,000	16.0	20.0

If the company were to recapitalize, debt would be issued, and the funds received would be used to repurchase stock. PizzaPalace is in the 40 percent state-plus-federal corporate tax bracket.

a. Now, to develop an example which can be presented to PizzaPalace's management to illustrate the effects of financial leverage, consider two hypothetical firms: Firm U, which uses no debt financing, and Firm L, which uses $10,000 of 12 percent debt. Both firms have $20,000 in assets, a 40 percent tax rate, and an expected EBIT of $3,000.

(1) Construct partial income statements, which start with EBIT, for the two firms.

(2) Now calculate ROE for both firms.

(3) What does this example illustrate about the impact of financial leverage on ROE?

b. (1) What is business risk? What factors influence a firm's business risk?

(2) What is operating leverage, and how does it affect a firm's business risk?

c. (1) What is meant by financial leverage and financial risk?

(2) How does financial risk differ from business risk?

d. Now consider the fact that EBIT is not known with certainty, but rather has the following probability distribution:

Economic State	Probability	EBIT
Bad	0.25	$2,000
Average	0.50	3,000
Good	0.25	4,000

Redo the Part a analysis for Firms U and L, but add basic earning power (BEP), return on investment (ROI), [defined as (Net income + Interest)/(Debt + Equity)], and the times-interest-earned (TIE) ratio to the outcome measures. Find the values for each firm in each state of the economy, and then calculate the expected values. Finally, calculate the standard deviation and coefficient of variation of ROE. What does this example illustrate about the impact of debt financing on risk and return?

e. How are financial and business risk measured in a stand-alone risk framework?

f. What does capital structure theory attempt to do? What lessons can be learned from capital structure theory?

g. With the above points in mind, now consider the optimal capital structure for PizzaPalace.

(1) What valuation equations can you use in the analysis?

(2) Could either the MM or the Miller capital structure theories be applied directly in this analysis, and if you presented an analysis based on these theories, how do you think the owners would respond?

h. (1) Describe briefly, without using any numbers, the sequence of events that would take place if PizzaPalace does recapitalize.

(2) What would be the new stock price if PizzaPalace recapitalized and used these amounts of debt: $250,000; $500,000; $750,000?

(3) How many shares would remain outstanding after recapitalization under each debt scenario?

(4) Considering only the levels of debt discussed, what is PizzaPalace's optimal capital structure?

i.   It is also useful to determine the effect of any proposed recapitalization on EPS. Calculate the EPS at debt levels of $0, $250,000, $500,000, and $750,000, assuming that the firm begins at zero debt and recapitalizes to each level in a single step. Is EPS maximized at the same level that maximizes stock price?

j.   Calculate the firm's WACC at each debt level. What is the relationship between the WACC and the stock price?

k.   Suppose you discovered that PizzaPalace had more business risk than you originally estimated. Describe how this would affect the analysis. What if the firm had less business risk than originally estimated?

l.   Is it possible to do an analysis exactly like the PizzaPalace analysis for most firms? Why or why not? What type of analysis do you think a firm should actually use to help set its optimal, or target, capital structure? What other factors should managers consider when setting the target capital structure?

CHAPTER 15
Capital Structure Decisions:
The Basics

- ■ Impact of leverage on returns
- ■ Business versus financial risk
- ■ Capital structure theory
- ■ Perpetual cash flow example
- ■ Setting the optimal capital structure in practice

Consider Two Hypothetical Firms

Firm U	Firm L
No debt	$10,000 of 12% debt
$20,000 in assets	$20,000 in assets
40% tax rate	40% tax rate

Both firms have same operating leverage, business risk, and EBIT of $3,000. They differ only with respect to use of debt.

Impact of Leverage on Returns

	Firm U	Firm L
EBIT	$3,000	$3,000
Interest	0	1,200
EBT	$3,000	$1,800
Taxes (40%)	1,200	720
NI	$1,800	$1,080
ROE	9.0%	10.8%

Why does leveraging increase return?

- Total dollar return to investors:
  - U: NI = $1,800.
  - L: NI + Int = $1,080 + $1,200 = $2,280.
  - Difference = $480.
- Taxes paid:
  - U: $1,200; L: $720.
  - Difference = $480.
- More EBIT goes to investors in Firm L.
- Equity $ proportionally lower than NI.

What is business risk?

- Uncertainty about future operating income (EBIT).

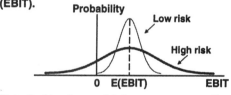

- Note that business risk focuses on operating income, so it ignores financing effects.

Factors That Influence Business Risk

- Uncertainty about demand (unit sales).
- Uncertainty about output prices.
- Uncertainty about input costs.
- Product and other types of liability.
- Degree of operating leverage (DOL).

What is operating leverage, and how does it affect a firm's business risk?

- Operating leverage is the use of fixed costs rather than variable costs.
- The higher the proportion of fixed costs within a firm's overall cost structure, the greater the operating leverage.

(More...)

- Higher operating leverage leads to more business risk, because a small sales decline causes a larger profit decline.

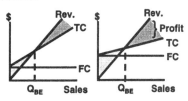

(More...)

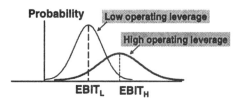

- In the typical situation, higher operating leverage leads to higher expected EBIT, but also increases risk.

Business Risk versus Financial Risk

- **Business risk:**
  - Uncertainty in future EBIT.
  - Depends on business factors such as competition, operating leverage, etc.
- **Financial risk:**
  - Additional business risk concentrated on common stockholders when financial leverage is used.
  - Depends on the amount of debt and preferred stock financing.

From a shareholder's perspective, how are financial and business risk measured in the stand-alone sense?

$$\frac{\text{Stand-alone}}{\text{risk}} = \frac{\text{Business}}{\text{risk}} + \frac{\text{Financial}}{\text{risk}} \cdot$$

Stand-alone risk = σ_{ROE}.

Business risk = $\sigma_{ROE(U)}$.

Financial risk = $\sigma_{ROE} - \sigma_{ROE(U)}$.

Now consider the fact that EBIT is not known with certainty. What is the impact of uncertainty on stockholder profitability and risk for Firm U and Firm L?

Firm U: Unleveraged

	Economy		
	Bad	Avg.	Good
Prob.	0.25	0.50	0.25
EBIT	$2,000	$3,000	$4,000
Interest	0	0	0
EBT	$2,000	$3,000	$4,000
Taxes (40%)	800	1,200	1,600
NI	$1,200	$1,800	$2,400

Firm L: Leveraged

	Economy		
	Bad	Avg.	Good
Prob.*	0.25	0.50	0.25
EBIT*	$2,000	$3,000	$4,000
Interest	1,200	1,200	1,200
EBT	$ 800	$1,800	$2,800
Taxes (40%)	320	720	1,120
NI	$ 480	$1,080	$1,680

*Same as for Firm U.

Firm U	Bad	Avg.	Good
BEP	10.0%	15.0%	20.0%
ROI*	6.0%	9.0%	12.0%
ROE	6.0%	9.0%	12.0%
TIE	∞	∞	∞
Firm L	Bad	Avg.	Good
BEP	10.0%	15.0%	20.0%
ROI*	8.4%	11.4%	14.4%
ROE	4.8%	10.8%	16.8%
TIE	1.7x	2.5x	3.3x

*ROI = (NI + Interest)/Total financing.

Profitability Measures:

	U	L
E(BEP)	15.0%	15.0%
E(ROI)	9.0%	11.4%
E(ROE)	9.0%	10.8%

Risk Measures:

	U	L
σ_{ROE}	2.12%	4.24%
CV_{ROE}	0.24	0.39
E(TIE)	∞	2.5x

Conclusions

- Basic earning power = BEP = EBIT/Total assets is unaffected by financial leverage.

- L has higher expected ROI and ROE because of tax savings.

- L has much wider ROE (and EPS) swings because of fixed interest charges. Its higher expected return is accompanied by higher risk. (More...)

- In a stand-alone risk sense, Firm L's stockholders see much more risk than Firm U's.

  - U and L: $\sigma_{ROE(U)}$ = 2.12%.

  - U: σ_{ROE} = 2.12%.

  - L: σ_{ROE} = 4.24%.

- L's financial risk is σ_{ROE} - $\sigma_{ROE(U)}$ = 4.24% - 2.12% = 2.12%. (U's is zero.)

(More...)

- For leverage to be positive (increase expected ROE), BEP must be > k_d.

- If k_d > BEP, the cost of leveraging will be higher than the inherent profitability of the assets, so the use of financial leverage will depress net income and ROE.

- In the example, E(BEP) = 15% while interest rate = 12%, so leveraging "works."

Capital Structure Theory

- MM theory
  - Zero taxes
  - Corporate taxes
  - Corporate and personal taxes
- Trade-off theory
- Signaling theory
- Debt financing as a managerial constraint

MM Theory: Zero Taxes

- MM prove, under a very restrictive set of assumptions, that a firm's value is unaffected by its financing mix.
- Therefore, capital structure is irrelevant.
- Any increase in ROE resulting from financial leverage is exactly offset by the increase in risk.

MM Theory: Corporate Taxes

- Corporate tax laws favor debt financing over equity financing.
- With corporate taxes, the benefits of financial leverage exceed the risks: More EBIT goes to investors and less to taxes when leverage is used.
- Firms should use almost 100% debt financing to maximize value.

MM Theory: Corporate and Personal Taxes

- Personal taxes lessen the advantage of corporate debt:
  - Corporate taxes favor debt financing.
  - Personal taxes favor equity financing.
- Use of debt financing remains advantageous, but benefits are less than under only corporate taxes.
- Firms should still use 100% debt.

Trade-off Theory

- MM theory ignores bankruptcy (financial distress) costs, which increase as more leverage is used.
- At low leverage levels, tax benefits outweigh bankruptcy costs.
- At high levels, bankruptcy costs outweigh tax benefits.
- An optimal capital structure exists that balances these costs and benefits.

Signaling Theory

- MM assumed that investors and managers have the same information.
- But, managers often have better information. Thus, they would:
  - Sell stock if stock is overvalued.
  - Sell bonds if stock is undervalued.
- Investors understand this, so view new stock sales as a negative signal.
- Implications for managers?

Debt Financing As a Managerial Constraint

- One agency problem is that managers can use corporate funds for non-value maximizing purposes.
- The use of financial leverage:
  - Bonds "free cash flow."
  - Forces discipline on managers.
- However, it also increases risk of financial distress.

Perpetual Cash Flow Example

Expected EBIT = $500,000; will remain constant over time.

Firm pays out all earnings as dividends (zero growth).

Currently is all-equity financed.

100,000 shares outstanding.

$P_0 = \$20$; $T = 40\%$.

Component Cost Estimates

Amount Borrowed (000)	k_d	k_s
$ 0	-	15.0%
250	10.0%	15.5
500	11.0	16.5
750	13.0	18.0
1,000	16.0	20.0

If company recapitalizes, debt would be issued to repurchase stock.

- The MM and Miller models cannot be applied here because several assumptions are violated.
  - k_d is not a constant.
  - Bankruptcy and agency costs exist.
- Theory provides some valuable insights, but because of invalid assumptions, direct real-world application is questionable.

Sequence of Events in a Recapitalization

- Firm announces the recapitalization.
- Investors reassess their views and estimate a new equity value.
- New debt is issued and proceeds are used to repurchase stock at the new equilibrium price.

(More...)

- $\dfrac{\text{Shares}}{\text{Bought}} = \dfrac{\text{Debt issued}}{\text{New price/share}}$.

- After recapitalization firm would have more debt but fewer common shares outstanding.

- An analysis of several debt levels is given next.

$D = \$250$, $k_d = 10\%$, $k_s = 15.5\%$.

$$S_1 = \frac{(\text{EBIT} - k_d D)(1 - T)}{k_s}$$

$$= \frac{[\$500 - 0.1(\$250)](0.6)}{0.155} = \$1,839.$$

$V_1 = S_1 + D_1 = \$1,839 + \$250 = \$2,089.$

$P_1 = \dfrac{\$2,089}{100} = \$20.89.$

$\dfrac{\text{Shares}}{\text{repurchased}} = \dfrac{\$250}{\$20.89} = 11.97.$

$\dfrac{\text{Shares}}{\text{remaining}} = n_1 = 100 - 11.97 = 88.03.$

Check on stock price:

$P_1 = \dfrac{S_1}{n_1} = \dfrac{\$1,839}{88.03} = \$20.89.$

Other debt levels treated similarly.

What is the firm's optimal amount of debt?

Debt	k_d	k_s	P
$250	10%	15.5%	$20.89
500	11	16.5	21.18
750	13	18.0	20.92

$500,000 of debt produces the highest stock price and thus is the best of the debt levels considered.

Calculate EPS at debt of $0, $250K, $500K, and $750K, assuming that the firm begins at zero debt and recapitalizes to each level in a single step.

Net income = NI = [EBIT - k_d D](1 - T).
EPS = NI/n.

D	NI	n	EPS
$ 0	$300	100.00	$3.00
250	285	88.03	3.24
500	267	76.39	3.50
750	242	64.15	3.77

- EPS continues to increase beyond the $500,000 optimal debt level.
- Does this mean that the optimal debt level is $750,000, or even higher?

Find the WACC at each debt level.

D	S	V	k_d	k_s	WACC
$ 0	$2,000	$2,000	--	15.0%	15.0%
250	1,839	2,089	10%	15.5	14.4
500	1,618	2,118	11.0	16.5	14.2
750	1,342	2,092	13.0	18.0	14.3

e.g. D = $250:

WACC = ($250/$2,089)(10%)(0.6)
        + ($1,839/$2,089)(15.5%)
      = 14.4%.

- The WACC is minimized at D = $500,000, the same debt level that maximizes stock price.

- Since the value of a firm is the present value of future operating income, the lowest discount rate (WACC) leads to the highest value.

How would higher or lower business risk affect the optimal capital structure?

- At any debt level, the firm's probability of financial distress would be higher. Both k_d and k_s would rise faster than before. The end result would be an optimal capital structure with less debt.

- Lower business risk would have the opposite effect.

Is it possible to do an analysis exactly like the one above for most firms?

- No. The analysis above was based on the assumption of zero growth, and most firms do not fit this category.

- Further, it would be very difficult, if not impossible, to estimate k_s with any confidence.

What type of analysis should firms conduct to help find their optimal, or target, capital structure?

- Financial forecasting models can help show how capital structure changes are likely to affect stock prices, coverage ratios, and so on.

(More...)

- Forecasting models can generate results under various scenarios, but the financial manager must specify appropriate input values, interpret the output, and eventually decide on a target capital structure.

- In the end, capital structure decision will be based on a combination of analysis and judgment.

15 - 43

What other factors would managers consider when setting the target capital structure?

- Debt ratios of other firms in the industry.

- Pro forma coverage ratios at different capital structures under different economic scenarios.

- Lender and rating agency attitudes (impact on bond ratings).

---

15 - 44

- Reserve borrowing capacity.

- Effects on control.

- Type of assets: Are they tangible, and hence suitable as collateral?

- Tax rates.

Donald Cheney, the CEO of Cheney Electronics, is concerned about his firm's level of debt financing. The company uses short-term debt to finance its temporary working capital needs, but it does not use any permanent (long-term) debt. Other electronics companies average about 30 percent debt, and Mr. Cheney wonders why the difference occurs, and what its effects are on stock prices. To gain some insights into the matter, he poses the following questions to you, his recently hired assistant:

a. *Business Week* recently ran an article on companies' debt policies, and the names Modigliani and Miller (MM) were mentioned several times as leading researchers on the theory of capital structure. Briefly, who are MM, and what assumptions are embedded in the MM and Miller models?

b. Assume that Firms U and L are in the same risk class, and that both have EBIT = $500,000. Firm U uses no debt financing, and its cost of equity is $k_{sU} = 14\%$. Firm L has $1 million of debt outstanding at a cost of $k_d = 8\%$. There are no taxes. Assume that the MM assumptions hold, and then:

   (1) Find V, S, k_s, and WACC for Firms U and L.

   (2) Graph (a) the relationships between capital costs and leverage as measured by D/V, and (b) the relationship between value and D.

c. Using the data given in Part b, but now assuming that Firms L and U are both subject to a 40 percent corporate tax rate, repeat the analysis called for in b(1) and b(2) under the MM with-tax model.

d. Now suppose investors are subject to the following tax rates: $T_d = 30\%$ and $T_s = 12\%$.

   (1) What is the gain from leverage according to the Miller model?

   (2) How does this gain compare to the gain in the MM model with corporate taxes?

   (3) What does the Miller model imply about the effect of corporate debt on the value of the firm, that is, how do personal taxes affect the situation?

e. What capital structure policy recommendations do the three theories (MM without taxes, MM with corporate taxes, and Miller) suggest to financial managers? Empirically, do firms appear to follow any one of these guidelines?

---

f. What are financial distress and agency costs? How does the addition of these costs change the MM and Miller models? (Express your answer in words, in equation form, and in graphical form.)

g. How are financial and business risk measured in a market risk framework?

h. What is the asymmetric information, or signaling, theory of capital structure?

i. What is the "pecking order" theory of capital structure?

CHAPTER 16
Capital Structure Decisions: Extensions

- MM and Miller models
- Hamada's equation
- Financial distress and agency costs
- Trade-off models
- Asymmetric information theory

Who are Modigliani and Miller (MM)?

- They published theoretical papers that changed the way people thought about financial leverage.
- They won Nobel prizes in economics because of their work.
- MM's papers were published in 1958 and 1963. Miller had a separate paper in 1977. The papers differed in their assumptions about taxes.

What assumptions underlie the MM and Miller models?

- Firms can be grouped into homogeneous classes based on business risk.
- Investors have identical expectations about firms' future earnings.
- There are no transactions costs.

(More...)

- All debt is riskless, and both individuals and corporations can borrow unlimited amounts of money at the risk-free rate.

- All cash flows are perpetuities. This implies perpetual debt is issued, firms have zero growth, and expected EBIT is constant over time.

(More...)

- MM's first paper (1958) assumed zero taxes. Later papers added taxes.

- No agency or financial distress costs.

- These assumptions were necessary for MM to prove their propositions on the basis of investor arbitrage.

MM with Zero Taxes (1958)

Proposition I:

$$V_L = V_U.$$

Proposition II:

$$k_{sL} = k_{sU} + (k_{sU} - k_d)(D/S).$$

Given the following data, find V, S, k_s, and WACC for Firms U and L.

Firms U and L are in same risk class.

$EBIT_{U,L}$ = $500,000.

Firm U has no debt; k_{sU} = 14%.

Firm L has $1,000,000 debt at k_d = 8%.

The basic MM assumptions hold.

There are no corporate or personal taxes.

1. Find V_U and V_L.

$$V_U = \frac{EBIT}{k_{sU}} = \frac{\$500,000}{0.14} = \$3,571,429.$$

$$V_L = V_U = \$3,571,429.$$

Questions: What is the derivation of the V_U equation? Are the MM assumptions required?

2. Find the market value of Firm L's debt and equity.

$$V_L = D + S = \$3,571,429$$
$$\$3,571,429 = \$1,000,000 + S$$
$$S = \$2,571,429.$$

3. Find k_{sL}.

$k_{sL} = k_{sU} + (k_{sU} - k_d)(D/S)$

$= 14.0\% + (14.0\% - 8.0\%)\left(\dfrac{\$1,000,000}{\$2,571,429}\right)$

$= 14.0\% + 2.33\% = 16.33\%.$

---

4. Proposition I implies WACC = k_{sU}. Verify for L using WACC formula.

$WACC = w_d k_d + w_{ce} k_s = (D/V)k_d + (S/V)k_s$

$= \left(\dfrac{\$1,000,000}{\$3,571,429}\right)(8.0\%)$

$+ \left(\dfrac{\$2,571,429}{\$3,571,429}\right)(16.33\%)$

$= 2.24\% + 11.76\% = 14.00\%.$

Graph the MM relationships between capital costs and leverage as measured by D/V.

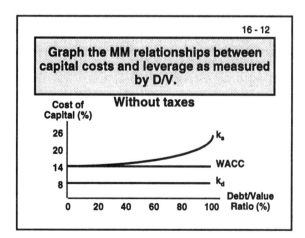

■The more debt the firm adds to its capital structure, the riskier the equity becomes and thus the higher its cost.

■Although k_d remains constant, k_s increases with leverage. The increase in k_s is exactly sufficient to keep the WACC constant.

Graph value versus leverage.

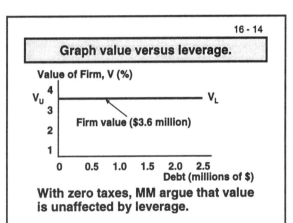

Value of Firm, V (%)

Firm value ($3.6 million)

Debt (millions of $)

With zero taxes, MM argue that value is unaffected by leverage.

Find V, S, k_s, and WACC for Firms U and L assuming a 40% corporate tax rate.

With corporate taxes added, the MM propositions become:

Proposition I:
$$V_L = V_U + TD.$$

Proposition II:
$$k_{sL} = k_{sU} + (k_{sU} - k_d)(1 - T)(D/S).$$

Notes About the New Propositions

1. When corporate taxes are added, $V_L \neq V_U$. V_L increases as debt is added to the capital structure, and the greater the debt usage, the higher the value of the firm.

2. k_{sL} increases with leverage at a slower rate when corporate taxes are considered.

---

1. Find V_U and V_L.

$$V_U = \frac{EBIT(1 - T)}{k_{sU}} = \frac{\$500,000(0.6)}{0.14} = \$2,142,857.$$

Note: Represents a 40% decline from the no taxes situation.

$$V_L = V_U + TD = \$2,142,857 + 0.4(\$1,000,000)$$
$$= \$2,142,857 + \$400,000$$
$$= \$2,542,857.$$

---

2. Find market value of Firm L's debt and equity.

$$V_L = D + S = \$2,542,857$$

$$\$2,542,857 = \$1,000,000 + S$$

$$S = \$1,542,857.$$

---

3. Find k_{sL}.

$k_{sL} = k_{sU} + (k_{sU} - k_d)(1 - T)(D/S)$

$= 14.0\% + (14.0\% - 8.0\%)(0.6)\left(\dfrac{\$1,000,000}{\$1,542,857}\right)$

$= 14.0\% + 2.33\% = 16.33\%.$

---

4. Find Firm L's WACC.

$WACC_L = (D/V)k_d(1 - T) + (S/V)k_s$

$= \left(\dfrac{\$1,000,000}{\$2,542,857}\right)(8.0\%)(0.6)$

$+ \left(\dfrac{\$1,542,857}{\$2,542,857}\right)(16.33\%)$

$= 1.89\% + 9.91\% = 11.80\%.$

When corporate taxes are considered, the WACC is lower for L than for U.

MM relationship between capital costs and leverage when corporate taxes are considered.

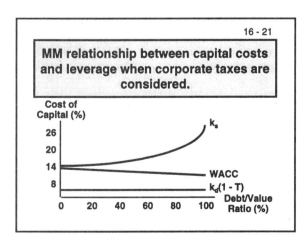

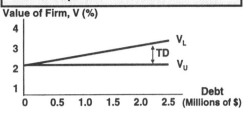

MM relationship between value and debt when corporate taxes are considered.

16 - 22

Value of Firm, V (%)

A graph with y-axis labeled from 1 to 4, x-axis labeled "Debt (Millions of $)" from 0 to 2.5. An upward sloping line labeled V_L and a horizontal line at 2 labeled V_U, with the gap between them labeled TD.

Under MM with corporate taxes, the firm's value increases continuously as more and more debt is used.

---

16 - 23

Assume investors have the following tax rates: T_d = 30% and T_s = 12%. What is the gain from leverage according to the Miller model?

Miller's Proposition I:

$$V_L = V_U + \left[1 - \frac{(1 - T_c)(1 - T_s)}{(1 - T_d)} \right] D.$$

T_c = corporate tax rate.
T_d = personal tax rate on debt income.
T_s = personal tax rate on stock income.

---

16 - 24

T_c = 40%, T_d = 30%, and T_s = 12%.

$$V_L = V_U + \left[1 - \frac{(1 - 0.40)(1 - 0.12)}{(1 - 0.30)} \right] D$$

$$= V_U + (1 - 0.75)D$$

$$= V_U + 0.25D.$$

Value rises with debt; each $100 increase in debt raises L's value by $25.

How does this gain compare to the gain in the MM model with corporate taxes?

If only corporate taxes, then

$$V_L = V_U + T_cD = V_U + 0.40D.$$

Here $100 of debt raises value by $40. Thus, personal taxes lowers the gain from leverage, but the net effect depends on tax rates.

(More...)

- If T_s declines, while T_c and T_d remain constant, the slope coefficient (which shows the benefit of debt) is decreased.

- A company with a low payout ratio gets lower benefits under the Miller model than a company with a high payout, because a low payout decreases T_s.

When Miller brought in personal taxes, the value enhancement of debt was lowered. Why?

1. Corporate tax laws favor debt over equity financing because interest expense is tax deductible while dividends are not.

(More...)

2. However, personal tax laws favor equity over debt because stocks provide both tax deferral and a lower capital gains tax rate.

3. This lowers the relative cost of equity vis-a-vis MM's no-personal-tax world and decreases the spread between debt and equity costs.

4. Thus, some of the advantage of debt financing is lost, so debt financing is less valuable to firms.

What does capital structure theory prescribe for corporate managers?

1. MM, No Taxes: Capital structure is irrelevant--no impact on value or WACC.

2. MM, Corporate Taxes: Value increases, so firms should use (almost) 100% debt financing.

3. Miller, Personal Taxes: Value increases, but less than under MM, so again firms should use (almost) 100% debt financing.

Do firms follow the recommendations of capital structure theory?

■ Firms don't follow MM/Miller to 100% debt. Debt ratios average about 40%.

■ However, debt ratios did increase after MM. Many think debt ratios were too low, and MM led to changes in financial policies.

Define financial distress and agency costs.

Financial distress: As firms use more and more debt financing, they face a higher probability of future financial distress, which brings with it lower sales, EBIT, and bankruptcy costs. Lowers value of stock and bonds.

(More...)

Agency costs: The costs of managers not behaving in the best interests of shareholders and the resulting costs of monitoring managers' actions. Lowers value of stock and bonds.

How do financial distress and agency costs change the MM and Miller models?

- MM/Miller ignored these costs, hence those models show firm value increasing continuously with leverage.
- Since financial distress and agency costs increase with leverage, such costs reduce the value of debt financing.

Here's a valuation model which includes financial distress and agency costs:

$$V_L = V_U + XD - \text{PV of expected fin. distress costs} - \text{PV of agency costs}.$$

- X represents either T_c in the MM model or the more complex Miller term.
- Now, optimal leverage involves a tradeoff between the tax benefits of debt and the costs associated with financial distress and agency.

Relationships between capital costs and leverage when financial distress and agency costs are considered.

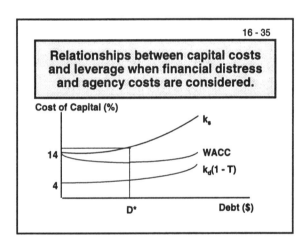

Relationship between value and leverage.

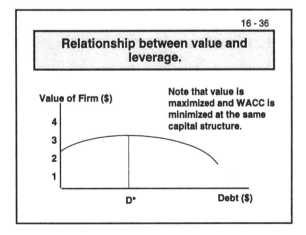

Note that value is maximized and WACC is minimized at the same capital structure.

How are financial and business risk measured in a market risk framework?

$$k_{sL} = k_{RF} + (k_M - k_{RF})b_U$$

$$+ (k_M - k_{RF})b_U(1 - T)(D/S)$$

$$= \begin{array}{c} \text{Pure} \\ \text{time} \\ \text{value} \end{array} + \begin{array}{c} \text{Business} \\ \text{risk} \\ \text{premium} \end{array} + \begin{array}{c} \text{Financial} \\ \text{risk} \\ \text{premium} \end{array} .$$

(Hamada's equation)

Hamada's equation for beta:

$$b_L = b_U + b_U(1 - T)(D/S)$$

$$= \begin{array}{c} \text{Unlevered} \\ \text{beta, which} \\ \text{reflects the} \\ \text{business} \\ \text{risk of the} \\ \text{firm} \end{array} + \begin{array}{c} \text{Increased} \\ \text{volatility of} \\ \text{the returns} \\ \text{to equity} \\ \text{due to the use} \\ \text{of debt} \end{array}$$

$$= \begin{array}{c} \text{Business} \\ \text{risk} \end{array} + \begin{array}{c} \text{Financial} \\ \text{risk} \end{array} .$$

What is the "pecking order theory" of capital structure?

■ Results of a survey by Donaldson and the asymmetric information theory.

■ Firms follow a specific financing order:
- First use internal funds.
- Next, draw on marketable securities.
- Then, issue new debt.
- Finally, and only as a last resort, issue new common stock.

Does the pecking order theory make sense? Explain.
Is the pecking order theory consistent with the trade-off theory?

- It is consistent with the asymmetric information theory, in which managers avoid issuing equity.

- It is not consistent with trade-off theory.

What is the asymmetric information theory of capital structure?

- Theory recognizes that market participants do not have homogeneous expectations-- managers typically have better information than investors.

- Thus, financing actions are interpreted by investors as signals of managerial expectations for the future. (More...)

- Managers will issue new common stock only when no other alternatives exist or when the stock is overvalued.

- Investors recognize this, so new stock sales are treated as negative signals and stock price falls.

- Managers do not want to trigger a price decline, so firms maintain a reserve borrowing capacity.

Southeastern Steel Company (SSC) was formed 5 years ago to exploit a new continuous-casting process. SSC's founders, Donald Brown and Margo Valencia, had been employed in the research department of a major integrated-steel company, but when that company decided against using the new process (which Brown and Valencia had developed), they decided to strike out on their own. One advantage of the new process was that it required relatively little capital in comparison with the typical steel company, so Brown and Valencia have been able to avoid issuing new stock, and thus they own all of the shares. However, SCC has now reached the stage where outside equity capital is necessary if the firm is to achieve its growth targets yet still maintain its target capital structure of 60 percent equity and 40 percent debt. Therefore, Brown and Valencia have decided to take the company public. Until now, Brown and Valencia have paid themselves reasonable salaries but routinely reinvested all after-tax earnings in the firm, so dividend policy has not been an issue. However, before talking with potential outside investors, they must decide on a dividend policy.

Assume that you were recently hired by Arthur Adamson & Company (AA), a national consulting firm, which has been asked to help SSC prepare for its public offering. Martha Millon, the senior AA consultant in your group, has asked you to make a presentation to Brown and Valencia in which you review the theory of dividend policy and discuss the following questions.

a. (1) What is meant by the term "dividend policy"?

   (2) The terms "irrelevance," "bird-in-the-hand," and "tax preference" have been used to describe three major theories regarding the way dividend policy affects a firm's value. Explain what these terms mean, and briefly describe each theory.

   (3) What do the three theories indicate regarding the actions management should take with respect to dividend policy?

   (4) Explain the relationships between dividend policy, stock price, and the cost of equity under each dividend policy theory by constructing two graphs such as those shown in Figure 17-1. Dividend payout should be placed on the X axis.

   (5) What results have empirical studies of the dividend theories produced? How does all this affect what we can tell managers about dividend policy?

b. Discuss (1) the information content, or signaling, hypothesis, (2) the clientele effect, and (3) their effects on dividend policy.

c. (1) Assume that SSC has an $800,000 capital budget planned for the coming year. You have determined that its present capital structure (60 percent equity and 40 percent debt) is optimal, and its net income is forecasted at $600,000. Use the residual dividend model approach to determine SSC's total dollar dividend and payout ratio. In the process, explain what the residual dividend model is. Then, explain what would happen if net income were forecasted at $400,000, or at $800,000.

   (2) In general terms, how would a change in investment opportunities affect the payout ratio under the residual payment policy?

   (3) What are the advantages and disadvantages of the residual policy? (Hint: Don't neglect signaling and clientele effects.)

d. What is a dividend reinvestment plan (DRIP), and how does it work?

e. Describe the series of steps that most firms take in setting dividend policy in practice.

f. What are stock repurchases? Discuss the advantages and disadvantages of a firm's repurchasing its own shares.

g. What are stock dividends and stock splits? What are the advantages and disadvantages of stock dividends and stock splits?

CHAPTER 17
Distributions to Shareholders:
Dividends and Repurchases

- Theories of investor preferences
- Signaling effects
- Residual model
- Dividend reinvestment plans
- Stock repurchases
- Stock dividends and stock splits

What is "dividend policy"?

- It's the decision to pay out earnings versus retaining and reinvesting them. Includes these elements:

    1. High or low payout?

    2. Stable or irregular dividends?

    3. How frequent?

    4. Do we announce the policy?

Do investors prefer high or low payouts? There are three theories:

- Dividends are irrelevant: Investors don't care about payout.

- Bird-in-the-hand: Investors prefer a high payout.

- Tax preference: Investors prefer a low payout, hence growth.

Dividend Irrelevance Theory

- Investors are indifferent between dividends and retention-generated capital gains. If they want cash, they can sell stock. If they don't want cash, they can use dividends to buy stock.
- Modigliani-Miller support irrelevance.
- Theory is based on unrealistic assumptions (no taxes or brokerage costs), hence may not be true. Need empirical test.

Bird-in-the-Hand Theory

- Investors think dividends are less risky than potential future capital gains, hence they like dividends.
- If so, investors would value high payout firms more highly, i.e., a high payout would result in a high P_0.

Tax Preference Theory

- Retained earnings lead to capital gains, which are taxed at lower rates than dividends: 28% maximum vs. up to 39.6%. Capital gains taxes are also deferred.
- This could cause investors to prefer firms with low payouts, i.e., a high payout results in a low P_0.

Implications of 3 Theories for Managers

Theory	Implication
Irrelevance	Any payout OK
Bird-in-the-hand	Set high payout
Tax preference	Set low payout

But which, if any, is correct???

Possible Stock Price Effects

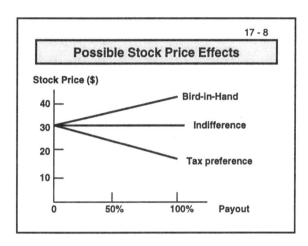

Possible Cost of Equity Effects

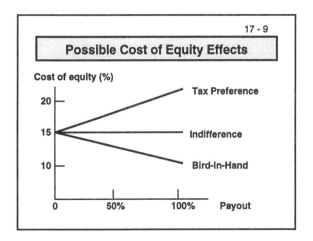

Which theory is most correct?

- Empirical testing has not been able to determine which theory, if any, is correct.
- Thus, managers use judgment when setting policy.
- Analysis is used, but it must be applied with judgment.

What's the "information content," or "signaling," hypothesis?

- Managers hate to cut dividends, so won't raise dividends unless they think raise is sustainable. So, investors view dividend increases as *signals* of management's view of the future.
- Therefore, a stock price increase at time of a dividend increase could reflect higher expectations for future EPS, not a desire for dividends.

What's the "clientele effect"?

- Different groups of investors, or clienteles, prefer different dividend policies.
- Firm's past dividend policy determines its current clientele of investors.
- Clientele effects impede changing dividend policy. Taxes & brokerage costs hurt investors who have to switch companies.

What's the "residual dividend model"?

- Find the retained earnings needed for the capital budget.

- Pay out any leftover earnings (the residual) as dividends.

- This policy minimizes flotation and equity signaling costs, hence minimizes the WACC.

Data for SSC

- Capital budget: $800,000. Given.

- Target capital structure: 40% debt, 60% equity. Want to maintain.

- Forecasted net income: $600,000.

- How much of the $600,000 should we pay out as dividends?

Of the $800,000 capital budget, 0.6($800,000) = $480,000 must be equity to keep at target capital structure. [0.4($800,000) = $320,000 will be debt.]

With $600,000 of net income, the residual is $600,000 - $480,000 = $120,000 = dividends paid.

Payout ratio = $120,000/$600,000
= 0.20 = 20%.

How would a drop in NI to $400,000 affect the dividend? A rise to $800,000?

- NI = $400,000: Need $480,000 of equity, so should retain the whole $400,000. Dividends = 0.

- NI = $800,000: Dividends = $800,000 - $480,000 = $320,000. Payout = $320,000/$800,000 = 40%.

How would a change in investment opportunities affect dividend under the residual policy?

- Fewer good investments would lead to smaller capital budget, hence to a higher dividend payout.

- More good investments would lead to a lower dividend payout.

Advantages and Disadvantages of the Residual Dividend Policy

- Advantages: Minimizes new stock issues and flotation costs.
- Disadvantages: Results in variable dividends, sends conflicting signals, increases risk, and doesn't appeal to any specific clientele.
- Conclusion: Consider residual policy when setting target payout, but don't follow it rigidly.

What's a "dividend reinvestment plan (DRIP)"?

- Shareholders can automatically reinvest their dividends in shares of the company's common stock. Get more stock than cash.
- There are two types of plans:
  - Open market
  - New stock

Open Market Purchase Plan

- Dollars to be reinvested are turned over to trustee, who buys shares on the open market.
- Brokerage costs are reduced by volume purchases.
- Convenient, easy way to invest, thus useful for investors.

New Stock Plan

- Firm issues new stock to DRIP enrollees, keeps money and uses it to buy assets.
- No fees are charged, plus sells stock at discount of 5% from market price, which is about equal to flotation costs of underwritten stock offering.

Optional investments sometimes possible, up to $150,000 or so.

Firms that need new equity capital use new stock plans.

Firms with no need for new equity capital use open market purchase plans.

Most NYSE listed companies have a DRIP. Useful for investors.

Setting Dividend Policy

- Forecast capital needs over a planning horizon, often 5 years.
- Set a target capital structure.
- Estimate annual equity needs.
- Set target payout based on the residual model.
- Generally, some dividend growth rate emerges. Maintain target growth rate if possible, varying capital structure somewhat if necessary.

Stock Repurchases

Repurchases: Buying own stock back from stockholders.

Reasons for repurchases:

- As an alternative to distributing cash as dividends.
- To dispose of one-time cash from an asset sale.
- To make a large capital structure change.

Advantages of Repurchases

- Stockholders can tender or not.
- Helps avoid setting a high dividend that cannot be maintained.
- Repurchased stock can be used in takeovers or resold to raise cash as needed.
- Income received is capital gains rather than higher-taxed dividends.
- Stockholders may take as a positive signal-- management thinks stock is undervalued.

Disadvantages of Repurchases

- May be viewed as a negative signal (firm has poor investment opportunities).
- IRS could impose penalties if repurchases were primarily to avoid taxes on dividends.
- Selling stockholders may not be well informed, hence be treated unfairly.
- Firm may have to bid up price to complete purchase, thus paying too much for its own stock.

Stock Dividends vs. Stock Splits

- Stock dividend: Firm issues new shares in lieu of paying a cash dividend. If 10%, get 10 shares for each 100 shares owned.

- Stock split: Firm increases the number of shares outstanding, say 2:1. Sends shareholders more shares.

Both stock dividends and stock splits increase the number of shares outstanding, so "the pie is divided into smaller pieces."

Unless the stock dividend or split conveys information, or is accompanied by another event like higher dividends, *the stock price falls so as to keep each investor's wealth unchanged.*

But splits/stock dividends may get us to an "optimal price range."

When should a firm consider splitting its stock?

- There's a widespread belief that the *optimal price range* for stocks is $20 to $80.
- Stock splits can be used to keep the price in the optimal range.
- Stock splits generally occur when management is confident, so are interpreted as *positive signals*.

BLUEPRINTS: CHAPTER 18
ISSUING SECURITIES, REFUNDING OPERATIONS, AND OTHER TOPICS

Randy's, a family-owned restaurant chain operating in Alabama, has grown to the point where expansion throughout the entire Southeast is feasible. The proposed expansion would require the firm to raise about $15 million in new capital. Because Randy's currently has a debt ratio of 50 percent, and also because the family members already have all their personal wealth invested in the company, the family would like to sell common stock to the public to raise the $15 million. However, the family does want to retain voting control. You have been asked to brief the family members on the issues involved by answering the following questions:

a. What agencies regulate securities markets?

b. What are some of the decisions faced by firms needing external financing?

c. Would the stock sale be an initial public offering (IPO)? What would be the advantages to the family members of having the firm go public? Would there be any disadvantages? If you were a key employee, but not a family member, or a potential key employee being interviewed as a part of the expansion process, how would the decision affect you?

d. What does it mean for a stock to be listed? Do you think that Randy's stock would be listed shortly after the company goes public? If not, where would the stock trade?

e. What is a rights offering? Would it make sense for Randy's to use a rights offering to raise the $15 million? Even if you do not think a rights offering should be employed, could one be used?

f. What is the difference between a private placement and a public offering? What are the advantages and disadvantages of each type of placement? Which type would be most suitable for Randy's?

g. What is meant by going private? Assume for the sake of this question that Randy's previously went public. What are the advantages and disadvantages of the firm's going private?

h. (1) Would Randy's be likely to sell the $15 million of stock by itself or through an investment banker?

(2) If an investment banker were used, would the sale most likely be on the basis of a competitive bid or a negotiated deal?

(3) If it were a negotiated deal, would it most likely be done on a best efforts or an underwritten basis? In each case, explain your answer.

i. Without doing any calculations, describe the procedure by which the company and its investment banker would determine the price at which the stock would be offered to the public.

j. Suppose the decision were made to issue 1.5 million shares at $10 per share. What would be the net amount raised if the flotation cost on the issue were 18 percent? What if the firm were already publicly owned and the flotation costs were 9 percent? Would there be a difference in costs between a best efforts and an underwritten offering?

k. What are some of the factors a firm should consider when deciding whether to issue long-term debt or equity?

l. Describe the key features of the following securities:

(1) Project financing

(2) Securitization

m. Under what conditions would a firm exercise a bond's call provision?

CHAPTER 18
Issuing Securities, Refunding Operations, and Other Topics

- Regulation and Investment Banking
- Public versus Private Ownership
- Debt Securities
- Factors Influencing Long-Term Financing Decisions
- Refunding Operations

What agencies regulate securities markets?

- The Securities and Exchange Commission (SEC) regulates:
  - Interstate public offerings.
  - National stock exchanges.
  - Trading by corporate insiders.
  - The corporate proxy process.
- The Federal Reserve Board controls margin requirements.   (More...)

- States control the issuance of securities within their boundaries.
- The securities industry, through the exchanges and the National Association of Securities Dealers (NASD), takes actions to ensure the integrity and credibility of the trading system.
- Why is it important that securities markets be tightly regulated?

What are some of the decisions faced by firms needing external financing?

- Stage I Decisions
  - Amount to be raised
  - Type(s) of securities to be used
  - Competitive bid versus a negotiated deal
  - Selection of an investment banker

(More...)

- Stage II Decisions
  - Reevaluating the initial decisions
  - Best efforts versus an underwritten deal
  - Banker's compensation and other expenses
  - Setting the offering price
- Selling Procedures
- Shelf Registrations

When is a stock sale an initial public offering (IPO)?

- A firm goes public through an IPO when the stock is offered to the public for the first time.

- Randy's is currently privately held.

- Selling stock to the public would make the company publicly held.

Why would Randy's consider going public?

- **Advantages of going public**
  - Current stockholders can diversify.
  - Liquidity is increased.
  - Easier to raise capital in the future.
  - Going public establishes firm value.
  - Makes it more feasible to use stock as employee incentives.

    (More...)

- **Disadvantages of Going Public**
  - Must file numerous reports.
  - Operating data must be disclosed.
  - Officers must disclose holdings.
  - Special "deals" to insiders will be more difficult to undertake.
  - A small new issue will not be actively traded, so market-determined price may not reflect true value.

How would the decision to go public affect key employees?

- If key employees own stock or options, they would know the true worth of these securities.
- Stock can be sold much more easily.
- It becomes easier to create employee incentive plans.

Could the founding stockholders sell some of their own shares when the firm goes public?

- Yes, but investment bankers would not like it. Would send negative signal to potential purchasers.

- Still, it's not uncommon for founding stockholders to sell some shares to diversify their personal holdings.

What is meant by "listing?" Would a small firm likely be listed?

- A listed stock is traded on an organized exchange.

- It's unlikely that a small firm's stock would be listed. Small firms trade in the OTC market.

- Today, even some larger firms are choosing to remain unlisted.

What is a rights offering? Would it make sense for a small firm that is going public to use a rights offering?

- A rights offering occurs when current shareholders get the first right to buy new shares.

- Would not make sense for a firm that is going public. If current stockholders wanted to buy shares, they wouldn't go public.

Differentiate between a private placement and a public offering.

- In a private placement, securities are sold to a few investors rather than to the public at large.

- In a public offering, securities are offered to the public through investment bankers. (Note that a private placement could also utilize investment bankers.)

(More...)

- Privately placed stock is not registered, so sales must be to "sophisticated" (high net worth) investors.

- Send out "offering memorandum" with 20-30 pages of data and information, prepared by securities lawyers.

- Buyers certify that they meet net worth/income requirements and they will not sell to unqualified investors.

What is meant by going private?

- Going private is the reverse of going public.
- Typically, the firm's managers team up with a small group of outside investors and purchase all of the publicly held shares of the firm.
- The new equity holders usually use a large amount of debt financing, so such transactions are called leveraged buyouts (LBOs).

Advantages of Going Private

- Gives managers greater incentives and more flexibility in running the company.

- Removes pressure to report high earnings in the short run.

- After several years as a private firm, owners typically go public again. Firm is presumably operating more efficiently and sells for more.

Disadvantages of Going Private

- Firms that have recently gone private are normally leveraged to the hilt, so it's difficult to raise new capital.

- A difficult period that normally could be weathered might bankrupt the company.

Would companies going public use a negotiated deal or a competitive bid?

- A negotiated deal.
  - The competitive bid process is only feasible for large issues by major firms. Even here, the use of bids is rare for equity issues.
  - It would cost investment bankers too much to learn enough about the company to make an intelligent bid.

Would the sale be on an underwritten or best efforts basis?

- Most offerings are underwritten.
- In very small, risky deals, the investment banker may insist on a best efforts basis.
- On an underwritten deal, the price is not set until
  - Investor interest is assessed.
  - Oral commitments are obtained.

Describe how an IPO would be priced.

- Since the firm is going public, there is no established price.
- The banker would examine market data on similar companies.
- Price set to place the firm's P/E and M/B ratios in line with publicly traded firms in the same industry having similar risk and growth prospects.

(More...)

- On the basis of all relevant factors, the investment banker would determine a ballpark equilibrium price.
- The offering price would be set somewhat lower to increase demand and to insure that the issue will sell out.

(More...)

- There is an inherent conflict of interest, because the banker has an incentive to set a low price:
  - to make brokerage customers happy.
  - to make it easy to sell the issue.
- Firm would like price to be high.
- Note that original owners generally sell only a small part of their stock, so if price increases, they benefit.
- Later offerings easier if first goes well.

Suppose a firm issued 1.5 million shares at $10 per share. What would be the net amount raised if flotation costs on the issue were 18%?

- Gross proceeds: $15 million.
- But, flotation costs of IPO would be about 18% or $2.7 million.
- The firm would net about $12.3 million from the sale.

What would be the net proceeds if the firm were already publicly owned and flotation costs were 9%?

- If the firm were already publicly owned, flotation costs would be much less, about 9% or about $1.4 million, because a market price for the stock would already have been established.
- Now the firm would net about $13.6 million.

Would there be a difference in costs between a best efforts and an underwritten offering?

- The investment bankers are exposed to more risk on underwritten deals, and hence will charge a price for assuming this risk.
- If the firm absolutely has to have the money to meet a commitment, it will want a guaranteed price and will use an underwritten sale.

What factors influence long-term financing decisions?

- Capital structure considerations
- Maturity matching
- Information asymmetries
- Amount of financing required
- Availability of collateral
- Current and prospective capital costs

Describe the following items:

- Project financing
- Securitization

■ Project financings are used to finance a specific large capital project. Sponsors provide the equity capital, while the rest of the project's capital is supplied by lenders and/or lessors who do not have recourse.

(More...)

■ Securitization is the process whereby financial instruments that were previously illiquid are converted to a form that creates greater liquidity. Examples are bonds backed by mortgages, auto loans, credit card loans (asset-backed), and so on.

Under what conditions would a firm exercise a bond call provision?

■ If interest rates have fallen since the bond was issued, the firm can replace the current issue with a new, lower coupon rate bond.

■ However, there are costs involved in refunding a bond issue. For example,
- The call premium.
- Flotation costs on the new issue.

(More...)

■ The NPV of refunding compares the interest savings benefit with the costs of the refunding. A positive NPV indicates that refunding today would increase the value of the firm.

■ However, it interest rates are expected to fall further, it may be better to delay refunding until some time in the future.

BLUEPRINTS: CHAPTER 19
LEASE FINANCING

Lewis Securities Inc. has decided to acquire a new market data and quotation system for its Richmond home office. The system receives current market prices and other information from several on-line data services, then either displays the information on a screen or stores it for later retrieval by the firm's brokers. The system also permits customers to call up current quotes on terminals in the lobby.

The equipment costs $1,000,000, and, if it were purchased, Lewis could obtain a term loan for the full purchase price at a 10 percent interest rate. The equipment is classified as a special-purpose computer, so it falls into the MACRS 3-year class. If the system were purchased, a 4-year maintenance contract could be obtained at a cost of $20,000 per year, payable at the *beginning* of each year. The equipment would be sold after 4 years, and the best estimate of its residual value at that time is $100,000. However, since real-time display system technology is changing rapidly, the actual residual value is uncertain.

As an alternative to the borrow-and-buy plan, the equipment manufacturer informed Lewis that Consolidated Leasing would be willing to write a 4-year guideline lease on the equipment, including maintenance, for payments of $280,000 at the *beginning* of each year. Lewis's marginal federal-plus-state tax rate is 40 percent. You have been asked to analyze the lease-versus-purchase decision, and in the process to answer the following questions:

a. (1) Who are the two parties to a lease transaction?

   (2) What are the four primary types of leases, and what are their characteristics?

   (3) How are leases classified for tax purposes?

   (4) What effect does leasing have on a firm's balance sheet?

   (5) What effect does leasing have on a firm's capital structure?

b. (1) What is the present value cost of owning the equipment? (Hint: Set up a time line which shows the net cash flows over the period t = 0 to t = 4, and then find the PV of these net cash flows, or the PV cost of owning.)

   (2) Explain the rationale for the discount rate you used to find the PV.

c. What is Lewis's present value cost of leasing the equipment? (Hint: Again, construct a time line.)

d. What is the net advantage to leasing (NAL)? Does your analysis indicate that Lewis should buy or lease the equipment? Explain.

---

e. Now assume that the equipment's residual value could be as low as $0 or as high as $200,000, but that $100,000 is the expected value. Since the residual value is riskier than the other cash flows in the analysis, this differential risk should be incorporated into the analysis. Describe how this could be accomplished. (No calculations are necessary, but explain how you would modify the analysis if calculations were required.) What effect would increased uncertainty about the residual value have on Lewis's lease-versus-purchase decision?

f. The lessee compares the cost of owning the equipment with the cost of leasing it. Now put yourself in the lessor's shoes. In a few sentences, how should you analyze the decision to write or not write the lease?

g. (1) Assume that the lease payments were actually $300,000 per year, that Consolidated Leasing is also in the 40 percent tax bracket, and that it also forecasts a $100,000 residual value. Also, to furnish the maintenance support, Consolidated would have to purchase a maintenance contract from the manufacturer at the same $20,000 annual cost, again paid in advance. Consolidated Leasing can obtain an expected 10 percent pre-tax return on investments of similar risk. What would Consolidated's NPV and IRR of leasing be under these conditions?

(2) What do you think the lessor's NPV would be if the lease payment were set at $280,000 per year? (Hint: The lessor's cash flows would be a "mirror image" of the lessee's cash flows.)

h. Lewis's management has been considering moving to a new downtown location, and they are concerned that these plans may come to fruition prior to the expiration of the lease. If the move occurs, Lewis would buy or lease an entirely new set of equipment, and hence management would like to include a cancellation clause in the lease contract. What impact would such a clause have on the riskiness of the lease from Lewis's standpoint? From the lessor's standpoint? If you were the lessor, would you insist on changing any of the lease terms if a cancellation clause were added? Should the cancellation clause contain any restrictive covenants and/or penalties of the type contained in bond indentures or provisions similar to call premiums?

CHAPTER 19
Lease Financing

- Types of leases
- Tax treatment of leases
- Effects on financial statements
- Lessee's analysis
- Lessor's analysis
- Other issues in lease analysis

Who are the two parties to a lease transaction?

- The lessee, who uses the asset and makes the lease, or rental, payments.
- The lessor, who owns the asset and receives the rental payments.
- Note that the lease decision is a financing decision for the lessee and an investment decision for the lessor.

What are the four primary lease types?

- Operating lease
  - Short-term and normally cancelable
  - Maintenance usually included
- Financial lease
  - Long-term and normally noncancelable
  - Maintenance usually not included
- Sale and leaseback
- Combination lease

How are leases treated for tax purposes?

- Leases are classified by the IRS as either guideline or nonguideline.
- For a guideline lease, the entire lease payment is deductible to the lessee.
- For a nonguideline lease, only the imputed interest payment is deductible.
- Why should the IRS be concerned about lease provisions?

How does leasing affect a firm's balance sheet?

- For accounting purposes, leases are classified as either capital or operating.
- Capital leases must be shown directly on the lessee's balance sheet.
- Operating leases, sometimes referred to as off-balance sheet financing, must be disclosed in the footnotes.
- Why are these rules in place?

What impact does leasing have on a firm's capital structure?

- Leasing is a substitute for debt.
- As such, leasing uses up a firm's debt capacity.
- Assume a firm has a 50/50 target capital structure. Half of its assets are leased. How should the remaining assets be financed?

Assume that Lewis Securities plans to acquire some new equipment having a 4-year useful life.

- If the equipment is leased:
  - Firm could obtain a 4-year lease which includes maintenance.
  - Lease meets IRS guidelines to expense lease payments.
  - Rental payment would be $280,000 at the beginning of each year.

- Other information:
  - Equipment cost: $1,000,000.
  - Loan rate on equipment = 10%.
  - Marginal tax rate = 40%.
  - 3-year MACRS life.
  - If company borrows and buys, 4 year maintenance contract costs $20,000 at beginning of each year.
  - Residual value at t = 4: $100,000.

Time Line: After-Tax Cost of Owning (In Thousands)

	0	1	2	3	4
AT loan pmt		-60	-60	-60	-1,060
Dep shld		132	180	60	28
Maint	-20	-20	-20	-20	
Tax sav	8	8	8	8	
RV					100
Tax					-40
NCF	-12	60	108	-12	-972

■ Note the depreciation shield in each year equals the depreciation expense times the lessee's tax rate. For Year 1, the depreciation shield is

$330,000(0.40) = $132,000.

■ The present value of the cost of owning cash flows, when discounted at 6%, is -$639,267.

Why use 6% as the discount rate?

■ Leasing is similar to debt financing.
- The cash flows have relatively low risk; most are fixed by contract.
- Therefore, the firm's 10% cost of debt is a good candidate.

■ The tax shield of interest payments must be recognized, so the discount rate is

10%(1 - T) = 10%(1 - 0.4) = 6.0%.

Time Line: After-Tax Cost of Leasing (In Thousands)

	0	1	2	3	4
Lease pmt	-280	-280	-280	-280	
Tax sav	112	112	112	112	
NCF	-168	-168	-168	-168	

PV cost of leasing @ 6% = -$617,066.

19 - 13

What is the net advantage to leasing (NAL)?

- NAL = PV cost of leasing - PV cost of owning
  = - $617,066 - (-$639,267)
  = $22,201.

- Should the firm lease or buy the equipment? Why?

19 - 14

- Note that we have assumed the company will not continue to use the asset after the lease expires; that is, project life is the same as the term of the lease.

- What changes to the analysis would be required if the lessee planned to continue using the equipment after the lease expired?

19 - 15

Assume the RV could be $0 or $200,000, with an expected value of $100,000. How could this risk be reflected?

- The discount rate applied to the residual value inflow (a positive CF) should be increased to account for the increased risk.

- All other cash flows should be discounted at the original 6% rate.

(More...)

- If the residual value were included as an outflow (a *negative* CF) in the cost of leasing cash flows, the increased risk would be reflected by applying a lower discount rate to the residual value cash flow.

- Again, all other cash flows have relatively low risk, and hence would be discounted at the 6% rate.

What effect would increased uncertainty about the residual value have on the lessee's decision?

- The lessor owns the equipment when the lease expires.

- Therefore, residual value risk is passed from the lessee to the lessor.

- Increased residual value risk makes the lease more attractive to the lessee.

How should the lessor analyze the lease transaction?

- To the lessor, writing the lease is an investment.

- Therefore, the lessor must compare the return on the lease investment with the return available on alternative investments of similar risk.

Assume the following data for Consolidated Leasing, the lessor:

- $300,000 rental payment instead of $280,000.

- All other data are the same as for the lessee.

Time Line: Lessor's Analysis (In Thousands)

	0	1	2	3	4
Cost	-1,000				
Dep shld		132	180	60	28
Maint	-20	-20	-20	-20	
Tax sav	8	8	8	8	
Lse pmt	300	300	300	300	
Tax	-120	-120	-120	-120	
RV					100
RV tax					-40
NCF	-832	300	348	228	88

- The NPV of the net cash flows, when discounted at 6%, is $21,875.

- The IRR is 7.35%.

- Should the lessor write the lease? Why?

Find the lessor's NPV if the lease payment were $280,000.

- With lease payments of $280,000, the lessor's cash flows would be equal, but opposite in sign, to the lessee's NAL.
- Thus, lessor's NPV = -$22,201.
- If all inputs are symmetrical, leasing is a zero-sum game.
- What are the implications?

What impact would a cancellation clause have on the lease's riskiness from the lessee's standpoint? From the lessor's standpoint?

- A cancellation clause would lower the risk of the lease to the lessee but raise the lessor's risk.
- To account for this, the lessor would increase the annual lease payment or else impose a penalty for early cancellation.

Other Issues in Lease Analysis

- Do higher residual values make leasing less attractive to the lessee?
- Is lease financing more available or "better" than debt financing?
- Is the lease analysis presented here applicable to real estate leases? To auto leases?

(More...)

■ **Would spreadsheet models be useful in lease analyses?**

■ **What impact do tax laws have on the attractiveness of leasing? Consider the following provisions:**

  ● Investment tax credit (when available)

  ● Tax rate differentials between the lessee and the lessor

  ● Alternative minimum tax (AMT)

Numerical analyses often indicate that owning is less costly than leasing. Why, then, is leasing so popular?

■ **Provision of maintenance services.**

■ **Risk reduction for the lessee.**

  ● Project life

  ● Residual value

  ● Operating risk

■ **Portfolio risk reduction enables lessor to better bear these risks.**

19E - 1

Chapter 19 Extension

- ■ Percentage return analysis
- ■ Leverage lease analysis
- ■ Feedback effect on capital budgeting

19E - 2

An alternative to the NAL is to find the percentage return on the lease.

- ■ NAL measures the dollar advantage of leasing versus borrowing and buying. A positive NAL indicates leasing.

- ■ The IRR of the incremental cash flows represents the rate of return on the lease. It must be compared to the after-tax cost of debt to find the better alternative.

19E - 3

Combine the Leasing and Owning CFs (In Thousands)

	0	1	2	3	4
Lease	-168	-168	-168	-168	
- Own	-12	60	108	-12	-972
ΔCF	-156	-288	-276	-156	972

What do the incremental CFs tell us about the economics of the leasing?

- The IRR of the incremental cash flow stream, 7.23%, represents the rate of return from leasing versus owning and borrowing.

- Because the after-tax cost of debt is less than the return from leasing, leasing is the best alternative.

- Both the NAL and IRR methods lead to the same lease versus buy decision. Why?

Now assume that the lessor can leverage the lease.

- The lessor can borrow $500,000 of the $1,000,000 purchase price with a 4-year loan costing 10%.

- For simplicity, assume that only interest is paid until maturity in 4 years, when the full principal is due.

Time Line: Leveraged Lease (In Thousands)

	0	1	2	3	4
Lse CF	-832	300	348	228	88
Loan	500				
AT Int		-30	-30	-30	-30
Prin pmt					-500
NCF	-332	270	318	198	-442

Leveraged Lease (Continued)

- The NPV of the leveraged lease, when discounted at 6%, is $21,875.
- Note that the NPV is unchanged. This is because the loan cost is the same as the discount rate.
- However, the $21,875 leveraged NPV requires an investment of only $500,000, as opposed to $1,000,000 with the unleveraged lease. (More...)

- Thus, with a $1 million investment, the lessor could finance two such leases and obtain double the amount of NPV: 2($21,875) = $43,750 in profit.
- With the leveraged lease, we get two IRRs: -3.5% and +29.6%. The MIRR of the leverage lease is about 6%.
- However, leveraging increases the risk to the lessor, so the decision to leverage involves a risk/return tradeoff.

Feedback Effects on Capital Budgeting

- If the cost of leasing is less than the cost of debt, it is possible that leasing might make a previously rejected project acceptable.
- If all projects could be leased, the firm's cost of capital should use the cost of leasing in place of the cost of debt. (More...)

- If only one project can be leased, the true NPV of the project (if leased) is the NPV based on the "regular" cost of capital plus the lease's NAL.

- If neither of the two extreme positions hold, no simple rule can be used to incorporate "feedback" effects.

Paul Duncan, financial manager of Edusoft Inc., is facing a dilemma. The firm was founded five years ago to provide educational software for the rapidly expanding primary and secondary school markets. Although Edusoft has done well, the firm's founder believes that an industry shakeout is imminent. To survive, Edusoft must grab market share now, and this will require a large infusion of new capital.

Because he expects earnings to continue rising sharply and looks for the stock price to follow suit, Mr. Duncan does not think it would be wise to issue new common stock at this time. On the other hand, interest rates are currently high by historical standards, and with the firm's B rating, the interest payments on a new debt issue would be prohibitive. Thus, he has narrowed his choice of financing alternatives to two securities: (1) bonds with warrants or (2) convertible bonds. As Duncan's assistant, you have been asked to help in the decision process by answering the following questions:

a. How does preferred stock differ from both common equity and debt?

b. What is a call option? How can a knowledge of call options help a financial manager to better understand warrants and convertibles?

c. One of the firm's alternatives is to issue a bond with warrants attached. EduSoft's current stock price is $20, and its investment banker estimates that the cost of a 20-year, annual coupon bond without warrants would be 12 percent. The bankers suggest attaching 50 warrants, each with an exercise price of $25, to each $1,000 bond. It is estimated that each warrant, when detached and traded separately, would have a value of $3.

   (1) What coupon rate should be set on the bond with warrants if the total package is to sell for $1,000?

   (2) Suppose the bonds were issued and the warrants immediately traded on the open market for $5 each. What would this imply about the terms of the issue? Did the company "win" or "lose"?

   (3) When would you expect the warrants to be exercised? Assume they have a 10-year life; that is, they expire 10 years after issue.

   (4) Will the warrants bring in additional capital when exercised? If so, how much, and what type of capital?

(5) Since warrants lower the cost of the accompanying debt issue, shouldn't all debt be issued with warrants? What is the expected return to the holders of the bond with warrants (or the expected cost to the company) if the warrants are expected to be exercised in five years, when EduSoft's stock price is expected to be $36.75? How would you expect the cost of the bond with warrants to compare with the cost of straight debt? With the cost of common stock?

d. As an alternative to the bond with warrants, Mr. Duncan is considering convertible bonds. The firm's investment bankers estimate that EduSoft could sell a 20-year, 10.5 percent annual coupon, callable convertible bond for its $1,000 par value, whereas a straight-debt issue would require a 12 percent coupon. The convertibles would be call protected for 5 years, the call price would be $1,100, and the company would probably call the bonds as soon as possible after their conversion value exceeds $1,200. Note, though, that the call must occur on an issue date anniversary. EduSoft's current stock price is $20, its last dividend was $1.48, and the dividend is expected to grow at a constant 8 percent rate. The convertible could be converted into 40 shares of EduSoft stock at the owner's option.

(1) What conversion price is built into the bond?

(2) What is the convertible's straight-debt value? What is the implied value of the convertibility feature?

(3) What is the formula for the bond's expected conversion value in any year? What is its conversion value at Year 0? At Year 10?

(4) What is meant by the "floor value" of a convertible? What is the convertible's expected floor value at Year 0? At Year 10?

(5) Assume that EduSoft intends to force conversion by calling the bond as soon as possible after its conversion value exceeds 20 percent above its par value, or 1.2($1,000) = $1,200. When is the issue expected to be called? (Hint: Recall that the call must be made on an anniversary date of the issue.)

(6) What is the expected cost of capital for the convertible to EduSoft? Does this cost appear to be consistent with the riskiness of the issue?

e. EduSoft's market value capital structure is as follows (in millions of dollars):

Debt	$ 50
Equity	50
	$100

If the company raises $20 million in additional capital by selling (1) convertibles or (2) bonds with warrants, what would its WACC be, and how would those figures compare with its current WACC? EduSoft's tax rate is 40 percent.

f. Mr. Duncan believes that the costs of both the bond with warrants and the convertible bond are close enough to one another to call them even, and also consistent with the risks involved. Thus, he will make his decision based on other factors. What are some of the factors which he should consider?

CHAPTER 20
Hybrid Financing: Preferred Stock, Warrants, and Convertibles

- ■ Types of hybrid securities
  - ● Preferred stock
  - ● Warrants
  - ● Convertibles
- ■ Features and risk
- ■ Cost of capital to issuers

How does preferred stock differ from common stock and debt?

- ■ Preferred dividends are specified by contract, but they may be omitted without placing the firm in default.
- ■ Most preferred stocks prohibit the firm from paying common dividends when the preferred is in arrears.
- ■ Usually cumulative up to a limit.

(More...)

- ■ Some preferred stock is perpetual, but most new issues have sinking fund or call provisions which limit maturities.
- ■ Preferred stock has no voting rights, but may require companies to place preferred stockholders on the board (sometimes a majority) if the dividend is passed.
- ■ Is preferred stock closer to debt or common stock? What is its risk to investors? To issuers?

What are the advantages and disadvantages of preferred stock financing?

- ■ **Advantages**
  - ● Dividend obligation not contractual
  - ● Avoids dilution of common stock
  - ● Avoids large repayment of principal
- ■ **Disadvantages**
  - ● Preferred dividends not tax deductible, so typically costs more than debt
  - ● Increases financial leverage, and hence the firm's cost of common equity

What is a call option?

A call option is a contract that gives the holder the right, but not the obligation, to buy some defined asset at a specified price within some specified period of time.

What is the relationship between call options, warrants, and convertibles?

- ■ A warrant is a long-term call option.
- ■ A convertible consists of a fixed rate bond (or preferred stock) plus a long-term call option.

Given the following facts, what coupon rate must be set on a bond with warrants if the total package is to sell for $1,000?

- $P_0 = \$20$.
- k_d of 20-year annual payment bond without warrants = 12%.
- 50 warrants with an exercise price of $25 each are attached to bond.
- Each warrant's value is estimated to be $3.

Step 1: Calculate V_{Bond}

$$V_{Package} = V_{Bond} + V_{Warrants} = \$1,000.$$

$$V_{Warrants} = 50(\$3) = \$150.$$

$$V_{Bond} + \$150 = \$1,000$$

$$V_{Bond} = \$850.$$

Step 2: Find Coupon Payment and Rate

20	12	-850		1000
N	I/YR	PV	PMT	FV

Solve for payment = 100

Therefore, the required coupon rate is $100/$1,000 = 10%.

If after issue the warrants immediately sell for $5 each, what would this imply about the value of the package?

■ At issue, the package was actually worth

$V_{Package} = \$850 + 50(\$5) = \$1,100,$

which is $100 more than the selling price.

(More...)

■ The firm could have set lower interest payments whose PV would be smaller by $100 per bond, or it could have offered fewer warrants and/or set a higher exercise price.

■ Under the original assumptions, current stockholders would be losing value to the bond/warrant purchasers.

Assume that the warrants expire 10 years after issue. When would you expect them to be exercised?

■ Generally, a warrant will sell in the open market at a premium above its value if exercised (it can't sell for less).

■ Therefore, warrants tend not to be exercised until just before expiration.

(More...)

- In a stepped-up exercise price, the exercise price increases in steps over the warrant's life. Because the value of the warrant falls when the exercise price is increased, step-up provisions encourage in-the-money warrant holders to exercise just prior to the step-up.

- Since no dividends are earned on the warrant , holders will tend to exercise voluntarily if a stock's payout ratio rises enough.

Will the warrants bring in additional capital when exercised?

- When exercised, each warrant will bring in the exercise price, $25.

- This is equity capital and holders will receive one share of common stock per warrant.

- The exercise price is typically set some 20% to 30% above the current stock price when the warrants are issued.

Because warrants lower the cost of the accompanying debt issue, should all debt be issued with warrants?

No. As we shall see, the warrants have a cost which must be added to the coupon interest cost.

What is the expected return to the bond-with-warrant holders (and cost to the issuer) if the warrants are expected to be exercised in 5 years when P = $36.75?

- The company will exchange stock worth $36.75 for one warrant plus $25. The opportunity cost to the company is $36.75 - $25.00 = $11.75 per warrant.
- Bond has 50 warrants, so the opportunity cost per bond = 50($11.75) = $587.50.

(More...)

- Here are the cash flows on a time line:

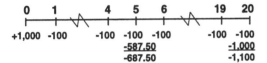

Input the cash flows into a calculator to find IRR = 14.7%. This is the pre-tax cost of the bond and warrant package.

(More...)

- The cost of the bond with warrants package is higher than the 12% cost of straight debt because part of the expected return is from capital gains, which are riskier than interest income.

- The cost is lower than the cost of equity because part of the return is fixed by contract.

(More...)

- When the warrants are exercised, there is a wealth transfer from existing stockholders to exercising warrant holders.
- But, bondholders previously transferred wealth to existing stockholders, in the form of a low coupon rate, when the bond was issued.

- At the time of exercise, either more or less wealth than expected may be transferred from the existing shareholders to the warrant holders, depending upon the stock price.
- At the time of issue, on a risk-adjusted basis, the expected cost of a bond-with-warrants issue is the same as the cost of a straight-debt issue.

Assume the following convertible bond data:

- 20-year, 10.5% annual coupon, callable convertible bond will sell at its $1,000 par value; straight debt issue would require a 12% coupon.
- Call protection = 5 years and call price = $1,100. Call the bonds when conversion value > $1,200, but the call must occur on the issue date anniversary.
- $P_0 = \$20$; $D_0 = \$1.48$; $g = 8\%$.
- Conversion ratio = CR = 40 shares.

What conversion price (P_c) is built into the bond?

$$P_c = \frac{\text{Par value}}{\text{\# Shares received}}$$

$$= \frac{\$1,000}{40} = \$25.$$

Like with warrants, the conversion price is typically set 20%-30% above the stock price on the issue date.

What is (1) the convertible's straight debt value and (2) the implied value of the convertibility feature?

Straight debt value:

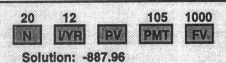

20	12		105	1000
N	I/YR	PV	PMT	FV

Solution: -887.96

Implied Convertibility Value

■ Because the convertibles will sell for $1,000, the implied value of the convertibility feature is

$1,000 - $887.96 = $112.04.

■ The convertibility value corresponds to the warrant value in the previous example.

What is the formula for the bond's expected conversion value in any year?

Conversion value = $CV_t = CR(P_0)(1 + g)^t$.

t = 0

$CV_0 = 40(\$20)(1.08)^0 = \$800.$

t = 10

$CV_{10} = 40(\$20)(1.08)^{10}$
$= \$1,727.14.$

What is meant by the floor value of a convertible? What is the floor value at t = 0? At t = 10?

- The floor value is the higher of the straight debt value and the conversion value.
- Straight debt value$_0$ = \$887.96.
- CV_0 = \$800.

Floor value at Year 0 = \$887.96.

- Straight debt value$_{10}$ = \$915.25.
- CV_{10} = \$1,727.14.

Floor value$_{10}$ = \$1,727.14.

- A convertible will generally sell above its floor value prior to maturity because convertibility constitutes a call option that has value.

If the firm intends to force conversion on the first anniversary date after CV > $1,200, when is the issue expected to be called?

8	-800	0	1200
N	I/YR	PV	PMT	FV

Solution: n = 5.27

Bond would be called at t = 6 since call must occur on anniversary date.

What is the convertible's expected cost of capital to the firm?

0	1	2	3	4	5	6

1,000	-105	-105	-105	-105	-105	-105

-1,269.50
-1,374.50

$CV_6 = 40(\$20)(1.08)^6 = \$1,269.50.$

Input the cash flows in the calculator and solve for IRR = 13.7%.

Does the cost of the convertible appear to be consistent with the costs of debt and equity?

- For consistency, need $k_d < k_c < k_s$.
- Why?

(More...)

■Check the values:

$k_d = 12\%$ and $k_c = 13.7\%$.

$$k_s = \frac{D_0(1 + g)}{P_0} + g = \frac{\$1.48(1.08)}{\$20} + 0.08$$

$$= 16.0\%.$$

Since k_c is between k_d and k_s, the costs are consistent with the risks.

WACC Effects

Assume the firm's tax rate is 40% and its debt ratio is 50%. Now suppose the firm is considering either:

    (1) issuing convertibles, or

    (2) issuing bonds with warrants.

Its new target capital structure will have 40% straight debt, 40% common equity and 20% convertibles or bonds with warrants. What effect will the two financing alternatives have on the firm's WACC?

Convertibles Step 1: Find the after-tax cost of the convertibles.

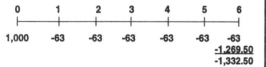

0	1	2	3	4	5	6
1,000	-63	-63	-63	-63	-63	-63
						-1,269.50
						-1,332.50

$INT(1 - T) = \$105(0.6) = \$63$.

With a calculator, find:

$k_c\,(AT) = IRR = 9.81\%$.

Convertibles Step 2: Find the after-tax cost of straight debt.

$$k_d (AT) = 12\%(0.06) = 7.2\%.$$

Convertibles Step 3: Calculate the WACC.

WACC (with convertibles) = 0.4(7.2%) + 0.2(9.81%) + 0.4(16%)

= 11.24%.

WACC (without convertibles) = 0.5(7.2%) + 0.5(16%)

= 11.60%.

■ Some notes:
- We have assumed that k_s is not affected by the addition of convertible debt.
- In practice, most convertibles are subordinated to the other debt, which muddies our assumption of $k_d = 12\%$ when convertibles are used.
- When the convertible is converted, the debt ratio would decrease and the firm's financial risk would decline.

Warrants Step 1: Find the after-tax cost of the bond with warrants.

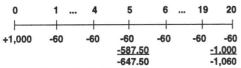

0	1 ...	4	5	6 ...	19	20
+1,000	-60	-60	-60	-60	-60	-60
			-587.50			-1,000
			-647.50			-1,060

INT(1 - T) = $100(0.60) = $60.

Warrants(Opportunity loss per warrant)
  = 50($11.75) = $587.50.

Solve for: k_w (AT) = 10.32%.

Warrants Step 2: Calculate the WACC if the firm uses warrants.

WACC (with warrants) = 0.4(7.2%) + 0.2(10.32%) + 0.4(16%) = 11.34%.

WACC (without warrants) = 0.5(7.2%) + 0.5(16%)

= 11.60%.

Besides cost, what other factors should be considered?

■ The firm's future needs for equity capital:
- Exercise of warrants brings in new equity capital.
- Convertible conversion brings in no new funds.
- In either case, new lower debt ratio can support more financial leverage. (More...)

---

20 - 40

■ **Does the firm want to commit to 20 years of debt?**

● Convertible conversion removes debt, while the exercise of warrants does not.

● If stock price does not rise over time, then neither warrants nor convertibles would be exercised. Debt would remain outstanding.

---

20 - 41

> **Recap the differences between warrants and convertibles.**

■ Warrants bring in new capital, while convertibles do not.

■ Most convertibles are callable, while warrants are not.

■ Warrants typically have shorter maturities than convertibles, and expire before the accompanying debt.

(More...)

---

20 - 42

■ Warrants usually provide for fewer common shares than do convertibles.

■ Bonds with warrants typically have much higher flotation costs than do convertible issues.

■ Bonds with warrants are often used by small start-up firms. Why?

20E - 1

Chapter 20 Extension

- Adjustable rate and market auction preferred stocks
- Reporting earnings when warrants or convertibles are outstanding
- Calling convertible issues
- Innovative new hybrids

20E - 2

What are some alternative types of preferred stock?

- In floating rate preferred, dividends are indexed to the rate on treasury securities (or some other rate). Excellent short-term investment for corporations:
  - Only 30% of dividends are taxable to corporations.
  - The floating rate generally keeps the issue trading near par. (More...)

20E - 3

- However, if the issuer is in poor financial condition, floating rate preferred stock may have too much credit risk to be held as a marketable security.
- With market auction preferred stock, an auction is held every seven weeks where buyers submit dividend rate bids. Thus, credit risk changes can be built into the yield and the stock price remains very close to par value.

How can earnings be reported when warrants and convertibles are used?

- **Basic EPS**
  - Based on the number of common shares actually outstanding.
- **Primary EPS**
  - Includes shares that would result from conversions and exercises likely to occur in the near future. **(More...)**

- **Diluted EPS**
  - Includes shares that would result from exercise of all outstanding warrants and conversion of all convertibles.
- **SEC requires firms to report both basic and diluted EPS.**
- **FASB requires firms to report basic EPS.**
- **Why should stock investors be concerned about how EPS is reported?**

When should convertible issues be called?

- **There are two possible situations:**
  - If the conversion value is less than the call price, call only if interest rates have fallen and new securities are less expensive.
  - If conversion value is greater than call price, call at first opportunity. **(More...)**

- The difference between the current stock price and conversion price constitutes an opportunity cost to existing stockholders.
- By calling at first opportunity, this cost is minimized.

■ Studies show that calls do not minimize wealth transfers, but rather are made later than indicated by theory.

- Perhaps to save near-term cash flow.
- Perhaps signaling value of future issues.

What new hybrid securities have recently been developed?

■ A new breed of preferred stock has been created that has appeal to both issuers and individual investors.

■ These issues have unusual names such as trust-oriented preferred securities (TOPrS) and monthly income preferred securities (MIPS).

(More...)

■ The new securities are tax deductible to the issuer.

- They are issued by a partnership or trust which then loans the proceeds to the company.
- Thus, the company technically makes interest rather than dividend payments.

■ The tax deductibility allows yields to be set higher than on conventional preferred.

Dan Barnes, financial manager of Ski Equipment Inc. (SKI), is excited, but apprehensive. The company's founder recently sold his 51 percent controlling block of stock to Kent Koren, who is a big fan of EVA (Economic Value Added). EVA is found by taking the after-tax operating profit and then subtracting the dollar cost of all the capital the firm uses:

$$EVA = NOPAT - Capital\ costs$$
$$= EBIT(1 - T) - WACC\ (Capital\ employed).$$

If EVA is positive, then the firm is creating value. On the other hand, if EVA is negative, the firm is not covering its cost of capital, and stockholders' value is being eroded. Koren rewards managers handsomely if they create value, but those whose operations produce negative EVAs are soon looking for work. Koren frequently points out that if a company can generate its current level of sales with less assets, it would need less capital. That would, other things held constant, lower capital costs and increase its EVA.

Shortly after he took control of SKI, Kent Koren met with SKI's senior executives to tell them of his plans for the company. First, he presented some EVA data which convinced everyone that SKI had not been creating value in recent years. He then stated, in no uncertain terms, that this situation must change. He noted that SKI's designs of skis, boots, and clothing are acclaimed throughout the industry, but something is seriously amiss elsewhere in the company. Costs are too high, prices are too low, or the company employs too much capital, and he wants SKI's managers to correct the problem or else.

Barnes has long felt that SKI's working capital situation should be studied--the company may have the optimal amounts of cash, securities, receivables, and inventories, but it may also have too much or too little of these items. In the past, the production manager resisted Dan's efforts to question his holdings of raw materials inventories, the marketing manager resisted questions about finished goods, the sales staff resisted questions about credit policy (which affects accounts receivable), and the treasurer did not want to talk about her cash and securities balances. Koren's speech made it clear that such resistance would no longer be tolerated.

Dan also knows that decisions about working capital cannot be made in a vacuum. For example, if inventories could be lowered without adversely affecting operations, then less capital would be required, the dollar cost of capital would decline, and EVA would increase. However, lower raw materials inventories might lead to production slowdowns and higher costs, while lower finished goods inventories might lead to the loss of profitable sales. So, before inventories are changed, it will be necessary to study operating as well as financial effects. The situation is the same with regard to cash and receivables. Following are some ratios for SKI:

	SKI	Industry
Current	1.75	2.25
Quick	0.83	1.20
Debt/assets	58.76%	50.00%
Turnover of cash and securities	16.67	22.22
Days sales outstanding	45.00	32.00
Inventory turnover	4.82	7.00
Fixed assets turnover	11.35	12.00
Total assets turnover	2.08	3.00
Profit margin on sales	2.07%	3.50%
Return on equity (ROE)	10.45%	21.00%

a. Dan plans to use the preceding ratios as the starting point for discussions with SKI's operating executives. He wants everyone to think about the pros and cons of changing each type of current asset and how changes would interact to affect profits and EVA. Based on the data in the table, does SKI seem to be following a relaxed, moderate, or restricted working capital policy?

b. How can one distinguish between a relaxed but rational working capital policy and a situation where a firm simply has a lot of current assets because it is inefficient? Does SKI's working capital policy seem appropriate?

c. What might SKI do to reduce its cash and securities without harming operations?

d. What is "float," and how is it affected by the firm's cash manager (treasurer)?

In an attempt to better understand SKI's cash position, Dan developed a cash budget. Data for the first two months of the year are shown at the end of this mini case. (Note that Dan's preliminary cash budget does not account for interest income or interest expense.) He has the figures for the other months, but they are not shown in this mini case.

e. Should depreciation expense be explicitly included in the cash budget? Why or why not?

f. In his preliminary cash budget, Dan has assumed that all sales are collected and, thus, that SKI has no bad debts. Is this realistic? If not, how would bad debts be dealt with in a cash budgeting sense? (Hint: Bad debts will affect collections but not purchases.)

g. Dan's cash budget for the entire year, although not given here, is based heavily on his forecast for monthly sales. Sales are expected to be extremely low between May and September but then increase dramatically in the fall and winter. November is typically the firm's best month, when SKI ships equipment to retailers for the holiday season. Interestingly, Dan's forecasted cash budget indicates that the company's cash holdings will exceed the targeted cash balance every month except for October and November, when shipments will be high but collections will not be coming in until later. Based on the ratios in the first table, does it appear that SKI's target cash balance is appropriate? In addition to possibly lowering the target cash balance, what actions might SKI take to better improve its cash management policies, and how might that affect its EVA?

h. What reasons might SKI have for maintaining a relatively high amount of cash?

i. What are the three categories of inventory costs? If the company takes steps to reduce its inventory, what effect would this have on the various costs of holding inventory?

j. Is there any reason to think that SKI may be holding too much inventory? If so, how would that affect EVA and ROE?

k. If the company reduces its inventory without adversely affecting sales, what effect should this have on the company's cash position (1) in the short run and (2) in the long run? Explain in terms of the cash budget and the balance sheet.

l. Dan knows that SKI sells on the same credit terms as other firms in its industry. Use the ratios presented in the first table to explain whether SKI's customers pay more or less promptly than those of its competitors. If there are differences, does that suggest that SKI should tighten or loosen its credit policy? What four variables make up a firm's credit policy, and in what direction should each be changed by SKI?

m. Does SKI face any risks if it tightens its credit policy?

n. If the company reduces its DSO without seriously affecting sales, what effect would this have on its cash position (1) in the short run and (2) in the long run? Answer in terms of the cash budget and the balance sheet. What effect should this have on EVA in the long run?

	Nov	Dec	Jan	Feb	Mar	Apr
I. COLLECTIONS AND PURCHASES WORKSHEET						
(1) Sales (gross)	$71,218	$68,212.00	$65,213.00	$52,475.00	$42,909	$30,524
Collections						
(2) During month of sale (0.2)(0.98)(month's sales)			12,781.75	10,285.10		
(3) During first month after sale 0.7(previous month's sales)			47,748.40	45,649.10		
(4) During second month after sale 0.1(sales 2 months ago)			7,121.80	6,821.20		
(5) Total collections (Lines 2 + 3 + 4)			$67,651.95	$62,755.40		
Purchases						
(6) 0.85(forecasted sales 2 months from now)		$44,603.75	$36,472.65	$25,945.40		
(7) Payments (1-month lag)			44,603.75	36,472.65		
II. CASH GAIN OR LOSS FOR MONTH						
(8) Collections (from Section I)			$67,651.95	$62,755.40		
(9) Payments for purchases (from Section I)			44,603.75	36,472.65		
(10) Wages and salaries			6,690.56	5,470.90		
(11) Rent			2,500.00	2,500.00		
(12) Taxes						
(13) Total payments			$53,794.31	$44,443.55		
(14) Net cash gain (loss) during month (Line 8 - Line 13)			$13,857.64	$18,311.85		
III. CASH SURPLUS OR LOAN REQUIREMENT						
(15) Cash at beginning of month if no borrowing is done			$ 3,000.00	$16,857.64		
(16) Cumulative cash (cash at start + gain or - loss = Line 14 + Line 15)			16,857.64	35,169.49		
(17) Target cash balance			1,500.00	1,500.00		
(18) Cumulative surplus cash or loans outstanding to maintain $1,500 target cash balance (Line 16 - Line 17)			$15,357.64	$33,669.49		

21 - 1

CHAPTER 21
Current Asset Management

■ Alternative working capital policies
■ Cash management
■ Inventory management
■ Accounts receivable management

---

21 - 2

Basic Definitions

■ Gross working capital:
   Total current assets.
■ Net working capital:
   Current assets - Current liabilities.
■ Working capital policy:
   ● The level of each current asset.
   ● How current assets are financed.
   (More...)

---

21 - 3

■ Working capital management:
   Includes both establishing working capital policy and then the day-to-day control of:
   ● Cash
   ● Inventories
   ● Receivables
   ● Short-term liabilities

Selected Ratios for SKI Incorporated

	SKI	Industry
Current	1.75x	2.25x
Quick	0.83x	1.20x
Debt/Assets	58.76%	50.00%
Turnover of cash & securities	16.67x	22.22x
DSO (days)	45.00	32.00
Inv. turnover	4.82x	7.00x
F.A. turnover	11.35x	12.00x
T.A. turnover	2.08x	3.00x
Profit margin	2.07%	3.50%
ROE	10.45%	21.00%

How does SKI's working capital policy compare with the industry?

- Working capital policy is reflected in a firm's current ratio, quick ratio, turnover of cash and securities, inventory turnover, and DSO.

- These ratios indicate SKI has large amounts of working capital relative to its level of sales. Thus, SKI is following a relaxed (fat cat) policy.

Alternative Current Asset Investment Policies

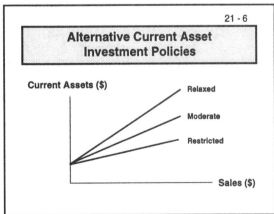

Is SKI inefficient or just conservative?

- A relaxed policy may be appropriate if it reduces risk more than profitability.

- However, SKI is much less profitable than the average firm in the industry. This suggests that the company probably has excessive working capital.

Cash Management: Cash doesn't earn interest, so why hold it?

- **Transactions:** Must have some cash to pay current bills.
- **Precaution:** "Safety stock." But lessened by credit line and marketable securities.
- **Compensating balances:** For loans and/or services provided.
- **Speculation:** To take advantage of bargains, to take discounts, and so on. Reduced by credit line, marketable securities.

What's the goal of cash management?

- To have sufficient cash on hand to meet the needs listed on the previous slide.

- However, since cash is a non-earning asset, to have not one dollar more.

Ways to Minimize Cash Holdings

- Use lockboxes.
- Insist on wire transfers from customers.
- Synchronize inflows and outflows.
- Use a remote disbursement account.

(More...)

- Increase forecast accuracy to reduce the need for a cash "safety stock."
- Hold marketable securities instead of a cash "safety stock."
- Negotiate a line of credit (also reduces need for a "safety stock").

What is float and how can it be affected by cash management?

- Net float is the difference between cash as shown on the firm's books and on its bank's books.
- If it takes SKI 1 day to deposit checks it receives and it takes its bank another day to clear those checks, SKI has 2 days of collections float.

- If it takes 6 days for the checks that SKI writes to clear and be deducted from SKI's account, SKI has 6 days of disbursement float.
- SKI's net float is the difference between the disbursement float and the collections float:

Net float = 6 days - 2 days = 4 days.

- If SKI wrote and received $1 million of checks per day, it would be able to operate with $4 million less working capital than if it had zero net float.

Cash Budget: The Primary Cash Management Tool

- Purpose: Uses forecasts of cash inflows, outflows, and ending cash balances to predict loan needs and funds available for temporary investment.
- Timing: Daily, weekly, or monthly, depending upon budget's purpose. Monthly for annual planning, daily for actual cash management.

Data Required for Cash Budget

1. Sales forecast.
2. Information on collections delay.
3. Forecast of purchases and payment terms.
4. Forecast of cash expenses: wages, taxes, utilities, and so on.
5. Initial cash on hand.
6. Target cash balance.

SKI's Cash Budget
for January and February

	Net Cash Flows	
	January	February
Collections	$67,651.95	$62,755.40
Purchases	$44,603.75	$36,472.65
Wages	6,690.56	5,470.90
Rent	2,500.00	2,500.00
Total payments	$53,794.31	$44,443.55
Net CF	$13,857.64	$18,311.85

Cash Budget (Continued)

	January	February
Cash at start	$ 3,000.00	$16,857.64
Net CF	13,857.64	18,311.85
Cumulative cash	$16,857.64	$35,169.49
Less: target cash	1,500.00	1,500.00
Surplus	$15,357.64	$33,669.49

Should depreciation be explicitly included in the cash budget?

- No. Depreciation is a noncash charge. Only cash payments and receipts appear on cash budget.
- However, depreciation does affect taxes, which do appear in the cash budget.

21 - 19

What are some other potential cash inflows besides collections?

- Proceeds from fixed asset sales.
- Proceeds from stock and bond sales.
- Interest earned.
- Court settlements.

21 - 20

How can interest earned or paid on short-term securities or loans be incorporated in the cash budget?

- Interest earned: Add line in the collections section.
- Interest paid: Add line in the payments section.
- Found as interest rate x surplus/loan line of cash budget for preceding month.
- Note: Interest on any other debt would need to be incorporated as well.

21 - 21

How could bad debts be worked into the cash budget?

- Collections would be reduced by the amount of bad debt losses.
- For example, if the firm had 3% bad debt losses, collections would total only 97% of sales.
- Lower collections would lead to lower surpluses and higher borrowing requirements.

SKI's forecasted cash budget indicates that the company's cash holdings will exceed the targeted cash balance every month, except for October and November.

- Cash budget indicates the company probably is holding too much cash.

- SKI could improve its EVA by either investing its excess cash in more productive assets or by paying it out to the firm's shareholders.

What reasons might SKI have for maintaining a relatively high amount of cash?

- If sales turn out to be considerably less than expected, SKI could face a cash shortfall.
- A company may choose to hold large amounts of cash if it does not have much faith in its sales forecast, or if it is very conservative.
- The cash may be there, in part, to fund a planned fixed asset acquisition.

Inventory Management: Categories of Inventory Costs

- Carrying Costs: Storage and handling costs, insurance, property taxes, depreciation, and obsolescence.
- Ordering Costs: Cost of placing orders, shipping, and handling costs.
- Costs of Running Short: Loss of sales, loss of customer goodwill, and the disruption of production schedules.

Effect of Inventory Size on Costs

Reducing the average amount of inventory held generally:

- Reduces carrying costs.
- Increases ordering costs.
- Increases probability of a stockout.

Is SKI holding too much inventory?

- SKI's inventory turnover (4.82) is considerably lower than the industry average (7.00). The firm is carrying a lot of inventory per dollar of sales.
- By holding excessive inventory, the firm is increasing its operating costs which reduces its NOPAT. Moreover, the excess inventory must be financed, so EVA is further lowered.

If SKI reduces its inventory, without adversely affecting sales, what effect will this have on its cash position?

- Short run: Cash will increase as inventory purchases decline.
- Long run: Company is likely to then take steps to reduce its cash holdings.

**Accounts Receivable Management:
Do SKI's customers pay more or less
promptly than those of its
competitors?**

- SKI's days' sales outstanding (DSO) of 45 days is well above the industry average (32 days).
- SKI's customers are paying less promptly.
- SKI should consider tightening its credit policy to reduce its DSO.

Elements of Credit Policy

- **Cash Discounts:** Lowers price. Attracts new customers and reduces DSO.
- **Credit Period:** How long to pay? Shorter period reduces DSO and average A/R, but it may discourage sales.

(More...)

- **Credit Standards:** Tighter standards reduce bad debt losses, but may reduce sales. Fewer bad debts reduces DSO.
- **Collection Policy:** Tougher policy will reduce DSO, but may damage customer relationships.

---

21 - 31

Does SKI face any risk if it tightens its credit policy?

YES! A tighter credit policy may discourage sales. Some customers may choose to go elsewhere if they are pressured to pay their bills sooner.

---

21 - 32

If SKI succeeds in reducing DSO without adversely affecting sales, what effect would this have on its cash position?

- Short run: If customers pay sooner, this increases cash holdings.
- Long run: Over time, the company would hopefully invest the cash in more productive assets, or pay it out to shareholders. Both of these actions would increase EVA.

BLUEPRINTS: CHAPTER 22
SHORT-TERM FINANCING

Bats and Balls (B&B) Inc., a baseball equipment manufacturer, is a small company with seasonal sales. Each year before the baseball season, B&B purchases inventory which is financed through a combination of trade credit and short-term bank loans. At the end of the season, B&B uses sales revenues to repay its short-term obligations. The company is always looking for ways to become more profitable, and senior management has asked one of its employees, Ann Taylor, to review the company's current asset financing policies. Putting together her report, Ann is trying to answer each of the following questions:

a. B&B tries to match the maturity of its assets and liabilities. Describe how B&B could adopt either a more aggressive or more conservative financing policy.

b. What are the advantages and disadvantages of using short-term credit as a source of financing?

c. Is it likely that B&B could make significantly greater use of accruals?

d. Assume that B&B buys on terms of 1/10, net 30, but that it can get away with paying on the 40th day if it chooses not to take discounts. Also, assume that it purchases $3 million of components per year, net of discounts. How much free trade credit can the company get, how much costly trade credit can it get, and what is the percentage cost of the costly credit? Should B&B take discounts?

e. What is commercial paper? Would it be feasible for B&B to finance with commercial paper?

f. Suppose B&B decided to raise an additional $100,000 as a 1-year loan from its bank, for which it was quoted a rate of 8 percent. What is the effective annual cost rate assuming (1) simple interest, (2) discount interest, (3) discount interest with a 10 percent compensating balance, and (4) add-on interest on a 12-month installment loan? For the first three of these assumptions, would it matter if the loan were for 90 days, but renewable, rather than for a year?

g. How large would the loan actually be in each of the cases in Part f?

h. What are the pros and cons of borrowing on a secured versus an unsecured basis?

CHAPTER 22
Short-Term Financing

- Working capital financing policies
- Accounts payable (trade credit)
- Commercial paper
- Short-term bank loans
- Secured short-term credit

Working Capital Financing Policies

- Maturity Matching: Matches the maturity of the assets with the maturity of the financing.
- Aggressive: Uses short-term (temporary) capital to finance some permanent assets.
- Conservative: Uses long-term (permanent) capital to finance some temporary assets.

Maturity Matching Financing Policy

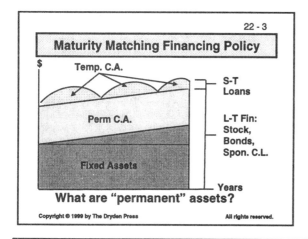

What are "permanent" assets?

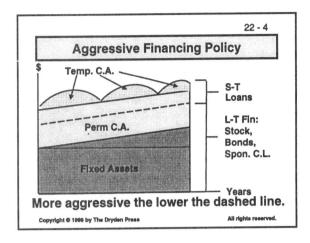

22 - 4

Aggressive Financing Policy

$

Temp. C.A.

Perm C.A.

Fixed Assets

S-T Loans

L-T Fin: Stock, Bonds, Spon. C.L.

Years

More aggressive the lower the dashed line.

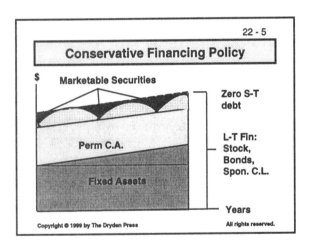

22 - 5

Conservative Financing Policy

$

Marketable Securities

Perm C.A.

Fixed Assets

Zero S-T debt

L-T Fin: Stock, Bonds, Spon. C.L.

Years

22 - 6

- The choice of working capital policy is a classic risk/return tradeoff.
- The aggressive policy promises the highest return but carries the greatest risk.
- The conservative policy has the least risk but also the lowest expected return.
- The moderate (maturity matching) policy falls between the two extremes.

What is short-term credit? What are the major sources?

- Short-term credit: Debt requiring repayment within one year.
- Major sources:
  - Accruals
  - Accounts payable (trade credit)
  - Commercial paper
  - Bank loans

- Short-term debt is riskier than long-term debt for the borrower.
  - Short-term rates may rise.
  - May have trouble rolling debt over.
- Advantages of short-term debt.
  - Typically lower cost.
  - Can get funds relatively quickly with low transactions costs.
  - Can repay without penalty.

Is there a cost to accruals? Do firms have much control over amount of accruals?

- Accruals are free in the sense that no explicit interest is charged.
- However, firms have little control over accrual levels, which are influenced more by industry custom, economic factors, and tax laws than by managerial actions.

What is trade credit?

- Trade credit is credit furnished by a firm's suppliers.
- Trade credit is often the largest source of short-term credit for small firms.
- Trade credit is spontaneous and relatively easy to get, but the cost can be high.

B&B buys $3,030,303 gross, or $3,000,000 net, on terms of 1/10, net 30. However, the firm pays on Day 40.

How much free and costly trade credit are they getting?

What is the cost of the costly trade credit?

Gross/Net Breakdown

- Company buys goods worth $3,000,000. That's the cash price.
- They must pay $30,303 more over the year if they forego the discount.
- Think of the extra $30,303 as a financing cost similar to the interest on a loan.
- Must compare that cost with the cost of alternative credit.

Net daily purchases = $3,000,000/360
= $8,333.

Payables level if discount is taken:
Payables = $8,333 (10) = $83,333.

Payables level if don't take discount:
Payables = $8,333 (40) = $333,333.

Credit Breakdown:
Total trade credit   = $333,333
Free trade credit   =   83,333
Costly trade credit = $250,000

Nominal Cost of Costly Trade Credit

Firm loses 0.01($3,030,303) = $30,303
of discounts to obtain $250,000 in
extra trade credit, so

$$k_{Nom} = \frac{\$30,303}{\$250,000} = 0.1212 = 12.12\%.$$

But the $30,303 in lost discounts is
paid all during the year, not just at
year-end, so the EAR is higher.

Nominal Cost Formula, 1/10, net 40

$$k_{Nom} = \frac{\text{Discount \%}}{1 - \text{Discount \%}} \times \frac{360}{\text{Days taken - Discount period}}$$

$$= \frac{1}{99} \times \frac{360}{30} = 0.0101 \times 12$$

$$= 0.1212 = 12.12\%.$$

Pays 1.01% 12 times per year.

Effective Annual Rate, 1/10, net 40

Periodic rate = 0.01/0.99 = 1.01%.

Periods/year = 360/(40 - 10) = 12.

$EAR = (1 + Periodic\ rate)^n - 1.0$
$= (1.0101)^{12} - 1.0 = 12.82\%.$

Commercial Paper (CP)

- CP are short term notes issued by large, strong companies. B&B could not issue CP; the company is too small.
- CP trades in the market at rates just above the T-bill rate.
- CP is bought by banks and other companies, then held as marketable securities for liquidity purposes.

A bank is willing to lend B&B $100,000 for 1 year at an 8 percent nominal rate. What is the EAR under the following five loans?

1. Simple annual interest, 1 year.
2. Simple interest, paid monthly.
3. Discount interest.
4. Discount interest with 10 percent compensating balance.
5. Installment loan, add-on, 12 months.

Why must we use Effective Annual Rates (EARs) to evaluate the loans?

- In our examples, the nominal (quoted) rate is 8% in all cases.

- We want to compare loan cost rates and choose the alternative with the lowest cost.

- Because the loans have different terms, we must make the comparison on the basis of EARs.

Simple Annual Interest, 1-Year Loan

"Simple interest" means not discount or add-on.

Interest = 0.08($100,000) = $8,000.

$$k_{Nom} = EAR = \frac{\$8,000}{\$100,000} = 0.08 = 8.0\%.$$

On a simple interest loan of one year, $k_{Nom} = EAR$.

Simple Interest, Paid Monthly

Monthly interest = (0.08/12)($100,000)
= $666.67.

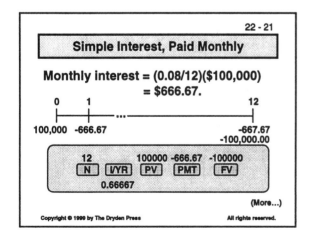

(More...)

---

k_{Nom} = (Monthly rate)(12)
    = 0.66667%(12) = **8.00%.**

$$EAR = \left(1 + \frac{0.08}{12}\right)^{12} - 1 = 8.30\%.$$

or: 8■NOM%, 12■P/YR, ■EFF% = 8.30%.

Note: If interest were paid quarterly, then:

$$EAR = \left(1 + \frac{0.08}{4}\right)^{4} - 1 = 8.24\%.$$

Daily, EAR = 8.33%.

8% Discount Interest, 1 Year

Interest deductible = 0.08($100,000)
                        = **$8,000.**
Usable funds   = $100,000 - $8,000
                        = **$92,000.**

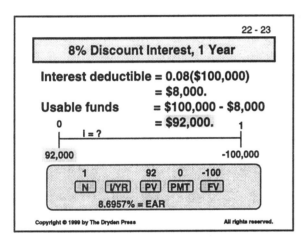

```
 0            I = ?              1
 |_____|
92,000                   -100,000
```

```
      1          92    0    -100
   [ N ] [I/YR] [PV] [PMT] [FV]
          8.6957% = EAR
```

Discount Interest (Continued)

$$\text{Amt. borrowed} = \frac{\text{Amount needed}}{1 - \text{Nominal rate (decimal)}}$$

$$= \frac{\$100,000}{0.92} = \$108,696.$$

Need $100,000. Offered loan with terms of 8% discount interest, 10% compensating balance.

$$\text{Face amount of loan} = \frac{\text{Amount needed}}{1 - \text{Nominal rate} - \text{CB}}$$

$$= \frac{\$100,000}{1 - 0.08 - 0.1} = \$121,951.$$

(More...)

Interest = 0.08 ($121,951) = $9,756.

$$\text{Cost} = \frac{\text{Interest paid}}{\text{Amount received}}.$$

$$\text{EAR} = \frac{\$9,756}{\$100,000} = 9.756\%.$$

EAR correct only if amount is borrowed for 1 year.

(More...)

8% Discount Interest with 10% Compensating Balance (Continued)

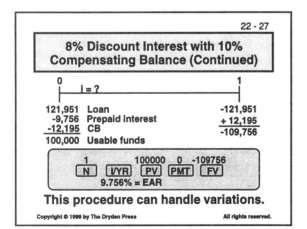

```
0          i = ?                          1
121,951    Loan                    -121,951
 -9,756    Prepaid interest        + 12,195
-12,195    CB                      -109,756
100,000    Usable funds
```

1		100000	0	-109756
N	I/YR	PV	PMT	FV

9.756% = EAR

This procedure can handle variations.

1-Year Installment Loan, 8% "Add-On"

Interest = 0.08($100,000) = $8,000.

Face amount = $100,000 + $8,000 = $108,000.

Monthly payment = $108,000/12 = $9,000.

Average loan outstanding = $100,000/2 = $50,000.

Approximate cost = $8,000/$50,000 = 16.0%.

(More...)

Installment Loan

To find the EAR, recognize that the firm has received $100,000 and must make monthly payments of $9,000. This constitutes an ordinary annuity as shown below:

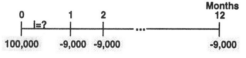

```
                                    Months
   0        1      2                  12
   |--------|------|-----...-----------|
   I=?
 100,000  -9,000 -9,000            -9,000
```

```
    12        100000  -9000    0
  [ N ] [ I/YR ] [ PV ] [ PMT ] [ FV ]
         1.2043% = rate per month
```

k_{Nom} = APR = (1.2043%)(12) = 14.45%.
EAR = $(1.012043)^{12}$ - 1 = 15.45%.

14.45 ■ NOM ⟶ enters nominal rate
12   ■ P/YR ⟶ enters 12 pmts/yr
      ■ EFF% = 15.4489 = 15.45%.

1 ■ P/YR to reset calculator.

What is a secured loan?

- In a secured loan, the borrower pledges assets as collateral for the loan.

- For short-term loans, the most commonly pledged assets are receivables and inventories.

- Securities are great collateral, but generally firms needing short-term loans generally do not have securities.

22E - 1

Chapter 22 Extension: Secured Short-Term Financing

- Accounts receivable financing
- Inventory financing

22E - 2

Important Legal Forms

- Security Agreement: Standard form under the Uniform Commercial Code. Specifies when lender can claim collateral if default occurs.
- UCC Form-1: Filed with Secretary of State to establish collateral claim. Prospective lenders will do a claims search, and won't make the loan if a prior UCC-1 has been filed.

22E - 3

What is the difference between pledging and factoring receivables?

- If receivables are pledged, the lender has recourse against both the original buyer of the goods and the borrower.
- When receivables are factored, they are generally sold, and the buyer (lender) has no recourse to the borrower.

What are three forms of inventory financing?

■ Blanket lien.

■ Trust receipt.

■ Warehouse receipt.

■ The form used depends on the type of inventory and situation at hand.

BLUEPRINTS: CHAPTER 23
WORKING CAPITAL MANAGEMENT: EXTENSIONS

Section 1: RECEIVABLES MANAGEMENT

Rich Jackson, a recent finance graduate, is planning to go into the wholesale building supply business with his brother, Jim, who majored in building construction. The firm would sell primarily to general contractors, and it would start operating next January. Sales would be slow during the cold months, rise during the spring, and then fall off again in the summer, when new construction in the area slows. Sales estimates for the first 6 months are as follows (in thousands of dollars):

January	$100
February	200
March	300
April	300
May	200
June	100

The terms of sale are net 30, but because of special incentives, the brothers expect 30 percent of the customers (by dollar value) to pay on the 10th day following the sale, 50 percent to pay on the 40th day, and the remaining 20 percent to pay on the 70th day. No bad debt losses are expected, because Jim, the building construction expert, knows which contractors are having financial problems.

a. Assume that, on average, the brothers expect annual sales of 18,000 items at an average price of $100 per item. (Use a 360-day year.)

   (1) What is the firm's expected days sales outstanding (DSO)?

   (2) What is its expected average daily sales (ADS)?

   (3) What is its expected average accounts receivable level?

   (4) Assume that the firm's profit margin is 25 percent. How much of the receivables balance must be financed? What would the firm's balance sheet figures for accounts receivable, notes payable, and retained earnings be at the end of one year if notes payable are used to finance the investment in receivables? Assume that the cost of carrying receivables had been deducted when the 25 percent profit margin was calculated.

   (5) If bank loans have a cost of 12 percent, what is the annual dollar cost of carrying the receivables?

---

b. What are some factors which influence (1) a firm's receivables level and (2) the dollar cost of carrying receivables?

c. Assuming that the monthly sales forecasts given previously are accurate, and that customers pay exactly as was predicted, what would the receivables level be at the end of each month? *To reduce calculations, assume that 30 percent of the firm's customers pay in the month of sale, 50 percent pay in the month following the sale, and the remaining 20 percent pay in the second month following the sale. Note that this is a different assumption than was made earlier.* Use the following format to answer Parts c and d:

Month	Sales	E.O.M. A/R	Quarterly Sales	ADS	DSO = (A/R)/(ADS)
Jan	$100	$ 70			
Feb	200	160			
Mar	300	250	$600	$6.67	37.5
Apr	$300				
May	200				
Jun	100				

d. What is the firm's forecasted average daily sales for the first 3 months? For the entire half-year? The days sales outstanding is commonly used to measure receivables performance. What DSO is expected at the end of March? At the end of June? What does the DSO indicate about customers' payments? Is DSO a good management tool in this situation? If not, why not?

e. Construct aging schedules for the end of March and the end of June (use the format given below). Do these schedules properly measure customers' payment patterns? If not, why not?

Age of Account (Days)	March A/R	%	June A/R	%
0 - 30	$210	84%		
31 - 60	40	16		
61 - 90	0	0	—	—
	$250	100%		

f. Construct the uncollected balances schedules for the end of March and the end of June. Use the format given below. Do these schedules properly measure customers' payment patterns?

March				June			
Month	Sales	Contribution to A/R	A/R-to-Sales Ratio	Month	Sales	Contribution to A/R	A/R-to-Sales Ratio
Jan	$100	$ 0	0%	Apr			
Feb	200	40	20	May			
Mar	300	210	70	Jun		—	—

g. Assume that it is now July of Year 1, and the brothers are developing pro forma financial statements for the following year. Further, assume that sales and collections in the first half-year matched the predicted levels. Using the Year 2 sales forecasts as shown next, what are next year's pro forma receivables levels for the end of March and for the end of June?

Month	Predicted Sales	Predicted A/R-to-Sales Ratio	Predicted Contribution to Receivables
Jan	$150	0%	$ 0
Feb	300	20	60
Mar	500	70	350
		Projected March 31 A/R balance =	$410
Apr	$400		
May	300		
Jun	200		
		Projected June 30 A/R balance =	___

h. Assume now that it is several years later. The brothers are concerned about the firm's current credit terms, which are now net 30, which means that contractors buying building products from the firm are not offered a discount, and they are supposed to pay the full amount in 30 days. Gross sales are now running $1,000,000 a year, and 80 percent (by dollar volume) of the firm's *paying* customers generally pay the full amount on Day 30, while the other 20 percent pay, on average, on Day 40. Two percent of the firm's gross sales end up as bad debt losses.

The brothers are now considering a change in the firm's credit policy. The change would entail (1) changing the credit terms to 2/10, net 20, (2) employing stricter credit standards before granting credit, and (3) enforcing collections with greater vigor than in the past. Thus, cash customers and those paying within 10 days would receive a 2 percent discount, but all others would have to pay the full amount after only 20 days. The brothers believe that the discount would both attract additional customers and encourage some existing customers to purchase more from the firm--after all, the discount amounts to a price reduction. Of course, these customers would take the discount and, hence, would pay in only 10 days. The net expected result is for sales to increase to $1,100,000; for 60 percent of the paying customers to take the discount and pay on the 10th day; for 30 percent to pay the full amount on Day 20; for 10 percent to pay late on Day 30; and for bad debt losses to fall from 2 percent to 1 percent of gross sales. The firm's operating cost ratio will remain unchanged at 75 percent, and its cost of carrying receivables will remain unchanged at 12 percent.

To begin the analysis, describe the four variables which make up a firm's credit policy, and explain how each of them affects sales and collections. Then use the information given in Part h to answer Parts i through n.

i. Under the current credit policy, what is the firm's days sales outstanding (DSO)? What would the expected DSO be if the credit policy change were made?

j. What is the dollar amount of the firm's current bad debt losses? What losses would be expected under the new policy?

k. What would be the firm's expected dollar cost of granting discounts under the new policy?

l. What is the firm's current dollar cost of carrying receivables? What would it be after the proposed change?

m. What is the incremental after-tax profit associated with the change in credit terms? Should the company make the change? (Assume a tax rate of 40 percent.)

	New	Old	Difference
Gross sales		$1,000,000	
Less discounts		0	
Net sales		$1,000,000	
Production costs		750,000	
Profit before credit costs and taxes		$ 250,000	
Credit-related costs:			
Carrying costs		8,000	
Bad debt losses		20,000	
Profit before taxes		$ 222,000	
Taxes (40%)		88,800	
Net income		$ 133,200	

n. Suppose the firm makes the change, but its competitors react by making similar changes to their own credit terms, with the net result being that gross sales remain at the current $1,000,000 level. What would the impact be on the firm's post-tax profitability?

Section II: INVENTORY MANAGEMENT

Andria Mullins, financial manager of Webster Electronics, has been asked by the firm's CEO, Fred Weygandt, to evaluate the company's inventory control techniques and to lead a discussion of the subject with the senior executives. Andria plans to use as an example one of Webster's "big ticket" items, a customized computer microchip which the firm uses in its laptop computer. Each chip costs Webster $200, and in addition it must pay its supplier a $1,000 setup fee on each order. Further, the minimum order size is 250 units; Webster's annual usage forecast is 5,000 units; and the annual carrying cost of this item is estimated to be 20 percent of the average inventory value.

Andria plans to begin her session with the senior executives by reviewing some basic inventory concepts, after which she will apply the EOQ model to Webster's microchip inventory. As her assistant, you have been asked to help her by answering the following questions:

a. Why is inventory management vital to the financial health of most firms?

b. What assumptions underlie the EOQ model?

c. Write out the formula for the total costs of carrying and ordering inventory, and then use the formula to derive the EOQ model.

d. What is the EOQ for custom microchips? What are total inventory costs if the EOQ is ordered?

e. What is Webster's added cost if it orders 400 units at a time rather than the EOQ quantity? What if it orders 600 per order?

f. Suppose it takes 2 weeks for Webster's supplier to set up production, make and test the chips, and deliver them to Webster's plant. Assuming certainty in delivery times and usage, at what inventory level should Webster reorder? (Assume a 52-week year, and assume that Webster orders the EOQ amount.)

g. Of course, there is uncertainty in Webster's usage rate as well as in delivery times, so the company must carry a safety stock to avoid running out of chips and having to halt production. If a 200-unit safety stock is carried, what effect would this have on total inventory costs? What is the new reorder point? What protection does the safety stock provide if usage increases, or if delivery is delayed?

h. Now suppose Webster's supplier offers a discount of 1 percent on orders of 1,000 or more. Should Webster take the discount? Why or why not?

i. For many firms, inventory usage is not uniform throughout the year, but, rather, follows some seasonal pattern. Can the EOQ model be used in this situation? If so, how?

j. How would these factors affect an EOQ analysis?

   (1) The use of just-in-time procedures.

   (2) The use of air freight for deliveries.

   (3) The use of a computerized inventory control system, wherein as units were removed from stock, an electronic system automatically reduced the inventory account and, when the order point was hit, automatically sent an electronic message to the supplier placing an order. The electronic system ensures that inventory records are accurate, and that orders are placed promptly.

   (4) The manufacturing plant is redesigned and automated. Computerized process equipment and state-of-the-art robotics are installed, making the plant highly flexible in the sense that the company can switch from the production of one item to another at a minimum cost and quite quickly. This makes short production runs more feasible than under the old plant setup.

CHAPTER 23
Working Capital Management: Extensions

- ■ Cash conversion cycle
- ■ Setting the target cash balance
- ■ Receivables management
  - ● Days sales outstanding (DSO)
  - ● Aging schedules
  - ● Payments pattern approach
- ■ EOQ model

Cash Conversion Cycle

The cash conversion cycle focuses on the time between payments made for materials and labor and payments received from sales:

Cash conversion cycle	=	Inventory conversion period	+	Receivables collection period	-	Payables deferral period

What does the cash conversion cycle tell us about working capital management?

Setting the Target Cash Balance

- ■ Theoretical models such as the Baumol model have been developed for use in setting target cash balances. The Baumol model is similar to the EOQ model, which will be discussed later.
- ■ Today, companies strive for zero cash balances and use borrowings or marketable securities as a reserve.
- ■ Monte Carlo simulation can be helpful in setting the target cash balance.

Receivables Monitoring

Assume the following sales estimates:

January	$100	April	$300
February	200	May	200
March	300	June	100

Terms of sale: Net 30.

Expected Collections

30% pay on Day 10 (month of sale).

50% pay on Day 40 (month after sale).

20% pay on Day 70 (2 months after sale).

Annual sales = 18,000 units @ $100/unit.

360-day year.

What is the firm's expected DSO and average daily sales (ADS)?

$$DSO = 0.30(10) + 0.50(40) + 0.20(70)$$
$$= 37 \text{ days.}$$

How does this compare with the firm's credit period?

$$ADS = \frac{18,000(\$100)}{360}$$
$$= \$5,000 \text{ per day.}$$

What is the expected average accounts receivable level? How much of this amount must be financed if the profit margin is 25%?

$$A/R = (DSO)(ADS) = 37(\$5,000)$$
$$= \$185,000.$$

$$0.75(\$185,000) = \$138,750.$$

If notes payable are used to finance the A/R investment, what does the firm's balance sheet look like?

A/R	$185,000	Notes payable	$138,750
		Retained earnings	46,250
			$185,000

If bank loans cost 12 percent, what is the annual dollar cost of carrying the receivables?

Cost of carrying receivables $= 0.12(\$138,750)$

$$= \$16,650.$$

In addition, there is an opportunity cost of not having the use of the profit component of the receivables.

What are some factors which influence a firm's receivables level?

- Receivables are a function of average daily sales and days sales outstanding.
- State of the economy, competition within the industry, and the firm's credit policy all influence a firm's receivables level.

What are some factors which influence the dollar cost of carrying receivables?

- The lower the profit margin, the higher the cost of carrying receivables, because a greater portion of each sales dollar must be financed.
- The higher the cost of financing, the higher the dollar cost.

What would the receivables level be at the end of each month?

A/R = 0.7(Sales in that month) +
0.2(Sales in previous month).

Month	Sales	A/R
Jan	$100	$ 70
Feb	200	160
Mar	300	250
April	300	270
May	200	200
June	100	110

23 - 13

What is the firm's forecasted average daily sales (ADS) for the first 3 months? For the entire half-year?

$$\text{Avg. Daily Sales} = \frac{\text{Total sales}}{\text{\# of days}} \cdot$$

1st Qtr: $600/90 = $6.67.
2nd Qtr: $600/90 = $6.67.

---

23 - 14

What DSO is expected at the end of March? At the end of June?

$$\text{DSO} = \frac{\text{A/R}}{\text{ADS}} \cdot$$

1st Qtr: $250/$6.67 = 37.5 days.
2nd Qtr: $110/$6.67 = 16.5 days.

---

23 - 15

What does the DSO indicate about customers' payments?

- It appears that customers are paying significantly faster in the second quarter than in the first.

- However, the receivables balances were created assuming a constant payment pattern, so the DSO is giving a false measure of payment performance.

- Underlying cause is seasonal variation.

Construct an aging schedule for the end of March and the end of June.

Age of Account (Days)	March A/R	%	June A/R	%
0 - 30	$210	84%	$ 70	64%
31-60	40	16	40	36
61-90	0	0	0	0
	$250	100%	$110	100%

Do aging schedules "tell the truth?"

Construct the uncollected balances schedules for the end of March and June.

Mos.	Sales	Contrib. to A/R	A/R to Sales
Jan	$100	$ 0	0%
Feb	200	40	20
Mar	300	210	70
End of Qtr. A/R		$250	90%

Mos.	Sales	Contrib. to A/R	A/R to Sales
Apr	$300	$ 0	0%
May	200	40	20
June	100	70	70
End of Qtr. A/R		$110	90%

Do the uncollected balances schedules properly measure customers' payment patterns?

■ The focal point of the uncollected balances schedule is the receivables -to-sales ratio.

■ There is no difference in this ratio between March and June, which tells us that there has been no change in payment pattern.

(More...)

■ The uncollected balances schedule gives a true picture of customers' payment patterns, even when sales fluctuate.

■ Any increase in the A/R to sales ratio from a month in one quarter to the corresponding month in the next quarter indicates a slowdown in payment.

■ The "bottom line" gives a summary of the changes in payment patterns.

Assume it is now July and you are developing pro forma financial statements for the following year.

Furthermore, sales and collections in the first half-year matched predicted levels. Using Year 2 sales forecasts, what are next year's pro forma receivables levels for the end of March and June?

March 31

Mos.	Predicted Sales	Predicted A/R to Sales Ratio	Predicted Contrib. to A/R
Jan	$150	0%	$ 0
Feb	300	20	60
Mar	500	70	350
Projected March 31 A/R balance			$410

June 30

Mos.	Predicted Sales	Predicted A/R to Sales Ratio	Predicted Contrib. to A/R
Apr	$400	0%	$ 0
May	300	20	60
June	200	70	140
Projected June 30 A/R balance			$200

What four variables make up a firm's credit policy?

- Cash discounts
- Credit period
- Credit standards
- Collection policy

Disregard any previous assumptions.

- Current credit policy:
  - Credit terms = Net 30.
  - Gross sales = $1,000,000.
  - 80% (of paying customers) pay on Day 30.
  - 20% pay on Day 40.
  - Bad debt losses = 2% of gross sales.
- Operating cost ratio = 75%.
- Cost of carrying receivables = 12%.

The firm is considering a change in credit policy.

- New credit policy:
  - Credit terms = 2/10, net 20.
  - Gross sales = $1,100,000.
  - 60% (of paying customers) pay on Day 10.
  - 30% pay on Day 20.
  - 10% pay on Day 30.
  - Bad debt losses = 1% of gross sales.

What is the DSO under the current and the new credit policies?

- Current:
  $DSO_O = 0.8(30) + 0.2(40)$
  $= 32$ days.
- New:
  $DSO_N = 0.6(10) + 0.3(20) + 0.1(30)$
  $= 15$ days.

What are bad debt losses under the current and the new credit policies?

- Current:
  $BDL_O = 0.02(\$1,000,000)$
  $\quad\quad = \$20,000.$
- New:
  $BDL_N = 0.01(\$1,100,000)$
  $\quad\quad = \$11,000.$

What are the expected dollar costs of discounts under the current and the new policies?

- $Discount_O = \$0.$

- $Discount_N = 0.6(0.02)(0.99)(\$1,100,000)$
  $\quad\quad = \$13,068.$

What are the dollar costs of carrying receivables under the current and the new policies?

- Costs of carrying receivables$_O$
  $=(\$1,000,000/360)(32)(0.75)(0.12)$
  $=\$8,000.$
- Costs of carrying receivables$_N$
  $=(\$1,100,000/360)(15)(0.75)(0.12)$
  $=\$4,125.$

23 - 31

What is the incremental after-tax profit associated with the change in credit terms?

	New	Old	Diff.
Gross sales	$1,100,000	$1,000,000	$100,000
Less: Disc.	13,068	0	13,068
Net sales	$1,086,932	$1,000,000	$ 86,932
Prod. costs	825,000	750,000	75,000
Profit before credit costs and taxes	$ 261,932	$ 250,000	$ 11,932

(More...)

23 - 32

	New	Old	Diff.
Profit before credit costs and taxes	$261,932	$250,000	$11,932
Credit-related costs:			
Carrying costs	4,125	8,000	(3,875)
Bad debts	11,000	20,000	(9,000)
Profit before taxes	$246,807	$222,000	$24,807
Taxes (40%)	98,723	88,800	9,923
Net income	$148,084	$133,200	$14,884

Should the company make the change?

23 - 33

Assume the firm makes the policy change, but its competitors react by making similar changes. As a result, gross sales remain at $1,000,000. How does this impact the firm's after-tax profitability?

Gross sales	$1,000,000
Less: discounts	11,880
Net sales	$ 988,120
Production costs	750,000
Profit before credit costs and taxes	$ 238,120
Credit costs:	
Carrying costs	3,750
Bad debt losses	10,000
Profit before taxes	$ 224,370
Taxes	89,748
Net Income	$ 134,622

- Before the new policy change, the firm's net income totaled $133,200.
- The change would result in a slight gain of $134,622 - $133,200 = $1,422.

Why is inventory management vital to the financial health of most firms?

- Insufficient inventories can lead to lost sales.
- Excess inventories means higher costs than necessary.
- Large inventories, but wrong items leads to both high costs and lost sales.
- Inventory management is more closely related to operations than to finance.

Assumptions of the EOQ Model

- All values are known with certainty and constant over time.
- Inventory usage is uniform over time.
- Carrying costs change proportionally with changes in inventory levels.
- All ordering costs are fixed.
- These assumptions do not hold in the "real world," so safety stocks are held.

Total Inventory Costs (TIC)

$$TIC = \begin{matrix} \text{Total} \\ \text{carrying} \\ \text{costs} \end{matrix} + \begin{matrix} \text{Total} \\ \text{ordering} \\ \text{costs} \end{matrix} = CP(Q/2) + F(S/Q).$$

C = Annual carrying costs (% of inv.).
P = Purchase price per unit.
Q = Number of units per order.
F = Fixed costs per order.
S = Annual usage in units.

Derive the EOQ model from the total cost equation

$$\frac{d(TIC)}{dQ} = \frac{CP}{2} - \frac{FS}{Q^2} = 0$$

$$Q^2 = \frac{2FS}{CP}$$

$$EOQ = Q^* = \sqrt{\frac{2FS}{CP}}.$$

Inventory Model Graph

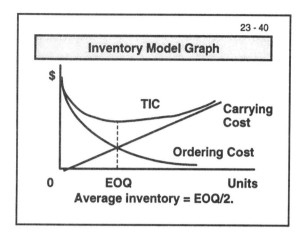

Average inventory = EOQ/2.

Assume the Following Data:

P = $200.
F = $1,000.
S = 5,000.
C = 0.2.
Minimum order size = 250.

What is the EOQ?

$$EOQ = \sqrt{\frac{2(\$1,000)(5,000)}{0.2(\$200)}}$$

$$= \sqrt{\frac{\$10,000,000}{40}}$$

$$= \sqrt{250,000} = 500 \text{ units.}$$

What are total inventory costs when the EOQ is ordered?

$$TIC = CP\left(\frac{Q}{2}\right) + F\left(\frac{S}{Q}\right)$$

$$= (0.2)(\$200)(500/2) + \$1,000(5,000/500)$$

$$= \$40(250) + \$1,000(10)$$

$$= \$10,000 + \$10,000 = \$20,000.$$

Additional Notes

- Average inventory = EOQ/2 = 500/2
  = 250 units.
- # of orders per year = S/EOQ
  = $5,000/500 = 10.
- At EOQ level, total carrying costs = total ordering costs.

What is the added cost if the firm orders 400 units or 600 units at a time rather than the EOQ?

400 units:

TIC = CP(Q/2) + F(S/Q)

= 0.2($200)(400/2) + $1,000(5,000/400)

= $8,000 + $12,500 = $20,500.

Added cost = $20,500 - $20,000 = $500.

600 units:

TIC = CP(Q/2) + F(S/Q)

= 0.2($200)(600/2) + $1,000(5,000/600)

= $12,000 +$8,333 = $20,333.

Added cost = $20,333 - $20,000 = $333.

Notes about EOQ

- At any quantity ≠ EOQ, total inventory costs are higher than necessary.
- The added cost of not ordering the EOQ is not large if the quantity ordered is close to EOQ.
- If Q < EOQ, then total carrying costs decrease, but ordering costs increase.
- If Q > EOQ, total carrying costs increase, but ordering costs decrease.

Suppose delivery takes 2 weeks. Assuming certainty in delivery and usage, at what inventory level should the firm reorder?

Weekly usage rate = 5,000/52
= 96 units.

If order lead time = 2 weeks, firm must reorder when:

Inventory level = 2(96) = 192 units.

Assume a 200-unit safety stock is carried. What effect would this have on total inventory costs?

Without safety stocks, the firm's total inventory costs = $20,000.

Cost of carrying additional 200 units
= CP(Safety stock)
= 0.2($200)(200) = $8,000.

Total inventory costs = $20,000 + $8,000
= $28,000.

Alternatively:

Average inventory = (500/2) + 200
= 450 units.

TIC = CP(Avg. Inv.) + F(S/Q)
= 0.2($200)(450) + $1,000(5,000/500)
= $18,000 + $10,000
= $28,000.

What is the new reorder point with the safety stock?

- ■ Reorder point = 200 + 192 = 392 units.
  - ● The firm's normal 96 unit usage could rise to 392/2 = 196 units per week.
  - ● Or the firm could operate for 392/96 = 4 weeks while awaiting delivery of an order.

Suppose the firm could receive a discount of 1% on orders of 1,000 or more. Should the firm take the discount?

Discount affects operating inventory only.
Discount price = $200(0.99) = $198.

TIC = CP(Q/2) + F(S/Q)
    = 0.2($198)(1,000/2) + $1,000(5,000/1,000)
    = $19,800 + $5,000 = $24,800.

(More...)

Savings = 0.01($200)(5,000)   = $10,000
Added costs = $24,800 - $20,000 = $ 4,800
Net savings = $10,000 - $4,800   = $ 5,200

Firm should take the discount.

Can the EOQ be used if there are seasonal variations?

- Yes, but it must be applied to shorter periods during which usage is approximately constant.

How would the following factors affect an EOQ analysis?

- Just-in-time system: Eliminates the need for using EOQ.
- Use of air freight for deliveries: Reduces the need for safety stock.
- Computerized inventory control system: Reduces safety stocks.
- Flexibility designed plants: Reduces inventory holdings of final goods.

Assume that you have just been hired as a financial analyst by Tropical Sweets Inc., a mid-sized California company that specializes in creating exotic candies from tropical fruits such as mangoes, papayas, and dates. The firm's CEO, George Yamaguchi, recently returned from an industry corporate executive conference in San Francisco, and one of the sessions he attended was on the pressing need for smaller companies to institute corporate risk management programs. Since no one at Tropical Sweets is familiar with the basics of derivatives and corporate risk management, Yamaguchi has asked you to prepare a brief report that the firm's executives could use to gain at least a cursory understanding of the topics.

To begin, you gathered some outside materials on derivatives and corporate risk management and used these materials to draft a list of pertinent questions that need to be answered. In fact, one possible approach to the paper is to use a question-and-answer format. Now that the questions have been drafted, you have to develop the answers.

a. Why might stockholders be indifferent whether or not a firm reduces the volatility of its cash flows?

b. What are six reasons risk management might increase the value of a corporation?

c. What is an option? What is the single most important characteristic of an option?

d. Options have a unique set of terminology. Define the following terms: (1) call option; (2) put option; (3) exercise price; (4) striking, or strike, price; (5) option price; (6) expiration date; (7) exercise value; (8) covered option; (9) naked option; (10) in-the-money call; (11) out-of-the-money call; and (12) LEAP.

e. Consider Tropical Sweets' call option with a $25 strike price. The following table contains historical values for this option at different stock prices:

Stock Price	Call Option Price
$25	$ 3.00
30	7.50
35	12.00
40	16.50
45	21.00
50	25.50

(1) Create a table which shows (a) stock price, (b) strike price, (c) exercise value, (d) option price, and (e) the premium of option price over exercise value.

(2) What happens to the premium of option price over exercise value as the stock price rises? Why?

f. In 1973, Fischer Black and Myron Scholes developed the Black-Scholes Option Pricing Model (OPM).

(1) What assumptions underlie the OPM?

(2) Write out the three equations that constitute the model.

(3) What is the value of the following call option according to the OPM?

Stock price = $27.00
Exercise price = $25.00
Time to expiration = 6 months
Risk-free rate = 6.0%
Stock return variance = 0.11

g. What impact does each of the following call option parameters have on the value of a call option?

(1) Current stock price

(2) Exercise price

(3) Option's term to maturity

(4) Risk-free rate

(5) Variability of the stock price

h. What is corporate risk management? Why is it important to all firms?

i. Risks that firms face can be categorized in many ways. Define the following types of risk: (1) speculative risks; (2) pure risks; (3) demand risks; (4) input risks; (5) financial risks; (6) property risks; (7) personnel risks; (8) environmental risks; (9) liability risks; and (10) insurable risks.

j. What are the three steps of corporate risk management?

k. What are some actions that companies can take to minimize or reduce risk exposures?

l. What is financial risk exposure? Describe the following concepts and techniques that can be used to reduce financial risks: (1) derivatives; (2) futures markets; (3) hedging; and (4) swaps.

m. Describe how commodity futures markets can be used to reduce input price risk.

24 - 1

CHAPTER 24
Derivatives and Risk Management

- Risk management and stock value maximization.
- Derivative securities.
- Fundamentals of risk management.
- Using derivatives to reduce interest rate risk.

---

24 - 2

Do stockholders care about volatile cash flows?

- If volatility in cash flows is not caused by systematic risk, then stockholders can eliminate the risk of volatile cash flows by diversifying their portfolios.
- Stockholders might be able to reduce impact of volatile cash flows by using risk management techniques in their own portfolios.

---

24 - 3

How can risk management increase the value of a corporation?

Risk management allows firms to:

- Have greater debt capacity, which has a larger tax shield of interest payments.
- Implement the optimal capital budget without having to raise external equity in years that would have had low cash flow due to volatility. (More...)

Risk management allows firms to:

■ **Avoid costs of financial distress.**
  - ●**Weakened relationships with suppliers.**
  - ●**Loss of potential customers.**
  - ●**Distractions to managers.**

■ **Utilize comparative advantage in hedging relative to hedging ability of investors.**

(More...)

Risk management allows firms to:

■ **Reduce borrowing costs by using interest rate swaps.**

Example: Two firms with different credit ratings, Hi and Lo:

Hi can borrow fixed at 11% and floating at LIBOR + 1%.

Lo can borrow fixed at 11.4% and floating at LIBOR + 1.5%.

(More...)

Hi wants fixed rate, but it will issue floating and "swap" with Lo. Lo wants floating rate, but it will issue fixed and swap with Hi. Lo also makes "side payment" of 0.45% to Hi.

CF to lender	-(LIBOR+1%)	-11.40%
CF Hi to Lo	-11.40%	+11.40%
CF Lo to Hi	+(LIBOR+1%)	-(LIBOR+1%)
CF Lo to Hi	+0.45%	-0.45%
Net CF	-10.95%	-(LIBOR+1.45%)

(More...)

Risk management allows firms to:

■ **Minimize negative tax effects due to convexity in tax code.**

Example: EBT of $50K in Years 1 and 2, total EBT of $100K,

Tax = $7.5K each year, total tax of $15.

EBT of $0K in Year 1 and $100K in Year 2,

Tax = $0K in Year 1 and $22.5K in Year 2.

What is an option?

An option is a contract which gives its holder the right, but not the obligation, to buy (or sell) an asset at some predetermined price within a specified period of time.

What is the single most important characteristic of an option?

■ **It does not obligate its owner to take any action. It merely gives the owner the right to buy or sell an asset.**

Option Terminology

- ■ Call option: An option to buy a specified number of shares of a security within some future period.
- ■ Put option: An option to sell a specified number of shares of a security within some future period.
- ■ Exercise (or strike) price: The price stated in the option contract at which the security can be bought or sold.

- ■ Option price: The market price of the option contract.
- ■ Expiration date: The date the option matures.
- ■ Exercise value: The value of a call option if it were exercised today = Current stock price - Strike price.

  Note: The exercise value is zero if the stock price is less than the strike price.

- ■ Covered option: A call option written against stock held in an investor's portfolio.
- ■ Naked (uncovered) option: An option sold without the stock to back it up.
- ■ In-the-money call: A call whose exercise price is less than the current price of the underlying stock.

- Out-of-the-money call: A call option whose exercise price exceeds the current stock price.

- LEAPs: Long-term Equity AnticiPation securities that are similar to conventional options except that they are long-term options with maturities of up to 2 1/2 years.

Consider the following data:

Stock Price	Call Option Price
$25	$ 3.00
30	7.50
35	12.00
40	16.50
45	21.00
50	25.50

Exercise price = $25.

Create a table which shows (a) stock price, (b) strike price, (c) exercise value, (d) option price, and (e) premium of option price over the exercise value.

Price of Stock (a)	Strike Price (b)	Exercise Value of Option (a) - (b)
$25.00	$25.00	$0.00
30.00	25.00	5.00
35.00	25.00	10.00
40.00	25.00	15.00
45.00	25.00	20.00
50.00	25.00	25.00

Table (Continued)

Exercise Value of Option (c)	Mkt. Price of Option (d)	Premium (d) - (c)
$ 0.00	$ 3.00	$ 3.00
5.00	7.50	2.50
10.00	12.00	2.00
15.00	16.50	1.50
20.00	21.00	1.00
25.00	25.50	0.50

What happens to the premium of the option price over the exercise value as the stock price rises?

- The premium of the option price over the exercise value declines as the stock price increases.
- This is due to the declining degree of leverage provided by options as the underlying stock price increases, and the greater loss potential of options at higher option prices.

What are the assumptions of the Black-Scholes Option Pricing Model?

- The stock underlying the call option provides no dividends during the call option's life.
- There are no transactions costs for the sale/purchase of either the stock or the option.
- k_{RF} is known and constant during the option's life.

(More...)

- Security buyers may borrow any fraction of the purchase price at the short-term risk-free rate.
- No penalty for short selling and sellers receive immediately full cash proceeds at today's price.
- Call option can be exercised only on its expiration date.
- Security trading takes place in continuous time, and stock prices move randomly in continuous time.

What are the three equations that make up the OPM?

$$V = P[N(d_1)] - Xe^{-k_{RF}t}[N(d_2)].$$

$$d_1 = \frac{\ln(P/X) + [k_{RF} + (\sigma^2/2)]t}{\sigma\sqrt{t}}$$

$$d_2 = d_1 - \sigma\sqrt{t}.$$

What is the value of the following call option according to the OPM? Assume: P = $27; X = $25; k_{RF} = 6%; t = 0.5 years: σ^2 = 0.11

$$V = \$27[N(d_1)] - \$25e^{-(0.06)(0.5)}[N(d_2)].$$

$$d_1 = \frac{\ln(\$27/\$25) + [(0.06 + 0.11/2)](0.5)}{(0.3317)(0.7071)}$$

$$= 0.5736.$$

$$d_2 = d_1 - (0.3317)(0.7071) = d_1 - 0.2345$$

$$= 0.5736 - 0.2345 = 0.3391.$$

$N(d_1) = N(0.5736) = 0.5000 + 0.2168$
    $= 0.7168.$
$N(d_2) = N(0.3391) = 0.5000 + 0.1327$
    $= 0.6327.$
Note: Values obtained from Table A-5 in text.

$V = \$27(0.7168) - \$25e^{-0.03}(0.6327)$
    $= \$19.3536 - \$25(0.97045)(0.6327)$
    $= \$4.0036.$

What impact do the following para-meters have on a call option's value?

- **Current stock price: Call option value increases as the current stock price increases.**
- **Exercise price: As the exercise price increases, a call option's value decreases.**

- **Option period: As the expiration date is lengthened, a call option's value increases (more chance of becoming in the money.)**
- **Risk-free rate: Call option's value tends to increase as k_{RF} increases (reduces the PV of the exercise price).**
- **Stock return variance: Option value increases with variance of the underlying stock (more chance of becoming in the money).**

What is corporate risk management?

Corporate risk management is the management of unpredictable events that would have adverse consequences for the firm.

Definitions of Different Types of Risk

- **Speculative risks:** Those that offer the chance of a gain as well as a loss.
- **Pure risks:** Those that offer only the prospect of a loss.
- **Demand risks:** Those associated with the demand for a firm's products or services.
- **Input risks:** Those associated with a firm's input costs. (More...)

- **Financial risks:** Those that result from financial transactions.
- **Property risks:** Those associated with loss of a firm's productive assets.
- **Personnel risk:** Risks that result from human actions.
- **Environmental risk:** Risk associated with polluting the environment.
- **Liability risks:** Connected with product, service, or employee liability.
- **Insurable risks:** Those which typically can be covered by insurance.

What are the three steps of corporate risk management?

Step 1. Identify the risks faced by the firm.

Step 2. Measure the potential impact of the identified risks.

Step 3. Decide how each relevant risk should be dealt with.

What are some actions that companies can take to minimize or reduce risk exposures?

■ Transfer risk to an insurance company by paying periodic premiums.

■ Transfer functions which produce risk to third parties.

■ Purchase derivatives contracts to reduce input and financial risks.

(More...)

■ Take actions to reduce the probability of occurrence of adverse events.

■ Take actions to reduce the magnitude of the loss associated with adverse events.

■ Avoid the activities that give rise to risk.

What is a financial risk exposure?

- Financial risk exposure refers to the risk inherent in the financial markets due to price fluctuations.
- Example: A firm holds a portfolio of bonds, interest rates rise, and the value of the bonds falls.

Financial Risk Management Concepts

- Derivative: Security whose value stems or is derived from the value of other assets. Swaps, options, and futures are used to manage financial risk exposures.
- Futures: Contracts which call for the purchase or sale of a financial (or real) asset at some future date, but at a price determined today. Futures (and other derivatives) can be used either as highly leveraged speculations or to hedge and thus reduce risk.

(More...)

- Hedging: Generally conducted where a price change could negatively affect a firm's profits.
  - Long hedge: Involves the purchase of a futures contract to guard against a price increase.
  - Short hedge: Involves the sale of a futures contract to protect against a price decline in commodities or financial securities.

(More...)

■ **Swaps:** Involve the exchange of cash payment obligations between two parties, usually because each party prefers the terms of the other's debt contract. Swaps can reduce each party's financial risk.

How can commodity futures markets be used to reduce input price risk?

The purchase of a commodity futures contract will allow a firm to make a future purchase of the input at today's price, even if the market price on the item has risen substantially in the interim.

24E - 1

Chapter 24 Extension:
Insurance and Bond Portfolio
Risk Management

- ■ Risk identification and measurement
- ■ Property loss, liability loss, and financial loss exposures
- ■ Bond portfolio risk management

24E - 2

How are risk exposures identified and measured?

- ■ Large corporations have risk management personnel which have the responsibility to identify and measure risks facing the firm.
- ■ Checklists are used to identify risks.
- ■ Small firms can obtain risk management services from insurance companies or risk management consulting firms.

24E - 3

Describe (1) "property" loss and (2) "liability" loss exposures.

- ■ Property loss exposures: Result from various perils which threaten a firm's real and personal properties.
  - ● Physical perils: Natural events
  - ● Social perils: Related to human actions
  - ● Economic perils: Stem from external economic events

■ **Liability loss exposures:** Result from penalties imposed when responsibilities are not met.

- Bailee exposure: Risks associated with having temporary possession of another's property while some service is being performed. (Cleaners ruin your new suit.)

- Ownership exposure: Risks inherent in the ownership of property. (Customer is injured from fall in store.)

- Business operation exposure: Risks arising from business practices or operations. (Airline sued following crash.)

- Professional liability exposure: Stems from the risks inherent in professions requiring advanced training and licensing. (Doctor sued when patient dies, or accounting firm sued for not detecting overstated profits.)

What actions can companies take to reduce property and liability exposures?

■ Both property and liability exposures can be accommodated by either self-insurance or passing the risk on to an insurance company.

■ The more risk passed on to an insurer, the higher the cost of the policy. Insurers like high deductibles, both to lower their losses and to reduce moral hazard.

How can diversification reduce business risk?

- By appropriately spreading business risk over several activities or operations, the firm can significantly reduce the impact of a single random event on corporate performance.

- Examples: Geographic and product diversification.

What is a financial risk exposure?

- Financial risk exposure refers to the risk inherent in the financial markets due to price fluctuations.

- Example: A firm holds a portfolio of bonds, interest rates rise, and the value of the bonds falls.

Financial risk management concepts:

- Duration: Average time to bondholders' receipt of cash flows, including interest and principal repayment. Duration is used to help assess interest rate and reinvestment rate risks.

- Immunization: Process of selecting durations for bonds in a portfolio such that gains or losses from reinvestment exactly match gains or losses from price changes.

Kimberly MacKenzie, president of Kim's Clothes Inc., a medium-sized manufacturer of women's casual clothing, is worried. Her firm has been selling clothes to Russ Brothers Department Store for more than ten years, and she has never experienced any problems in collecting payment for the merchandise sold. Currently, Russ Brothers owes Kim's Clothes $65,000 for spring sportswear that was delivered to the store just two weeks ago. Kim's concern was brought about by an article that appeared in yesterday's *Wall Street Journal* that indicated that Russ Brothers was having serious financial problems. Further, the article stated that Russ Brothers' management was considering filing for reorganization, or even liquidation, with a federal bankruptcy court.

Kim's immediate concern was whether or not her firm would collect its receivables if Russ Brothers went bankrupt. In pondering the situation, Kim also realized that she knew nothing about the process that firms go through when they encounter severe financial distress. To learn more about bankruptcy, reorganization, and liquidation, Kim asked Ron Mitchell, the firm's chief financial officer, to prepare a briefing on the subject for the entire board of directors. In turn, Ron asked you, a newly hired financial analyst, to do the groundwork for the briefing by answering the following questions:

a. (1) What are the major causes of business failure?

   (2) Do business failures occur evenly over time?

   (3) Which size of firm, large or small, is more prone to business failure? Why?

b. What key issues must managers face in the financial distress process?

c. What informal remedies are available to firms in financial distress? In answering this question, define the following terms:

   (1) Workout

   (2) Restructuring

   (3) Extension

   (4) Composition

   (5) Assignment

   (6) Assignee (trustee)

d. Briefly describe U.S. bankruptcy law, including the following terms:

   (1) Chapter 11

   (2) Chapter 7

   (3) Trustee

   (4) Voluntary bankruptcy

   (5) Involuntary bankruptcy

e. What are the major differences between an informal reorganization and reorganization in bankruptcy? In answering this question, be sure to discuss the following items:

   (1) Common pool problem

   (2) Holdout problem

   (3) Automatic stay

   (4) Cramdown

   (5) Fraudulent conveyance

f. What is a prepackaged bankruptcy? Why have prepackaged bankruptcies become more popular in recent years?

g. Briefly describe the priority of claims in a Chapter 7 liquidation.

h. Assume that Russ Brothers did indeed fail, and that it had the following balance sheet when it was liquidated (in millions of dollars):

Current assets	$40.0	Accounts payable	$10.0
Net fixed assets	5.0	Notes payable (to banks)	5.0
		Accrued wages	0.3
		Federal taxes	0.5
		State and local taxes	0.2
		Current liabilities	$16.0
		First mortgage	$ 3.0
		Second mortgage	0.5
		Subordinated debentures[a]	4.0
		Total long-term debt	$ 7.5
		Preferred stock	$ 1.0
		Common stock	13.0
		Paid-in capital	2.0
		Retained earnings	5.5
		Total equity	$21.5
Total assets	$45.0	Total claims	$45.0

[a]The debentures are subordinated to the notes payable.

The liquidation sale resulted in the following proceeds:

From sale of current assets	$14,000,000
From sale of fixed assets	2,500,000
Total receipts	$16,500,000

For simplicity, assume that there were no trustee's fees or any other claims against the liquidation proceeds. Also, assume that the mortgage bonds are secured by the entire amount of fixed assets. What would each claimant receive from the liquidation distribution?

CHAPTER 25
Bankruptcy, Reorganization, and Liquidation

- Financial distress process
- Federal bankruptcy law
- Reorganization
- Liquidation

What are the major causes of business failure?

- Economic factors
  - industry weakness
  - poor location/product
- Financial factors
  - too much debt
  - insufficient capital

Most failures occur because a number of factors combine to make the business unsustainable.

Do business failures occur evenly over time?

- A large number of businesses fail each year, but the number in any one year has never been a large percentage of the total business population.
- The failure rate of businesses has tended to fluctuate with the state of the economy.

What size firm, large or small, is more prone to business failure?

- Bankruptcy is more frequent among smaller firms.
- Large firms tend to get more help from external sources to avoid bankruptcy, given their greater impact on the economy.

What key issues must managers face in the financial distress process?

- Is it a temporary problem (technical insolvency) or a permanent problem caused by asset values below debt obligations (insolvency in bankruptcy)?
- Who should bear the losses?
- Would the firm be more valuable if it continued to operate or if it were liquidated?

(More...)

- Should the firm file for bankruptcy, or should it try to use informal procedures?
- Who would control the firm during liquidation or reorganization?

What informal remedies are available to firms in financial distress?

- Informal reorganization
- Informal liquidation
- Why might informal remedies be preferable to formal bankruptcy?
- What types of companies are most suitable for informal remedies?

Informal Bankruptcy Terminology

- Workout: Voluntary informal reorganization plan.
- Restructuring: Current debt terms are revised to facilitate the firm's ability to pay.
  - Extension: Creditors postpone the dates of required interest or principal payments, or both. Creditors prefer extension because they are promised eventual payment in full. (More...)

- Composition: Creditors voluntarily reduce their fixed claims on the debtor by either accepting a lower principal amount or accepting equity in lieu of debt repayment.
- Assignment: An informal procedure for liquidating a firm's assets. Title to the debtor's assets is transferred to a third party, called a trustee or assignee, and then the assets are sold off.

Describe the following terms related to U.S. bankruptcy law:

■ Chapter 11: Business reorganization guidelines.

■ Chapter 7: Liquidation procedures.

■ Trustee:
  ● Appointed to control the company when current management is incompetent or fraud is suspected.
  ● Used only in unusual circumstances. (More...)

■ Voluntary bankruptcy: A bankruptcy petition filed in federal court by the distressed firm's management.

■ Involuntary bankruptcy: A bankruptcy petition filed in federal court by the distressed firm's creditors.

What are the major differences between an informal reorganization and reorganization in bankruptcy?

■ Informal Reorganization:
  ● Less costly
  ● Relatively simple to create
  ● Typically allows creditors to recover more money and sooner.

  (More...)

- ■ **Reorganization in Bankruptcy**

  - ● **Avoids holdout problems.**

  - ● **Due to automatic stay provision, avoids common pool problem.**

  - ● **Interest and principal payments may be delayed without penalty until reorganization plan is approved.**

    (More...)

- ● **Permits the firm to issue debtor in possession (DIP) financing.**

- ● **Gives debtor exclusive right to submit a proposed reorganization plan for agreement from the parties involved.**

- ● **Reduces fraudulent conveyance problem.**

- ● **Cramdown if majority in each creditor class approve plan.**

What is a prepackaged bankruptcy?

- ■ **New type of reorganization**
  - ● **Combines the advantages of both formal and informal reorganizations.**
  - ● **Avoids holdout problems**
  - ● **Preserves creditors' claims**
  - ● **Favorable tax treatment.**
- ■ **Agreement to plan obtained from creditors prior to filing for bankruptcy.**
- ■ **Plan filed with bankruptcy petition.**

---

25 - 16

List the priority of claims in a Chapter 7 liquidation.

- Secured creditors.
- Trustee's administrative costs.
- Expenses incurred after involuntary case begun but before trustee appointed.
- Wages due workers within 3 months prior to filing.   (More...)

---

25 - 17

- Unpaid contributions to employee benefit plans that should have been paid within 6 months prior to filing.
- Unsecured claims for customer deposits.
- Taxes due.
- Unfunded pension plan liabilities.
- General (unsecured) creditors.
- Preferred stockholders.
- Common stockholders.

---

25 - 18

Liquidation Illustration Data (millions of $)

Creditor Claims:

Accounts payable	$10.0
Notes payable	5.0
Accrued wages	0.3
Federal taxes	0.5
State and local taxes	0.2
First mortgage	3.0
Second mortgage	0.5
Subordinated debentures*	4.0
	$23.5

*Subordinated to notes payable.   (More...)

Proceeds from liquidation:

From current assets	$14.0
From fixed assets*	2.5
Total receipts	$16.5

* All fixed assets pledged as collateral to mortgage holders.

Priority Distribution (millions of $)

Creditor	Claim	Distribution	Unsatisfied
Accrued wages	$0.3	$0.3	$0.0
Federal taxes	0.5	0.5	0.0
Other taxes	0.2	0.2	0.0
First mortgage	3.0	2.5	0.5
Second mortgage	0.5	0.0	0.5
	$4.5	$3.5	$1.0

Notes: (1) First mortgage receives entire proceeds from sale of fixed assets, leaving $0 for the second mortgage.
(2) $16.5 - $3.5 = $13.0 remains for distribution to general creditors.

General Creditor Distribution (millions of $)

Creditor	Remaining GC Claim	Initial Distrib.[a]	Final Amount[b]	Percent Received
Accounts payable	$10.0	$6.500	$6.500	65.0%
Notes payable	5.0	3.250	5.000	100.0
Accrued wages	0.0		0.300	100.0
Federal taxes	0.0		0.500	100.0
Other taxes	0.0		0.200	100.0
First mortgage	0.5	0.325	2.825	94.2
Second mortgage	0.5	0.325	0.325	65.0
Sub. deb.	4.0	2.600	0.850	21.2
	$20.0	$13.000	$16.500	

[a] Pro rata amount = $13/$20 = 0.65.
[b] Includes priority distribution and $1.75 transfer from subordinated debentures.

Other Motivations for Bankruptcy

- Normally, bankruptcy is motivated by serious current financial problems.
- However, some companies have used bankruptcy proceedings for other purposes:
  - To break union contracts
  - To hasten liability settlements

Some Criticisms of Bankruptcy Laws

- Critics contend that current (1978) bankruptcy laws are flawed.
- Too much value is siphoned off by lawyers, managers, and trustees.
- Companies that have no hope remain alive too long, leaving little for creditors when liquidation does occur.
- Companies in bankruptcy can hurt other companies in industry.

25E- 1

Chapter 25 Extension

- ■ MDA to predict bankruptcy
- ■ Recent business failures

25E- 2

What is MDA, and how can it be used to predict bankruptcy?

- ■ Multiple discriminant analysis (MDA) is a statistical technique similar to multiple regression.
- ■ It identifies the characteristics of firms that went bankrupt in the past.
- ■ Then, data from any firm can be entered into the model to assess the likelihood of future bankruptcy.

25E- 3

MDA Illustration

- ■ Assume you have the following 1997 data for 12 companies:
  - ● Current ratio
  - ● Debt ratio
- ■ Six of the companies (marked by Xs) went bankrupt in 1998 while six (marked by dots) remained solvent.

(More...)

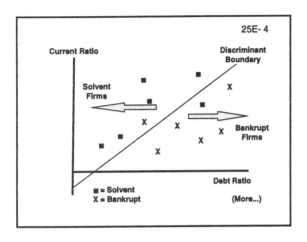

25E- 4

Current Ratio

Discriminant Boundary

Solvent Firms

Bankrupt Firms

Debt Ratio

■ = Solvent
X = Bankrupt

(More...)

25E- 5

■ The discriminant boundary, or Z line, statistically separates the bankrupt and solvent companies.

■ Note that two companies have been misclassified by the MDA program: One bankrupt company falls on the solvent (left) side and one solvent company falls on the bankrupt (right) side.

(More...)

25E- 6

■ Assume the equation for the boundary line is

Z = -2 + 1.5(Current ratio) - 5.0(Debt ratio).

■ Furthermore, if Z = -1 to +1, the future of the company is uncertain. If Z > 1, bankruptcy is unlikely; if Z < -1, bankruptcy is likely to occur.

Using MDA To Predict Bankruptcy

- Suppose Firm S has CR = 4.0 and DR = 0.40. Then,

  $$Z = -2 + 1.5(4.0) - 5.0(0.40) = +2.0,$$
  and firm is unlikely to go bankrupt.

- Suppose Firm B has CR = 1.5 and DR = 0.75. Then,

  $$Z = -2 + 1.5(1.5) - 5.0(0.75) = -3.5,$$
  and firm is likely to go bankrupt.

Some Final Points

- The most well-known bankruptcy prediction model is Edward Altman's five factor model.

- Such models tend to work relatively well, but only for the near term.

- The more similar the historical sample to the firm being evaluated, the better the prediction.

Smitty's Home Repair Company, a regional hardware chain which specializes in "do-it-yourself" materials and equipment rentals, is cash rich because of several consecutive good years. One of the alternative uses for the excess funds is an acquisition. Linda Wade, Smitty's treasurer and you boss, has been asked to place a value on a potential target, Hill's Hardware, a small chain which operates in an adjacent state, and she has enlisted your help.

The table below indicates Wade's estimates of Hill's earnings potential if it came under Smitty's management (in millions of dollars). The interest expense listed here includes the interest (1) on Hill's existing debt, (2) on new debt Smitty's would issue to help finance the acquisition, and (3) on new debt expected to be issued over time to help finance expansion within the new "H division," the code name given to the target firm. The retentions represent earnings that will be reinvested within the H division to help finance its growth.

Security analysts estimate Hill's beta to be 1.3. The acquisition would not change Hill's capital structure or tax rate. Wade realizes that Hill's Hardware also generates depreciation cash flows, but she believes that these funds would have to be reinvested within the division to replace worn-out equipment.

Wade estimates the risk-free rate to be 9 percent and the market risk premium to be 4 percent. She also estimates that net cash flows after 2002 will grow at a constant rate of 6 percent. Following are projections for sales and other items.

	1999	2000	2001	2002
Net sales	$60.0	$90.0	$112.5	$127.5
Cost of goods sold (60%)	36.0	54.0	67.5	76.5
Selling/administrative expense	4.5	6.0	7.5	9.0
Interest expense	3.0	4.5	4.5	6.0
Necessary retained earnings	0.0	7.5	6.0	4.5

Smitty's management is new to the merger game, so Wade has been asked to answer some basic questions about mergers as well as to perform the merger analysis. To structure the task, Wade has developed the following questions, which you must answer and then defend to Smitty's board.

a. Several reasons have been proposed to justify mergers. Among the more prominent are (1) tax considerations, (2) risk reduction, (3) control, (4) purchase of assets at below-replacement cost, (5) synergy, and (6) globalization. In general, which of the reasons are economically justifiable? Which are not? Which fit the situation at hand? Explain.

b. Briefly describe the differences between a hostile merger and a friendly merger.

c. Use the data developed previously to construct the H division's cash flow statements for 1999 through 2002. Why is interest expense deducted in merger cash flow statements, whereas it is not normally deducted in capital budgeting cash flow analysis? Why are earnings retentions deducted in the cash flow statement?

d. Conceptually, what is the appropriate discount rate to apply to the cash flows developed in Part c? What is your actual estimate of this discount rate?

e. What is the estimated terminal value of the acquisition; that is, what is the estimated value of the H division's cash flows beyond 2002? What is Hill's value to Smitty's? Suppose another firm were evaluating Hill's as an acquisition candidate. Would they obtain the same value? Explain.

f. Assume that Hill's has 10 million shares outstanding. These shares are traded relatively infrequently, but the last trade, made several weeks ago, was at a price of $9 per share. Should Smitty's make an offer for Hill's? If so, how much should it offer per share?

g. Assume that publicly traded companies in Hill's line of business have stock prices in the range of 5 to 6 times earnings before interest, taxes, depreciation, and amortization (EBITDA). Use the market multiple approach to value the target company.

h. There has been considerable research undertaken to determine whether mergers really create value, and, if so, how this value is shared between the parties involved. What are the results of this research?

i. What are the two methods of accounting for mergers?

j. What merger-related activities are undertaken by investment bankers?

k. What is a leveraged buyout (LBO)? What are some of the advantages and disadvantages of going private?

l. What are the major types of divestitures? What motivates firms to divest assets?

m. What are holding companies? What are their advantages and disadvantages?

CHAPTER 26
Mergers, LBOs, Divestitures, and Holding Companies

- Types of mergers
- Merger analysis
- Role of investment bankers
- LBOs, divestitures, and holding companies

What are some valid economic justifications for mergers?

- Synergy: Value of the whole exceeds sum of the parts. Could arise from:
  - Operating economies
  - Financial economies
  - Differential management efficiency
  - Taxes (use accumulated losses)

(More...)

- Break-up value: Assets would be more valuable if broken up and sold to other companies.

What are some questionable reasons for mergers?

- Diversification
- Purchase of assets at below replacement cost
- Acquire other firms to increase size, thus making it more difficult to be acquired

---

Differentiate between hostile and friendly mergers

- Friendly merger:
  - The merger is supported by the managements of both firms.

(More...)

- Hostile merger:
  - Target firm's management resists the merger.
  - Acquirer must go directly to the target firm's stockholders, try to get 51% to tender their shares.
  - Often, mergers that start out hostile end up as friendly, when offer price is raised.

DCF Valuation Analysis (In Millions)

Cash Flow Statements after Merger Occurs

	1999	2000	2001	2002
Net sales	$60.0	$90.0	$112.5	$127.5
Cost of goods sold (60%)	36.0	54.0	67.5	76.5
Selling/admin. expenses	4.5	6.0	7.5	9.0
Interest expense	3.0	4.5	4.5	6.0
EBT	$16.5	$25.5	$33.0	$36.0
Taxes (40%)	6.6	10.2	13.2	14.4
Net income	$9.9	$15.3	$19.8	$21.6
Retentions	0.0	7.5	6.0	4.5
Cash flow	$9.9	$7.8	$13.8	$17.1

Conceptually, what is the appropriate discount rate to apply to the target's cash flows?

- Estimated cash flows are residuals that belong to the shareholders of the acquiring firm.

- They are riskier than the typical capital budgeting cash flows, because including fixed interest charges increases the volatility.

(More...)

- Because the cash flows are equity flows, they should be discounted using a cost of equity rather than an overall cost of capital.

- Note that the cash flows reflect the target's business risk, not the acquiring company's.

- However, if the merger will affect the target's leverage and tax rate, then it will affect its financial risk.

Discount Rate Calculation

$$k_{s(Target)} = k_{RF} + (k_M - k_{RF})b_{Target}$$
$$= 9\% + (4\%)1.3 = 14.2\%.$$

How much faith should we place in the discount rate estimate?

■ **Not much, because:**

- ● The 1.3 beta is an estimate.
- ● Historical betas are questionable.
- ● The market risk premium is an estimate.
- ● The CAPM is based on questionable assumptions.

Discount Rate Calculation

$$\text{Terminal value} = \frac{(2002\ \text{Cash flow})(1+g)}{k_s - g}$$
$$= \frac{\$17.1(1.06)}{0.142 - 0.06}$$
$$= \$221.0 \text{ million.}$$

What Is the Value of the Target Firm? (In Millions)

	1999	2000	2001	2002
Annual cash flow	$9.9	$7.8	$13.8	$ 17.1
Terminal value	___	___	___	221.0
Net cash flow	$9.9	$7.8	$13.8	$238.1

$$\text{Value} = \frac{\$9.9}{(1.142)^1} + \frac{\$7.8}{(1.142)^2} + \frac{\$13.8}{(1.142)^3} + \frac{\$238.1}{(1.142)^4}$$

$$= \$163.9 \text{ million.}$$

Would another potential acquirer obtain the same value?

- No. The cash flow estimates would be different, both due to forecasting inaccuracies and to differential synergies.

- Further, a different beta estimate, financing mix, or tax rate would change the discount rate.

Assume the target company has 10 million shares outstanding. The stock last traded at $9 per share, which reflects the target's value on a stand-alone basis. How much should the acquiring firm offer?

Estimate of target's value = $163.9 million

Target's current value   = $ 90.0 million

Merger premium   = $ 73.9 million

Presumably, the target's value is increased by $73.9 million due to merger synergies, although realizing such synergies has been problematic in many mergers.

(More...)

- The offer could range from $9 to $163.9/10 = $16.39 per share.
- At $9, all merger benefits would go to the acquiring firm's shareholders.
- At $16.39, all value added would go to the target firm's shareholders.
- The graph on the next slide summarizes the situation.

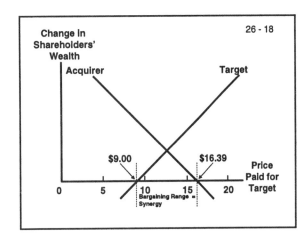

Points About Graph

- Nothing magic about crossover price.

- Actual price would be determined by bargaining. Higher if target is in better bargaining position, lower if acquirer is.

- If target is good fit for many acquirers, other firms will come in, price will be bid up. If not, could be close to $9.

(More...)

- Acquirer might want to make high "preemptive" bid to ward off other bidders, or low bid and then plan to go up. Strategy is important.

- Do target's managers have 51% of stock and want to remain in control?

- What kind of personal deal will target's managers get?

Assuming a market multiple of 5-6 times EBITDA, use the market multiple method to value the stock.

1999 EBITDA = $ 19.50 million
2002 EBITDA = __ 42.00__
$ 61.50 million
Divided by 2 = Average = $ 30.75 million

5 x Avg. EBITDA = $153.75 million
6 x Avg. EBITDA = $184.50 million

Which valuation method is better, DCF or market multiple?

Both methods have significant implementation problems.

- Confidence in DCF cash flow forecasts and discount rate is often low.
- Validity of market multiple method depends on comparability of firms and ability of EBITDA to capture synergies.
- Judgment is key to final valuation.

Do mergers really create value?

- According to empirical evidence, acquisitions do create value as a result of economies of scale, other synergies, and/or better management.
- Shareholders of target firms reap most of the benefits, that is, the final price is close to full value.
  - Target management can always say no.
  - Competing bidders often push up prices.

What are the two methods of accounting for mergers?

- Pooling of interests:
  - Assumes a merger among equals.
  - New balance sheet is merely the sum of the two existing balance sheets.
  - No income statement effects other than summing the two income statements.

(More...)

■ **Purchase:**

- The assets of the acquired firm are "written up" to reflect purchase price if it is greater than the net asset value.

- Goodwill is often created, which appears as an asset on the balance sheet.

- Common equity account is increased to balance assets and claims.

- Goodwill is amortized and expensed over time, thus reducing future reported earnings.

What are some merger-related activities of investment bankers?

- ■ Identifying targets
- ■ Arranging mergers
- ■ Developing defensive tactics
- ■ Establishing a fair value
- ■ Financing mergers
- ■ Arbitrage operations

What is a leveraged buyout (LB0)?

- ■ In an LBO, a small group of investors, normally including management, buys all of the publicly held stock, and hence takes the firm private.

- ■ Purchase often financed with debt.

- ■ After operating privately for a number of years, investors take the firm public to "cash out."

What are are the advantages and disadvantages of going private?

- ■ Advantages:
  - ● Administrative cost savings
  - ● Increased managerial incentives
  - ● Increased managerial flexibility
  - ● Increased shareholder participation
- ■ Disadvantages:
  - ● Limited access to equity capital
  - ● No way to capture return on investment

What are the major types of divestitures?

- ■ Sale of an entire subsidiary to another firm.
- ■ Spinning off a corporate subsidiary by giving the stock to existing shareholders.
- ■ Carving out a corporate subsidiary by selling a minority interest.
- ■ Outright liquidation of assets.

What motivates firms to divest assets?

- ■ Subsidiary worth more to buyer than when operated by current owner.
- ■ To settle antitrust issues.
- ■ Subsidiary's value increased if it operates independently.
- ■ To change strategic direction.
- ■ To shed money losers.
- ■ To get needed cash when distressed.

What are holding companies?

- A holding company is a corporation formed for the sole purpose of owning the stocks of other companies.

- In a typical holding company, the subsidiary companies issue their own debt, but their equity is held by the holding company, which, in turn, sells stock to individual investors.

What are the advantages and disadvantages of holding companies?

- Advantages:
  - Control with fractional ownership.
  - Isolation of risks.
- Disadvantages:
  - Partial multiple taxation.
  - Ease of enforced dissolution.

Citrus Products Inc. is a medium-sized producer of citrus juice drinks with groves in Indian River County, Florida. Until now, the company has confined its operations and sales to the United States, but its CEO, George Gaynor, wants to expand into Europe. The first step would be to set up sales subsidiaries in Spain and Portugal, then to set up a production plant in Spain, and, finally, to distribute the product throughout the European common market. The firm's financial manager, Ruth Schmidt, is enthusiastic about the plan, but she is worried about the implications of the foreign expansion on the firm's financial management process. She has asked you, the firm's most recently hired financial analyst, to develop a 1-hour tutorial package that explains the basics of multinational financial management. The tutorial will be presented at the next board of directors meeting. To get you started, Schmidt has supplied you with the following list of questions.

a. What is a multinational corporation? Why do firms expand into other countries?

b. What are the six major factors which distinguish multinational financial management from financial management as practiced by a purely domestic firm?

c. Consider the following illustrative exchange rates.

	U.S. Dollars Required to Buy One Unit of Foreign Currency
Spanish peseta	0.0075
Portuguese escudo	0.0063

(1) Are these currency prices direct quotations or indirect quotations?

(2) Calculate the indirect quotations for pesetas and escudos.

(3) What is a cross rate? Calculate the two cross rates between pesetas and escudos.

(4) Assume Citrus Products can produce a liter of orange juice and ship it to Spain for $1.75. If the firm wants a 50 percent markup on the product, what should the orange juice sell for in Spain?

(5) Now, assume Citrus Products begins producing the same liter of orange juice in Spain. The product costs 200 pesetas to produce and ship to Portugal, where it can be sold for 400 escudos. What is the dollar profit on the sale?

(6) What is exchange rate risk?

d. Briefly describe the current international monetary system. How does the current system differ from the system that was in place prior to August 1971?

e. What is a convertible currency? What problems arise when a multinational company operates in a country whose currency is not convertible?

f. What is the difference between spot rates and forward rates? When is the forward rate at a premium to the spot rate? At a discount?

g. What is interest rate parity? Currently, you can exchange 1 peseta for 0.0080 dollar in the 30-day forward market, and the risk-free rate on 30-day securities is 4 percent in both Spain and the United States. Does interest rate parity hold? If not, which securities offer the highest expected return?

h. What is purchasing power parity? If grapefruit juice costs $2.00 a liter in the United States and purchasing power parity holds, what should be the price of grapefruit juice in Portugal?

i. What impact does relative inflation have on interest rates and exchange rates?

j. Briefly discuss the international capital markets.

k. To what extent do average capital structures vary across different countries?

l. What is the impact of multinational operations on each of the following financial management topics?

(1) Cash management.

(2) Capital budgeting decisions.

(3) Credit management.

(4) Inventory management.

CHAPTER 27
Multinational Financial Management

- Factors that make multinational financial management different
- Exchange rates and trading
- International monetary system
- International financial markets
- Specific features of multinational financial management

What is a multinational corporation?

- A multinational corporation is one that operates in two or more countries.
- At one time, most multinationals produced and sold in just a few countries.
- Today, many multinationals have world-wide production and sales.

Why do firms expand into other countries?

- To seek new markets.
- To seek new supplies of raw materials.
- To gain new technologies.
- To gain production efficiencies.
- To avoid political and regulatory obstacles.
- To reduce risk by diversification.

What are the major factors that distinguish multinational from domestic financial management?

- Currency differences
- Economic and legal differences
- Language differences
- Cultural differences
- Government roles
- Political risk

Consider the following exchange rates:

	U.S. $ to buy 1 Unit
Spanish peseta	0.0075
Portuguese escudo	0.0063

Are these currency prices direct or indirect quotations?

Since they are prices of foreign currencies expressed in U.S. dollars, they are direct quotations.

What is an indirect quotation?

- An indirect quotation gives the amount of a foreign currency required to buy one U.S. dollar.
- Note than an indirect quotation is the reciprocal of a direct quotation.

Calculate the indirect quotations for pesetas and escudos.

	# of Units of Foreign Currency per U.S. $
Spanish peseta	133.3
Portuguese escudo	158.7

Peseta: 1/0.0075 = 133.3.
Escudo: 1/0.0063 = 158.7.

What is a cross rate?

■ A cross rate is the exchange rate between any two currencies not involving U.S. dollars.

■ In practice, cross rates are usually calculated from direct or indirect rates. That is, on the basis of U.S. dollar exchange rates.

Calculate the two cross rates between pesetas and escudos.

■ Cross rate $= \dfrac{Pesetas}{Dollar} \times \dfrac{Dollars}{Escudo}$

$= 133.3 \times 0.0063$
$= 0.84$ pesetas/escudo.

■ Cross rate $= \dfrac{Escudos}{Dollar} \times \dfrac{Dollars}{Peseta}$

$= 158.7 \times 0.0075$
$= 1.19$ escudos/peseta.

Note:

■ The two cross rates are reciprocals of one another.

■ They can be calculated by dividing either the direct or indirect quotations.

Assume the firm can produce a liter of orange juice and ship it to Spain for $1.75. If the firm wants a 50% markup on the product, what should the juice sell for in Spain?

Price = ($1.75)(1.50)(133.3 pesetas/$)

= 349.91 pesetas.

Now the firm begins producing the orange juice in Spain. The product costs 200 pesetas to produce and ship to Portugal, where it can be sold for 400 escudos. What is the dollar profit on the sale?

200 pesetas = 200(1.19) = 238 escudos.

400 - 238 = 162 escudos profit.

158.7 escudos = 1 U.S. dollar.

Dollar profit = 162/158.7 = $1.02.

What is exchange rate risk?

Exchange rate risk is the risk that the value of a cash flow in one currency translated from another currency will decline due to a change in exchange rates.

For example, in the last slide, a weakening escudo (strengthening dollar) would lower the dollar profit.

Describe the current and former international monetary systems.

- The current system is a floating rate system.
- Prior to 1971, a fixed exchange rate system was in effect.
  - The U.S. dollar was tied to gold.
  - Other currencies were tied to the dollar.

What is a convertible currency?

- A currency is convertible when the issuing country promises to redeem the currency at current market rates.
- Convertible currencies are traded in world currency markets.

What problems arise when a firm operates in a country whose currency is not convertible?

- It becomes very difficult for multi-national companies to conduct business because there is no easy way to take profits out of the country.
- Often, firms will barter for goods to export to their home countries.

What is the difference between spot rates and forward rates?

- A spot rate is the rate applied to buy currency for immediate delivery.
- A forward rate is the rate applied to buy currency at some agreed-upon future date.

When is the forward rate at a premium to the spot rate?

- If the U.S. dollar buys fewer units of a foreign currency in the forward than in the spot market, the foreign currency is selling at a premium.
- In the opposite situation, the foreign currency is selling at a discount.
- The primary determinant of the spot/forward rate relationship is relative interest rates.

What is interest rate parity?

Interest rate parity implies that investors should expect to earn the same return on similar-risk securities in all countries:

$$\frac{\text{Forward rate}}{\text{Spot rate}} = \frac{1 + k_h}{1 + k_f} \, .$$

Here,

k_h = periodic interest rate in the home country.
k_f = periodic interest rate in the foreign country.

Assume 1 peseta = $0.008 in the 30-day forward market and the Spanish and U.S. risk-free rate = 4%.

Does interest rate parity hold?

Forward rate = $0.008.
k_h = 4%/12 = 0.333%.
k_f = 4%/12 = 0.333%.

(More...)

$$\frac{\text{Forward rate}}{\text{Spot rate}} = \frac{1 + k_h}{1 + k_f}$$

$$\frac{0.0080}{\text{Spot rate}} = \frac{1.0033}{1.0033}$$

Spot rate = 0.0080.

If interest rate parity holds, the spot rate would be 0.0080 dollars/peseta. However, the observed spot rate is 0.0075 dollars/peseta.

Which 30-day security (U.S. or Spanish) offers the higher return?

■ Buy $1,000 worth of pesetas in the spot market:

1,000(133.333) = 133,333 pesetas.

■ Spanish investment returns 133,777 pesetas:

133,333(1.00333) = 133,777 pesetas.

(More...)

■ Buy contract today to exchange 133,777 pesetas in 30 days at forward rate of 0.008 dollars/peseta.

■ At end of 30 days, convert peseta investment to dollars:

133,777(0.008) = $1,070.22.

■ Calculate the rate of return:

$70.22/$1,000 = 7.02% per 30 days.

(More...)

■ U.S. 30-day rate is 0.33%, so Spanish securities at 7.02% offer the higher rate of return.

■ Note that a forward rate of 0.0075 would produce a rate of return of 0.33%:

133,777(0.0075) = $1,003.33.

$3.33/$1,000 = 0.33% per 30 days.

■ Traders would recognize the arbitrage opportunity; their actions would tend to move forward and spot rates to parity.

What is purchasing power parity?

Purchasing power parity implies that the level of exchange rates adjusts so that identical goods cost the same amount in different countries.

$$P_h = P_f(\text{Spot rate}),$$

or

$$\text{Spot rate} = P_h/P_f.$$

If grapefruit juice costs $2.00/liter in the U.S. and purchasing power parity holds, what is price in Portugal?

$$\text{Spot rate} = P_h/P_f.$$
$$\$0.0063 = \$2.00/P_f$$
$$P_f = \$2.00/\$0.0063$$
$$= 317.46 \text{ escudos.}$$

- Do interest rate and purchasing power parity hold exactly at any point in time?

What impact does relative inflation have on interest rates and exchange rates?

- Lower inflation leads to lower interest rates, so borrowing in low-interest countries may appear attractive to multinational firms.
- However, currencies in low-inflation countries tend to appreciate against those in high-inflation rate countries, so the true interest cost increases over the life of the loan.

Describe the international money and capital markets.

- Eurodollar markets
  - Dollars held outside the U.S.
  - Mostly Europe, but also elsewhere
- International bonds
  - Foreign bonds: Sold by foreign borrower, but denominated in the currency of the country of issue.
  - Eurobonds: Sold in country other than the one in whose currency it is denominated.

To what extent do capital structures vary across different countries?

- Early studies suggested that average capital structures varied widely among the large industrial countries.
- However, a recent study, which controlled for differences in accounting practices, suggests that capital structures are more similar across different countries than previously thought.

What is the impact of multinational operations on each of the following topics?

Cash Management

- Distances are greater.
- Access to more markets for loans and for temporary investments.
- Cash is often denominated in different currencies.

Capital Budgeting Decisions

- Foreign operations are taxed locally, and then funds repatriated may be subject to U.S. taxes.
- Foreign projects are subject to political risk.
- Funds repatriated must be converted to U.S. dollars, so exchange rate risk must be taken into account.

Credit Management

- Credit is more important, because commerce to lesser-developed countries often relies on credit.
- Credit for future payment may be subject to exchange rate risk.

Inventory Management

- Inventory decisions can be more complex, especially when inventory can be stored in locations in different countries.
- Some factors to consider are shipping times, carrying costs, taxes, import duties, and exchange rates.

Southeast Tile Distributors Inc. is a building tile wholesaler that originated in Atlanta but is now considering expansion throughout the region to take advantage of continued strong population growth. The company has been a "mom and pop" operation supplemented by part-time workers, so it currently has no corporate retirement plan. However, the firm's owner, Andy Johnson, believes that it will be necessary to start a corporate pension plan to attract the quality employees needed to make the expansion succeed. Andy has asked you, a recent business school graduate who has just joined the firm, to learn all that you can about pension funds, and then prepare a briefing paper on the subject. To help you get started, he sketched out the following questions:

a. How important are pension funds to the U.S. economy?

b. Define the following pension fund terms:

   (1) Defined benefit plan

   (2) Defined contribution plan

   (3) Profit sharing plan

   (4) Vesting

   (5) Portability

   (6) Fully funded; overfunded; underfunded

   (7) Actuarial rate of return

   (8) Employee Retirement Income Security Act (ERISA)

   (9) Pension Benefit Guarantee Corporation (PBGC)

c. What two organizations provide guidelines for reporting pension fund activities to stockholders? Describe briefly how pension fund data are reported in a firm's financial statements. (Hint: Consider both defined contribution and defined benefit plans.)

d. Assume that an employee joins the firm at age 25, works for 40 years to age 65, and then retires. The employee lives another 15 years, to age 80, and during retirement draws a pension of $20,000 at the end of each year. How much must the firm contribute annually (at year-end) over the employee's working life to fully fund the plan by retirement age if the plan's actuarial rate of return is 10 percent? Draw a graph which shows the value of the employee's pension fund over time. Why is real-world pension fund management much more complex than indicated in this illustration?

e. Discuss the risks to both the plan sponsor and plan beneficiaries under the three types of pension plans.

f. How does the type of pension plan influence decisions in each of the following areas:

(1) The possibility of age discrimination in hiring?

(2) The possibility of sex discrimination in hiring?

(3) Employee training costs?

(4) The militancy of unions when a company faces financial adversity?

g. What are the two components of a plan's funding strategy? What is the primary goal of a plan's investment strategy?

h. How can a corporate financial manager judge the performance of pension plan managers?

i. What is meant by "tapping" pension fund assets? Why is this action so controversial?

j. What has happened to the cost of retiree health benefits over the last decade? How are retiree health benefits reported to shareholders?

CHAPTER 28
Pension Plan Management

- Pension plan terminology
- Defined benefit versus defined contribution plans
- Pension fund investment tactics
- Retiree health benefits

How important are pension funds?

- They constitute the largest and fastest growing class of investors.
- They have about 50% of institutionally held long-term assets. (Other 50% held by insurance companies, mutual funds, S&Ls, banks, credit unions, etc.) Pension fund share is rising rapidly.

Pension Plan Terminology

- Defined benefit plan: Employer agrees to give retirees a specific benefit, generally a percentage of final salary.
- Defined contribution plan: Employer agrees to make specific payments into a retirement fund, frequently a mutual fund. Retirees' benefits depend on the investment performance of their own fund. 401(k) is the most common type.

(More...)

■ **Profit sharing plan:** Employer payments vary with the firm's profits. (Defined contribution, but as a percentage of profits).

■ **Vesting:** Gives the employee the right to receive pension benefits at retirement even if he/she leaves the company before retirement.

■ **Deferred vesting:** Pension rights are not vested for the first few years.

(More...)

■ **Portability:** A "portable" pension plan can be moved to another employer if the employee changes jobs.

■ **Fully funded:** Value of plan assets equals the present value of expected retirement benefits.

■ **Underfunded:** Plan assets are less than the PV of the benefits. An "unfunded liability" is said to exist.

■ **Overfunded:** The reverse of underfunded.

(More...)

■ **Actuarial rate of return:** The rate of return:

● used to find the PV of expected benefits (discount rate).

● at which the fund's assets are assumed to be invested.

■ **Employee Retirement Income Security Act (ERISA):** The federal law governing the administration and structure of corporate pension plans.

(More...)

---

28 - 7

■ **Pension Benefit Guarantee Corporation (PBGC):**

● A government agency created by ERISA to ensure that employees of firms which go bankrupt before their defined benefit plans are fully funded will receive some minimum level of benefits.

● However, for high income employees (i.e., airline pilots), PBGC pension payments are often less than those promised by the company.

28 - 8

Who establishes guidelines for reporting pension fund information on corporate financial statements?

■ Financial Accounting Standards Board (FASB), together with the SEC, establishes rules for reporting pension information.

■ Pension costs are huge, and assumptions have major effect on reported profits.

28 - 9

How are pension fund data reported in a firm's financial statements?

■ Defined Contribution Plan:

● The annual contribution is shown as a cost on the income statement.

● A note explains the entry.

■ Defined Benefit Plan:

● The plan's funding status must be reported directly on the balance sheet. (More...)

- The annual pension contribution (expense) is shown on the income statement.
- Details regarding the annual expense, along with the composition of the fund's assets, are reported in the notes section.
- The annual pension contribution is tied to the assumed actuarial rate of return: the greater the assumed return, the smaller the contribution.

Given the following data, how much must the firm contribute annually (at year-end) over the employee's working life to fully fund the plan by retirement age?

■ Data/Assumptions:
- Employee begins work at 25, will work 40 years until 65, and then retire.
- Employee will live another 15 years, to age 80, and will draw a pension of $20,000 per year.
- The plan's actuarial rate of return is 10%.

Step 1.	Determine the amount the firm must have in the plan at the time the employee retires. It is $152,122.

Input	15	10		20000	0
	N	I	PV	PMT	FV
Output			152,122		

Step 2: Determine the annual contribution during the employment years. With $152,122 to be accumulated, the answer is $343.71.

Input	40	10	0		152122
	N	I	PV	PMT	FV
Output				343.71	

Graph of Pension Fund Assets

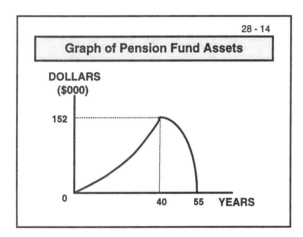

Pension fund management is much more complex than this illustration.

- Don't know how long the employee will work for the firm (the 40 years).
- Don't know what the annual pension payment will be (the $20,000).
- Don't know what rate of return the pension fund will earn (the 10%).
- A large number of employees creates complexities, but it also reduces the aggregate actuarial uncertainty.

What risks are borne by the plan sponsor and plan beneficiaries under the three types of pension plans?

■ Defined benefit plan: Most risk falls on the company, because it guarantees to pay a specific retirement benefit regardless of the firm's profitability or the return on the plan's assets.

(More...)

■ Defined contribution plan: Places more risk on employees, because benefits depend on the return performance of each employee's chosen investment fund.

■ Profit sharing: Most risk to employee, least to employer. Company doesn't pay into fund unless it has earnings, and employees bear investment risk.

What type of companies tend to have each type of plan?

■ Large, more mature companies (and governments) tend to use defined benefit plans.

■ New, start-up companies tend to use profit sharing plans.

■ Many older companies are shifting to defined contribution plans.

---

28 - 19

If a company uses either a defined contribution or a profit sharing plan, how are the assets administered?

- Usually set up as a 401(k) plan.

- Employees make tax-deductible contributions into one or more investment vehicles (often mutual funds) established by the company.

- Company may make independent or matching contributions.

---

28 - 20

Does the type of pension plan influence the possibility of age discrimination?

Defined benefit plans are more costly to firms when older workers are hired. The firm has a shorter time to accumulate the needed funds, hence must make larger annual contributions.

---

28 - 21

Does the type of pension plan influence the possibility of sex discrimination?

Since women live longer than men, female employees are more costly under defined benefit plans.

How does the type of pension plan influence employee training costs?

- Defined benefit plans encourage employees to stay with a single company, hence they reduce training costs.

- Vesting and portability facilitate job shifts, hence increase training costs.

Does the type of pension plan influence the militancy of unions when a company faces financial adversity?

Benefits paid under defined benefit plans are usually tied to the number of years worked and the final (or last few) year's salary. Therefore, unions are more likely to work with a firm to ensure its survival under a defined benefit plan.

What are the two components of a plan's funding strategy?

- How fast should any unfunded liability be reduced?

- What rate of return should be assumed in the actuarial calculations?

28 - 25

What is the primary goal of a plan's investment strategy?

- To structure the portfolio to minimize the risk of not achieving the assumed actuarial rate of return.

- But a low risk portfolio will mean low expected returns, which will mean larger annual contributions, which hurt profits.

---

28 - 26

How can a company judge the performance of it pension plan managers?

- Alpha analysis: Compare the realized return on the portfolio with the required return on the portfolio.

- Comparative analysis: Compare the manager's historical returns with other managers having the same investment objective (same risk profile).

---

28 - 27

What's meant by "tapping" pension fund assets?

- This occurs when a company terminates an overfunded defined benefit plan, uses a portion of the funds to purchase annuities which provide the promised pensions to employees, and then recovers the excess for use by the firm.

- First used by corporate raiders after takeovers, with proceeds used to pay down takeover debt.

Why is "tapping" controversial?

■ Some people believe that pension fund assets belong to employees, hence tapping "robs" employees. (Excess funds make it easier to bargain for higher benefits.)

■ Courts have ruled that defined benefit plan assets belong to the firm, so firms can recover these assets as long as this action does not jeopardize current employees' contractual benefits.

What has happened to the cost of retiree health benefits over the last decade?

Because of the increased number of retirees, longer life expectancies, and the dramatic escalation in health care costs over the last ten years, many firms are forecasting that retiree health care costs will be as high, or higher, than pension costs.

How are retiree health benefits reported to shareholders?

■ Before 1990, firms used pay-as-you-go procedures which concealed the true liability.

■ Now companies must set up reserves for retiree medical benefits.

■ Firms must report current expenses to account for vested future medical benefits.

■ The 1990 rule has forced companies to assess their retiree health care liability. Many are now cutting benefits.

HANJIN PARK